Survival Tips

If you are in the hell of a major depression or anxiety disorder and feel that you have reached your limit, here are three coping strategies that you can use right now:

> 1) **Set the intention to heal. Make the decision that you want to get well (even if you don't know how).**
>
> 2) **Reach out for support—to other people and to spirit.**
>
> 3) **Ask spirit (or your Higher Power) for the courage and endurance to stay in the pain until it repatterns.**

If you follow these three suggestions, while I cannot guarantee that you will get better (no one can know the future with certainty), my experience tells me that you will greatly maximize your chances of healing and of making a full recovery.

I know it's hard, but hang in there.
Take one day at a time.
Don't give up five minutes before the miracle.

Please feel free to photocopy or remove this page for your personal use.

More Advance Praise for
When Going Through Hell...Don't Stop!

"Congratulations on courageously telling your inspiring story. Anyone who has suffered from depression will be uplifted by it."
Harold H. Bloomfield, M.D., bestselling author of
How to Survive the Loss of a Love and *How to Heal Depression*

"Mr. Bloch's powerful imagery stunningly portrays the agony of depression as well as the hope that healing is possible."
Rea McDonnell, Ph.D., author of *God Is Close to the Brokenhearted*

"A comprehensive and down-to-earth approach for individuals who are struggling with depression, as well as for their families."
Vicki Vanderslice, M.S.W.

"A true survivor's guide that can be used by anyone who is undergoing a dark night of the soul experience. This book is also invaluable for the friend or caregiver of a person suffering from anxiety or depression."
Julie Weiss, Ph.D.

"A superb job. Combines a gripping narrative with a comprehensive self-help manual on healing from depression."
Cynthia Waller, R.N., psychiatric nurse

"Nothing speaks with more authority than the voice of experience. As one who has been there and back, Douglas has created a powerful and useful roadmap for others to follow. His book offers a beacon of hope for those who are still wandering in the darkness of depression."
Michael Moran, Senior Minister, Spiritual Life Center

When Going Through Hell....
Don't Stop!

A Survivor's Guide to Overcoming Anxiety and Clinical Depression

Douglas Bloch, M.A.

Pallas Communications

Portland, Oregon

ISBN 0-929671-02-3

Library of Congress Card Number: 99-091270

Printed in the United States of America

Published by Pallas Communications
4226 NE 23rd Avenue
Portland, Oregon 97211
503-284-2848

Cover Design by Helena Wolfe
Cover Illustration: "The Scream," by Edvard Munch

"There is not one of us in whom a devil does not dwell. At some time, at some point, that devil masters each of us. It is not having been in the dark house, but having left it, that counts."

Teddy Roosevelt

Dedicated to the loving memory of Anne Zimmerman
Although you could not save yourself,
your spirit lives on
in the lives of those whom you loved and served.

ACKNOWLEDGMENTS

I t takes a whole village to shepherd a person through a dark night of the soul. At least, that has been my experience. Without the care and concern of a legion of guardian angels, I would never have been lifted out of the black hole of depression.

My appreciation begins with the staff of the Sellwood Day Treatment Clinic, who provided a safe haven not only for myself, but for twenty to thirty other sufferers of mental illness during the winter of 1996 and 1997. These health care providers include clinic director Peter Grover; my psychiatrist, Allen Stark; therapists Pat Ritter, Victoria Peacock, Vicki Vanderslice, Mike Terry, Art Kovich, and Tracey Jones; and office manager Beth Morphew. Sadly, the day treatment program has now closed.

In addition to receiving expert professional help, I was blessed with courageous friends. Though not everyone had the fortitude to endure my agitated moods, there were those who chose to stand beside me—Stuart Warren, Ann Garrett, Joe Mitchell, Kathleen Herron, Cathy Brenner, Cynthia Waller, and Linda Larsen-Wheatley. During my darkest hours, Raeanne Lewman's loving massage gave me some small pleasure to look forward to once a week.

I also received tremendous support from the patients at day treatment. Evelyn, Kate, Terri, Lynette, Angela, Jacob, Chris, Leon, Robert, Mike, Todd and Tom—I bless you and pray that you, too, have found some relief from your torment.

My appreciation also goes to Terry Grant and Leslie Newman for your professional home health services.

I will forever be grateful to Marsha Nord for insisting that I would come out on the other side, and to Teresa Keane for teaching me the mindfulness techniques that allowed me to hold on, minute by minute, until help arrived.

This help took the form of the "God group," a group of spiritual friends who gathered together with me at the Living Enrichment Center over a six-month period and held a vision of healing and wellness for me. They are Mary Manin Morrissey and Eddy Marie Crouch (who initiated the meetings), Pat Ritter, Dennis McClure, Victoria Etchemendy, Judy Swensen, Sally Brunell, Stuart Warren, Joan Bloch, Michael Moran, Ann Garrett, Dianne Pharo, Mark and Tracy Sione, Adele Zimmerman, Sally Rutis, and Jon Merritt.

Thanks to Phonesis McEachim and Araline Cate, whose bodywork helped me to stabilize once the depression lifted.

Last but not least, my deepest thanks go to Joan Christine Bridgman—for being such a loyal friend and caregiver (thank you for all those lifesaving walks in Forest Park), and to Joan Bloch for giving our marriage a second chance.

❖ ❖ ❖ ❖

Six weeks after my remission began, I was guided to begin work on this book. At that point, a new crew of helpers appeared to aid and abet the literary process. The first of these were the Reverend Michael Moran and my late therapist, Anne Zimmerman, who first encouraged me to tell my story. Once I became well enough to write, Teresa Keane enthusiastically stepped in as my primary editor and gave generously of her time as well as of her professional expertise. I am also appreciative of Phineas Warren's suggestion that I create a mini self-help manual to follow the book's personal narrative.

In addition, the following people agreed to read and comment on early drafts of the manuscript: Miki Barnes, Joan Bridgman, Deanna Byrne, Araline Cate, Al Coffman, Eddy Marie Crouch, Larry Dossey, Chip Douglas, Bob Edelstein, Jim Eddy, John Engelsman, Victoria Etchemendy, Elliot Geller, Penny Gerharter, Joel Goleb, Beth Hahn, Heather Hannum, Jim Hunzicker, Lee Judy, Ann Kelley, Tonia Larson, Lynne Massie, Dennis McClure, Rhea McDonnell, Philip Mostow, Michael Moran, Marsha Nord, Tracy Pilch, Luella Porter, Pat Ritter, Bruce Robinson, Al Siebert, Vicki Vanderslice,

Julie Weiss, Linda Larsen-Wheatley, and Adele Zimmerman. Thank you all for your invaluable feedback.

I am especially grateful to Brian Litt, who, at key points in the manuscript's evolution, offered cogent advice on how to improve the book's organization and structure. Helen Tevlin, Ph.D., became my "technical advisor" and provided helpful feedback about the accuracy and precision of the clinical information I presented.

Thanks go to the Multnomah County Library for providing me with a plethora of books on the subject of depression and for answering all of my research questions. I also wish to pay tribute to William Styron, Martha Manning, Tracy Thompson, Elizabeth Wurtzel, Susanna Kaysen, Russell Hampton, Jan Dravecky, and Andrew Solomon, whose personal accounts of their struggles with depression informed me that I was not alone.

Throughout the two years of writing, my therapist Pat Ritter and my Master Mind group (Joan Bloch, Stuart Warren, Ann Garrett, Jon Merritt, Judy Swensen, Beth Hahn and John Brown) helped me to maintain my emotional stability and serenity.

I also wish to acknowledge my wonderful mathematics students from the Portland Public Schools who gave me an outlet for daily one-on-one service which balanced the introspective process of writing. My calico cat and muse, Athena, kept me company and watched over the creative process from her perch on top of the file cabinet.

My partner Joan assured me, as she has with my prior works, that if spirit had called me to tell my story, then someone needed to hear it. Helena Wolfe provided her invaluable expertise in designing and formatting the book.

Finally, I give thanks to God, my Higher Power, who I believe (on some level) orchestrated the whole affair—my divorce, my breakdown, my recovery, and ultimately the creation of this narrative. If this work has been a part of Your greater plan, I hope that I have been a worthy teller of Your good news.

Other inspirational books by Douglas Bloch

Words That Heal:
Affirmations and Meditations for Daily Living

Listening to Your Inner Voice:
Discover the Truth Within You and Let It Guide Your Way

I Am With You Always:
A Treasury of Inspirational Quotations, Poems and Prayers

Positive Self-Talk for Children:
Teaching Self-Esteem Through Affirmations

Contents

Sidebars

Part One

Part Two

INTRODUCTION

"Anyone who survives a test is obliged to tell his story."
Elie Wiesel, author and survivor of the Nazi concentration camps

T his is the story of one person's descent into hell. I have written it for myself and for others (as well as their loved ones and caregivers) who find themselves in a similar kind of predicament.

The inferno in which I dwelled was not an external hell. I was not lost at sea nor was I a prisoner of war. The enemies were not "out there"—rather the concentration camp resided in my own mind. I suffered from the hell of a major depression.

Although the depressive episode that I describe in this book began in the summer of 1996, its roots extended far into my past. Like alcoholism and heart disease, depression runs in families and is a multigenerational disorder. If one parent has suffered from depression there is a 25 percent chance that a child will develop the illness; if both parents are depressed, the risk rises to 75 percent.

Although I have never formally investigated my genealogy, I know that the illness has run rampant in my family for at least three generations. Five of my family members have suffered from chronic depression; one developed an eating disorder and another a gambling addiction. One uncle died of starvation in the midst of a depressive episode. My mother suffered two major depressive episodes in a three-year period before she was saved at the eleventh hour by electroconvulsive therapy (ECT). I strongly suspect that both of my grandmothers lived with untreated depression all of their lives.*

---

* The tendency of depression to run in families is probably a combination of both genetic predisposition and family culture. Through observing and imprinting on family dynamics, children learn ways of coping that support or impede mental health. (An example of the latter is the well-documented phenomenon of "learned helplessness."

Compounding my genetic predisposition towards depression was the trauma surrounding my birth. I was born three weeks early, emerging from the womb underweight and "undercooked"—i.e., with slightly underdeveloped digestive and nervous systems. For the first two weeks of my life, I had severe colic, a result of my inability to tolerate the prepared milk formulas that were fed me (as a rule, mothers in the 1950s did not breastfeed their children). In my agony, I screamed my eyes out, unable to sleep for nights on end. Just as I was getting over this disaster, both of my legs were placed in solid casts for six months—a therapy considered normal protocol for straightening out a pair of "pigeon-toed" feet.

I never did fully recover from this difficult entry into the world.* During my formative years, I became excessively introverted, high-strung, and fearful. Things improved somewhat when I entered school and channeled my nervous energy into academic pursuits. Nonetheless, I lived my life in a thinly veiled state of hypervigilance—a clear sign of anxiety as well as of latent depression.**

Although one may be genetically and temperamentally predisposed to depression, it normally takes a stressor (personal loss, illness, financial setback, etc.) to activate the illness. A person with a low susceptibility to depression can endure a fair amount of mental or emotional stress and not become ill. A person with a high degree of vulnerability, however, has only a thin cushion of protection. The slightest insult to the system can initiate a depressive episode.

During my freshman year in college in 1967, I encountered many such stressors. A combination of homesickness, living under the cloudy skies of Rochester, New York, and dealing with the fallout of the Vietnam War initiated my first descent into major depression. Although I was able to limp my way through college with decent grades (and a bachelor's degree in psychology), I left too bummed out and disillusioned (both with myself and society) to continue on to graduate school.

---

* Ironically, the name "Douglas" literally means "black or dark waters."

** My latent depression, though missed by my parents and teachers, was spotted by a perceptive counselor who recommended that I see a psychiatrist. Unfortunately, no one acted on his recommendation.

Statistics show that once a person has experienced a major depression, there is a 50 percent likelihood that the illness will strike again. The odds were borne out when, at the ages of 26 and 33, I experienced two additional episodes, each being triggered by the loss of a love relationship. The first breakdown led to a four-month stay in a halfway house in Berkeley, California; the second resulted in a one-month residence in a well-known New York psychiatric hospital. Fortunately, I was able to emerge from these ordeals relatively intact. (I later described the movement from trauma to recovery as *breakup, breakdown, breakthrough.*) In 1984, I moved to Portland, Oregon, bought a house, got married, found a good therapist, and began my present writing career. By the late eighties I was sure that I had left the dark house forever.

In 1990, however, my marriage began to unravel when my wife was diagnosed with post traumatic stress disorder (PTSD), surfacing from incidents of sexual abuse in her past. Our separation in 1993 initiated a slow crumbling of my psyche which culminated in February 1996, when the divorce became final. My mental decline was further exacerbated by recurrent bouts of cellulitis—a strep infection of the soft tissue in my lower right leg—for which I was hospitalized and given massive doses of antibiotics. (Streptococcal bacteria have since been linked to anxiety attacks and obsessive-compulsive disorders.*) Shortly afterwards, I developed chronic insomnia, a malady that had preceded my previous depressive episodes.

By the summer of 1996, I was, in the words of a friend, "barely limping along." Although previous trials of antidepressants had been unsuccessful, on the advice of a psychiatrist, I decided to try a new Prozac-related medication which had recently been approved by the FDA. Instead of calming me down, however, the drug catapulted me into an "agitated depression"—a state of acute anxiety which alternated with dark, suicidal feelings of despair.

---

* I experienced four additional bouts of cellulitis which further exacerbated my emotional symptoms. For further information on the link between microbes and mental illness, see Part Two, Section 3: "The Roots of Depression."

In the pages that follow, I will share my struggle with and ultimate recovery from this life-threatening depressive illness. While the current protocol for treating depression focuses on the use of antidepressant medication to balance brain chemistry, this path did not work for me. What I needed, and what I eventually received for my deliverance, was a spiritual healing.

It is the purpose of this narrative to document, for myself and others, the exact nature of this miraculous cure. In addition to my personal story, I have written a series of informational sidebars and a mini self-help manual (following the narrative) that address a number of *practical coping strategies* for dealing with depression and anxiety. * Some of the topics include:

- How do I know if I am clinically depressed?
- How can I set up a survival "life raft" that will keep me afloat until help comes?
- How can I cope with the symptoms of intense agitation?
- Why should I stay alive when I've lost hope?
- What do I do when I start to catastrophize about the future?
- Where do I turn if standard medical treatment doesn't work?
- What does it take to be a survivor?
- Once I have recovered from an episode of depression, what can I do to stay well and avoid relapse?
- If a friend or loved one is depressed, how can I best support him or her?

These self-help pointers were taken, not from a psychiatry textbook, but from my own experience in overcoming depression. They emerged from the crucible of struggle and torment.

I have also included reproductions of paintings, by history's great artists that visually depict the various states of mind I experienced. By providing words and images that stimulate both sides of the brain, I hope to give the reader a complete picture of the journey from depression to recovery.

---

* You can either read the sidebars alongside the story or return to them after you complete the narrative.

Although my story focuses on healing from a depressive illness, I believe that many of its principles can be applied to anyone who is undergoing a "dark night of the soul"—i.e., relentless *emotional* or *physical* pain that appears to have no end. It is my deepest wish that the lessons learned from my suffering may give you or a loved one the hope and inspiration to fight on in your darkest hours.

Douglas Bloch
August 26, 1999
Portland, Oregon

CHAPTER ONE

THE DESCENT INTO HELL

*"The journey to higher awareness is not a direct flight.
Challenges, struggles and tests confront the traveler along the way.
Eventually, no matter who you are or how far you have come along the
path, you must experience your 'dark night of the soul.' "*
Douglas Bloch, *Words That Heal*

T he notebook by the side of my bed was finally being put
to use. Given to me by a friend so that I could record my
dreams, the lined yellow paper had remained untouched
for months, as my sleeping medication made dream recollection all
but impossible.

"Oh, well, " I mused. "It won't matter much after today."

I looked out the window. It was another of those oppressive
Oregon winter skies that moves in like an unwanted house guest at
the beginning of November and doesn't depart until the first of July.
The black clouds overhead mirrored those inside my head. I was
suffering from a mental disorder known as clinical depression.

Slowly, I reached for the pen and began to write.

To my friends and family,   November 12, 1996

I know that this is wrong, but I can no longer endure the pain
of living with this mental illness. Further hospitalizations will not
help, as my condition is too deep-seated and advanced to uproot.
On some deeper level, I know that my work on the planet is finished, and that it is time to move on.

Douglas

I reached over for the bottle of pills that I had secretly saved for this occasion, slowly twisted off the cap and imagined the sweet slumber that awaited me. My reverie was interrupted by a loud knock at the door.

"Who can that be?" I wondered. "Can't a man commit suicide in peace?"

I turned over in bed and spied my friend Stuart entering the living room.

"Just thought I'd check in and see if you made it off to day treatment," he said cheerfully as he made his way to the bedroom.

I quickly hid the pills, wondering if I should tell Stuart about my note. Meanwhile, I could feel the stirrings of another anxiety attack. It began with the involuntary twitching of my legs, then violent shaking, until my whole body went into convulsions. Not able to contain the huge amount of energy that was surging through me, I jumped out of bed and began to pace. Back and forth, back and forth I stumbled across the living room, hitting myself in the head and screaming, "Electric shock for Douglas Bloch. Electric shock for Douglas Bloch."

❖ ❖ ❖ ❖

I had not always been so disturbed. Just ten weeks earlier, on September 4, 1996, I had taken a new Prozac-related medication in the hopes of alleviating a two-year, chronic, low-grade depression which was brought on by a painful divorce and a bad case of writer's block. Instead of mellowing me out, however, the drug produced an adverse reaction—a state of intense agitation that catapulted me into the psychiatric ward of a local hospital.

It soon became clear that taking this antidepressant created a permanent shift in my body/mind. Before ingesting the drug, I felt crummy, but not crazy; emotionally down, but still able to function. My suffering was intense—but not enough to disable me, not enough to make me suicidal. Now, I had entered a whole new realm of torment. The drug's assault on my brain caused something inside me to snap, sending me into an emotional freefall and creating a life-threatening biochemical disorder. The closest analogy I can use to describe my state is that I was on a bad LSD trip—except that I didn't "come down" after the customary eight hours. In fact, the nightmare was just beginning.

There were two things about my predicament that made it different from anything I had ever experienced—the sheer intensity of the pain and its seeming nonstop assault on my nervous system. During my hospitalization, I discovered that my official diagnosis was "major depression" combined with a "generalized anxiety disorder." Here is what I learned when I asked my doctor about these terms.

Major Depression
*"If there is hell on earth, it is to be found in the heart
of a melancholy man."*
Robert Burton, seventeenth-century English scholar

Before I describe my own experience of major depression (also known as clinical depression), I would like to delineate the difference between the medical term "clinical depression" and the word "depression" as it is used by most people. Folks say they are depressed when they experience some disappointment or personal setback—e.g., the stock market drops, they fail to get a raise, or there's trouble at home with the kids. While I would never want to minimize anyone's pain, clinical depression takes this kind of suffering to a whole new level, making these hurts look like a mild sunburn.

Major depression can be distinguished from "the blues" of everyday life in that a depressive illness is a "whole body" disorder, involving one's physiology, biochemistry, mood, thoughts, and behavior. It affects the way you eat and sleep, the way you think and feel about yourself, others and the world. Clinical depression is not a passing blue mood or a sign of personal weakness. Subtle changes inside the brain's chemistry create a terrible malaise in the body-mind-spirit that can affect every dimension of one's being.

Diagnostic Criteria for a Major Depressive Episode

A depressive illness is a "whole body" illness, involving one's body, mood, thoughts and behavior. It affects the way you eat and sleep, the way you feel about yourself and think about things. It is not a passing blue mood or a sign of personal weakness.

Depressive illnesses come in different forms, the most serious of which is major depression. The following criteria for major depression are taken from the Diagnostic and Statistical Manual of Mental Disorders (DSM-IV). If you or someone you know fits these criteria, seek professional help.

A. Five or more of these symptoms should be present during the same two-week period and represent a change from previous functioning.
1. Depressed mood most of the day
2. Markedly diminished interest in pleasure
3. Significant change in appetite, leading to weight loss or weight gain
4. Insomnia or hypersomnia (too much sleep) nearly every day
5. Psychomotor agitation or retardation nearly every day
6. Fatigue or loss of energy nearly every day
7. Feelings of worthlessness or excessive or inappropriate guilt
8. Diminished ability to think or concentrate, or indecisiveness
9. Recurrent thoughts of death, recurrent suicidal thoughts without a specific plan, suicide attempts, or specific plans for committing suicide

B. In addition, these symptoms cause clinically significant distress or impairment in social, occupational or other important areas of functioning.

On the facing page, I have listed the official symptoms of major depression, taken from the Diagnostic and Statistical Manual of Mental Disorders (DSM-IV), the official diagnostic resource of the mental health profession. Describing how depression actually feels, however—especially to someone who has never "been there"—is not so straightforward. If I told you that I had been held hostage, put in solitary confinement and beaten, you might receive a graphic image of my suffering. But how does one describe a "black hole of the soul" where the tormentors are invisible?

I remember seeing a diagram in my high school biology class depicting what happens when you put your hand on a hot stove. The nerve receptors in the skin send a message up the arm and spinal column to the brain, which interprets the situation as "Ouch, that's hot!" The brain then sends a message back down the spine telling the hand to remove itself from the burner. All of this takes place in a fraction of a second.

The pain of depression is not so easy to track. It cannot be described as stabbing, shooting or burning; neither can its sensations be localized to any one part of the body. It is an all-encompassing malignancy—a crucifying pain that slowly permeates every fiber of one's being. Being consumed by depression is not like being gored by a bull; it is more akin to being eaten alive by an army of starving termites.

When one is clinically depressed, the capacity for (and the memory of) pleasure vanishes. The best that one can hope for is a kind of "negative happiness" that results from the temporary absence of distress. Life fluctuates between the horrible and the miserable. A sense of humor, that wonderful analgesic that existed even among some concentration camp prisoners, is completely absent. (Many friends marked the beginning of my depression as when I lost the ability to laugh.)

Even though depression is called a mood disorder, mood is only one of the many bodily functions that are disrupted by a disorganized, misfiring brain. Eating and sleeping are disrupted (along

"Melancholy," by Edvard Munch

When asked by Art Buchwald whether his depression was improved by being in the country, William Styron replied:

> It's all the same. You're carrying the thing around with you. It's like a crucifixion. It doesn't matter where you are; nothing in the outer world can alter it. You could be in the sublimest place you could possibly imagine. For example, [Mike] Wallace went down to St. Martin which is a wonderfully attractive place. But he had his darkest moments there.

As Styron knew only too well, there is little respite from the hell of a major depression. You cannot curl up in bed with a few good videos, drink chicken soup and expect to feel better in seven to ten days. Unlike most physical ailments, depression does not improve with rest. Being alone in bed actually makes matters worse, as the mind turns further inward and tortures itself with imaginary demons.

I felt as if some sadist were twisting my arm behind my back and would not relent even after I yelled "Uncle!" With each unfolding day, the pain seemed to increase. I complained to my friends, "This is the worst I've ever felt!"

"But that's what you say every day," they countered.

It didn't matter. There was something freshly horrible about the pain, as if I were being kicked in the stomach once every minute.

I felt as if someone had created a cruel parody of Psalm 139 in which David says to God, "*Where can I go from your spirit? Or where can I flee from your presence? If I ascend into heaven you are there...If I take the wings of the morning and dwell in the uttermost parts of the sea, even there your hand shall lead me and your right hand shall hold me...*" except that in depression it is not God, but the Devil who follows you everywhere. And there is no escape.*

Generalized Anxiety Disorder

"There may be no rest for the wicked, but compared to the rest that anxious people get, the wicked undoubtedly have a pastoral life."
Russell Hampton, *The Far Side of Despair*

*"If you're facing terror every day,
it's gonna bring Hannibal to his knees."*
Jim Ballenger, a leading expert on anxiety

Although no one knows exactly why, a great number of depressions are also accompanied by anxiety. In one study, 85 percent of those with major depression were also diagnosed with generalized anxiety disorder (see symptoms on the following page) while 35 percent had symptoms of a panic disorder. Because they so often go hand in hand, anxiety and depression are considered the fraternal twins of mood disorders.

---

* Not all depressions are this severe. People can be mildly to moderately depressed or suffer from low-grade, chronic depression known as "dysthymia." To learn more about the many other types of depression, refer to Part Two, Section 2: "The Many Faces of Depression."

Diagnostic Criteria for Generalized Anxiety Disorder

How do you know if you are suffering from clinical anxiety? The following criteria are taken from the Diagnostic and Statistical Manual of Mental Disorders (DSM-IV). If you, or someone you know is experiencing these symptoms seek professional assistance.

A. Excessive anxiety and worry occurring more days than not for at least six months.
B. Difficulty in controlling the worry and anxiety.
C. The anxiety and worry are associated with three (or more) of the following six symptoms:
1. Restlessness or feeling keyed up or on edge
2. Being easily fatigued
3. Difficulty concentrating or mind going blank
4. Irritability
5. Muscle tension
6. Sleep disturbances (difficulty falling or staying asleep, or restless, unsatisfying sleep)
D. The anxiety, worry, or physical symptoms cause clinically significant distress or impairment in social, occupational or other important areas of functioning.
E. The disturbance is not due to the direct physiological effects of a substance (e.g., a drug abuse or a medication) or a general medical condition (e.g., hyperthyroidism).

Believed to be caused in part by a malfunction of brain chemistry, generalized anxiety is not the normal apprehension that one feels before taking a test or awaiting the outcome of a biopsy. A person with an anxiety disorder suffers from what President Franklin Roosevelt called "fear itself." For a reason that is only partially known, the brain's fight-or-flight mechanism becomes activated, even when no real threat exists. Being chronically anxious is like being stalked by an imaginary tiger. The feeling of being in danger never goes away.

Even more than the depression, it was my anxiety and agitation that became the defining symptoms of my illness. Like epileptic seizures, a series of frenzied anxiety attacks would descend upon me without warning. My body was possessed by a chaotic, demonic force which led to my shaking, pacing and violently hitting myself across the chest or in the head. This self-flagellation seemed to provide a physical outlet for my invisible torment, as if I were letting steam out of a pressure cooker.

The force of my symptoms was so great that I considered the possibility that I might be possessed by some malevolent demon. I remembered the film "The Exorcist" and set up an appointment with a priest who specialized in satanic possession. After taking a thorough case history and questioning me about my religious beliefs, the priest concluded that I was not possessed by the Devil.

"It certainly feels that way," I replied.

I then consulted a psychiatrist who told me that my symptoms were not those of a panic disorder. I did not experience palpitations, pounding heart, sweating, trembling, shortness of breath, chest pain, fear of dying, etc. The word "agitation" was the closest I could come to describing the feeling of wanting to jump out of my skin. Hence my disorder was eventually diagnosed as "agitated depression."

Agitated depression is not a good diagnosis to have. Clinicians have observed that when anxiety occurs "comorbidly" with depression, the symptoms of *both* the depression and anxiety are more severe compared to when those disorders occur independently.

Moreover, the symptoms of the depression take longer to resolve, making the illness more chronic and more resistant to treatment. Finally, depression exacerbated by anxiety has a much higher suicide rate than depression alone. (In one study, 92 percent of depressed patients who had attempted suicide were also plagued by severe anxiety.*) Like alcohol and barbiturates, depression and anxiety are a deadly combination when taken together.

In addition to physical agitation, my anxiety was accompanied by obsessively rhyming voices. In my book *Words That Heal*, I suggested that people rhyme their affirmations because "words that rhyme make a more powerful impression on the subconscious than blank verse." Now, my own subconscious had decided, in a malicious way, to take my advice to heart. Rhymes such as "electric shock for Douglas Bloch," "the River Styx in '96," and "suicidal ideation is a hit across the nation" flooded my mind.** When my anxiety became extreme, I shouted these rhymes out loud, further upsetting myself and those around me. Although I did not actually hear these verses—they were more like obsessive thoughts—their presence led my doctors to give me a final diagnosis of *agitated depression with psychotic features*.

Because my anxiety emerged from a disordered brain it, like the depression, was outside my conscious control. Yet virtually everyone—my friends, family, men's group members, and even health professionals—interpreted the anxiety as some sort of "acting out" that I could modify at will; they did not understand that I was sick. Some people even became angry and abusive in response to my distress. The most dramatic illustration of this occurred on the night of my first hospitalization.

The day had begun with a major anxiety attack, an aftershock from the overly anxious reaction to an antidepressant I had taken

---

* Clinical Psychiatry News 27(6):25, 1999.

** The rhyme "electric shock for Douglas Bloch" was an allusion to ECT, electroconvulsive therapy.

More than any other image, Edvard Munch's "The Scream" depicts
the out-of-control anxiety that was threatening to destroy me.

two days earlier. At my request, my ex-wife Joan telephoned the on-call psychiatrist who advised that I hospitalize myself, given the extremity of my symptoms. It took most of the day for my managed care insurance to pre-certify my admission, so that by the time we left for the hospital it was already late in the evening.

As Joan and I made our way out the Sunset Highway, my terror escalated as I recalled the trauma of my previous psychiatric hospitalizations. Five blocks from the unit, realizing that history was about to repeat itself, I attempted to jump out of the car and was prevented only by the automatic door locks which Joan activated from the driver's side.

We arrived on the psychiatric ward at midnight, and after being searched and having my belongings confiscated, I was led to a stark, barren room with a hospital cot and a glaring overhead light.

"What did you expect?" the night nurse commented, when she saw the distress on my face.

From her tone of voice, I could sense that order, not compassion, was this woman's priority. She spoke in carefully measured phrases, as if competing with a metronome to see who could keep the most exact beat.

"Isn't there a reading lamp here?" I asked timidly. "It helps me to relax if I can curl up in bed with a book."

"Lamps are not allowed in the rooms," she replied. "We can't risk having our patients strangle themselves with the cord."

Pondering that morbid remark, I asked the nurse for a tranquilizer to help me get to sleep.

"You don't need medication," she replied in a clinical voice. "Take some deep breaths and try to control yourself."

"I'd like to, but I can't," I responded. That is why I was admitted to the hospital—because I'm out of control. Please call the psychiatrist and ask him to order me a sleeping pill."

Big Nurse was unmoved. My anxiety escalated and I began to pace the floor. "Whack! Whack!" I hit myself in the head, then across the chest.

"If you can't restrain yourself," she warned in a high-pitched voice, "I'm going to call security and tell them to strap you down."

Upon hearing these words my mind raced forward to a scene of being forcibly put in a straightjacket. I felt myself suffocating, and was filled with terror. My worst fear was about to come true—I was going to die in a mental hospital. I spotted a bottle of tranquilizers that was sitting unattended at the nurse's station and moved towards it. "I'd rather get it over with now than die of fright," I decided.

Fortunately, Joan was still on the unit. Sensing my distress, she grabbed me by the arm and escorted me for a long walk around the ward. When we returned, the on-call psychiatrist had ordered a 50-milligram tablet of Mellaril (an antipsychotic tranquilizer in the same

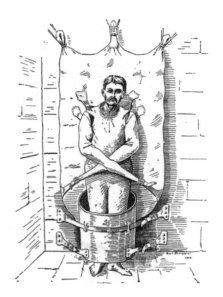

This illustration depicts two types of restraints commonly used in 19th-century hospitals. Modern day methods are more humane and are used only when a person is a danger to himself or others.

family as Thorazine) for me. With a prayer of thanksgiving, I gulped down the medicine.

Even with the Mellaril, I still felt a bit agitated, and so I asked Joan to rock me to sleep. When the nurse made her rounds a few hours later, she spotted Joan and became livid. "What are you doing here?" she howled. "I thought I told you to leave!" At that moment, I realized that the notorious Nurse Ratched (from the book and movie *One Flew Over the Cuckoo's Nest*) was not just a fictional character.

Unfortunately, this experience was repeated two months later in a different hospital. My anxiety in the new environment was exacerbated by the fact that I was residing in a locked unit. The only outdoor space available for exercise was a small courtyard surrounded by barbed wire. Here, restless patients took their smoke breaks. The air was so full of secondhand smoke, that I could hardly breathe, let alone jog or run in place. My exercise options all but eliminated, I paced back and forth in the halls for hours at a time.

One day, upon witnessing my agitation, a mental health therapist took me aside.

"Why don't you practice the cognitive therapy techniques you learned in your behavior modification group?" he asked.

"I think a Klonopin would be more effective." (Klonopin is an anti-seizure medication which is also used to treat anxiety.)

"You can control your thoughts and your behaviors without medication," he insisted.

"Don't you understand?" I replied emphatically. "I AM NOT IN CONTROL OF MY NERVOUS SYSTEM. I AM NOT IN CONTROL OF MY NERVOUS SYSTEM."

Instead of a straightjacket, the nurses and therapist decided to put me in the "quiet room"—a euphemism for a padded cell with no windows. "Just what a claustrophobic needs to calm his anxiety," I mused.

Such lack of compassion on the part of trained professionals shows their ignorance of a basic medical fact—that in *extreme* cases of anxiety, the agitation *chemically interferes* with the brain's ability to hold positive thoughts over a sustained period.

❁   ❁   ❁   ❁

It was not until six months later that the legitimacy of my symptoms was validated by a savvy nurse-practitioner who taught stress-reduction to patients with chronic pain. "When your brain gets wacked out to this extreme," Teresa advised, "you literally need to *burn off* those agitating chemicals; I recommend intense exercise." Following her counsel, whenever my anxiety began to escalate, I ran down to my neighborhood pool and swam a mile or more until I dropped. (I called this ritual "swimming for my life.")

Meanwhile, I was living in the inferno, a concentration camp of the mind. I felt as if my brain were being batted back and forth by two drunken Ping-Pong players—one named anxiety and the other called depression. I had never believed that hell was a place you went to after death, but rather a state of consciousness that one could experience here on earth. Now I had the living proof. About four months after my first hospitalization, my psychiatrist asked, "Douglas, are you afraid that if these symptoms persist, you will become chronically mentally ill?"

"What do you mean?" I replied incredulously. *"I already am chronically mentally ill."*

For the first few days after my release, I maintained a shaky stability. I returned to work, hoping that the focus of a job would alleviate my anxiety. Instead, my moods turned inexorably downward. With each passing day, I felt more and more fragile. Early morning awakenings (a classic symptom of depression) intensified. My depressive moods blackened. The anxiety attacks, which had begun sporadically, increased in frequency to two to three times a week. I was less and less able to concentrate on my sales job, crying at the slightest upset. Like the Bizarro Superman I used to read about in the comic books, I felt as if the old Douglas had been replaced by some malfunctioning impersonator.

My predicament brings up a pertinent question that has enormous social implications—what happens to a person who is incapacitated by clinical depression? Where does he or she go when he reaches the point that he can no longer cope? There are no halfway houses for depressives, although with seventeen million Americans suffering from depression, you would think there would be. Neither are there any 12-step groups called Depressives Anonymous. Many people in the throes of depression "tough it out" and continue their daily routine in spite of the incredible pain, becoming what William Styron calls "the walking wounded." I did not have that luxury. The symptoms of my anxiety were simply too extreme for me to be on my own.

Although I had many wonderful friends, they were busy with their jobs and family obligations and could not monitor me throughout the day. (It is also easy for friends to get burned out caring for someone who is clinically depressed.)* My ex-wife Joan had moved in with me in September to become my caretaker, but was actively looking for a full-time job. This crisis was too big to be handled by friends and family alone—I needed the support of a therapeutic community.

During my previous depressive episodes, I had stumbled across two such environments. In 1976, I spent four months residing at

---

* To find out what friends and family can do, please refer to Part Two, Section 8: "When Someone You Love Is Depressed."

"The Sleep of Reason Produces Monsters," by Francisco de Goya.

Berkeley Place, Inc., a halfway house that transitioned hospitalized patients back into the community. (Although I had no history of hospitalization, I was allowed to stay because I was homeless.) Then, in 1983, my parents admitted me to New York Hospital for a one-month stay (at that time, a month was considered a short-term stint). During these respites my symptoms significantly improved, and by the time of my discharge I was on the mend. I believe that each of these institutions saved my life.

Now, however, it was 1996. With managed care insurance companies in charge of mental health treatment, the landscape was anything but patient-friendly. I consulted a number of psychiatrists and psychotherapists in the hopes of getting healed through outpatient therapy, but none of them would work with me. "You're too agitated and out of control to benefit from therapy," they said. "You should spend at least four to six weeks in a residential setting in order to get stabilized." The prescription was sound, but it over-looked a critical point—psychiatric hospitals no longer provided long-term care. Beginning with the 1960s, each decade has seen a gradual reduction of inpatient time allotted to the mentally ill.

For example, in the mid '60's I knew a woman who suffered from schizophrenia and who spent *two years* getting well at McLean, Harvard's famous psychiatric teaching hospital.* In *The Far Side of Despair*, author Russell Hampton recounts his *six-month* hospitaliza-tion for anxiety and depression during the early 1970s. In 1985, author William Styron spent *six weeks* in a hospital recovering from a major depressive episode. By the time my crisis hit, the average stay had been reduced to *seventy-two hours*. Even McLean, champion of milieu therapy, had switched over to short-term treatment.

"Slit your wrists and a hospital will have to take you in," a friend advised when I told him of my predicament.

"If it were only that easy," I replied, as I thought of my ex-roommate Dan, whom I had met during my first hospitalization. A high school physics teacher in his mid-thirties, Dan had been ad-mitted after his wife found him wandering in the woods with a gun, threatening to blow his brains out.

"What is your treatment plan?" I asked over breakfast.

"I don't know," he replied with an apathetic look on his face. "I get discharged later today."

"But you're not ready to leave!" I said incredulously. "You were only admitted last night!"

"I can't help it. My insurance company said my time is up."

As he predicted, Dan was discharged later that afternoon, less than twenty-four hours after he was admitted. I frequently think of him, wondering if he is still alive, in spite of the system that failed him.**

---

* Many celebrities have resided at McLean—including Sylvia Plath, Robert Lowell, Ray Charles, and singer James Taylor, who wrote about the experience in his first album. Novelist Susanna Kaysen also recounts her stay at McLean in the book *Girl, Interrupted*.

** Not only patients, but psychiatrists are becoming increasingly frustrated with a managed health care system that puts profits above the welfare of the individual. One psychiatrist told me that he is forced to treat many of his severely ill patients—who at one time would have been hospitalized—on an outpatient basis.

As I struggled to find someone (or someplace) to be my caregiver, I imagined the ideal healing environment for someone in Dan's or my state—a restful, peaceful asylum in the country modeled after the old health sanatoriums of Europe. Here is the vision that came to me:

> This center is designed to treat the whole person, combining the best of medical treatment (antidepressants and/ or ECT) with alternative care—diet, exercise, light therapy, acupuncture, vitamin and mineral supplementation, prayer, psychotherapy, group therapy, vocational counseling, etc. Unlike traditional hospitals, the entire facility is a place of beauty. The buildings are open and spacious with plenty of natural light. Soothing classical music fills the air and gorgeous works of art decorate the hallways and walls of the patient's rooms. Nutritious meals are served using fresh foods from the ground's organic gardens. Various forms of physical therapy such as massage and whirlpools provide relaxation for patients and staff. Puppies and kittens are available for everyone to love. In short, the center provides a holistic "therapeutic milieu," the goal of which is to return the individual to society as soon as possible, but not before he or she is ready.

Aside from its role in reducing the human suffering caused by mental illness, such a facility might well pay for itself by reducing the $43.7 billion annual cost that depression places on the U.S. economy.

Unfortunately, the only institution that remotely resembled my fantasy was the world-famous Menninger Clinic in Topeka, Kansas. While Menninger had an excellent reputation, the price tag was daunting—$30,000 for a month's stay—an amount that no insurance would cover. Moreover, I was scared of being transplanted to the Midwest without friends or family support. For the next five months I agonized about whether to take the radical step of going to Menninger.*

Just as I was about to give up hope, I learned of a residential clinic that seemed to fit my needs. Springbrook, a drug and alcohol rehabilitation center located forty-five miles southwest of Portland, had everything I had hoped for—a minimum 28-day residency (with a possible 60 day extension); group and individual therapy; recreational therapy that included a gym, a weight room and access to a city pool; a beautifully manicured twenty-five acre campus with walking paths; a balanced diet consisting of excellent food provided by Marriott Food Service (the only complaints about the food are that the servings are too big); and 12-step spiritual orientation. Finally (this is the most amazing fact), in most cases insurance companies would pay for 50 to 80 percent of the treatment cost.

There was, however, a small catch—one had to be an alcoholic or a drug addict to be admitted.

"I'm not an addict," I explained to the admissions officer over the phone, "but I am in as much pain as one."

"I'm afraid that you don't meet our criteria," she replied.

"But I read in your brochure that you treat people for depression."

"Only if you have chemical dependency as your primary diagnosis."

"Let me understand this," I said, pondering the absurdity of the situation. "If I were to self-medicate with drugs or alcohol to nullify the pain of my depression, and consequently developed an addiction, I would be able to pursue long-term recovery in an elaborate treatment center. But if I choose a healthier outcome and resist the temptation to abuse myself, I am limited to a 72-hour stay in the local psych ward." **

---

* Looking back, I am convinced that if long-term residential care had been available to me (as it was in 1976 and 1983), my recent illness would have resolved far sooner. The absence of adequate facilities for people suffering from extreme depression and anxiety is a major failing of our mental health care system.

** I recently learned that guitarist Eric Clapton plans to raise $5 million for a drug and alcohol recovery center. Perhaps one day a famous depressive will start a treatment center for people with mood disorders.

"I see your point," she said sympathetically, "but I have to abide by our policy."

I had heard of people slipping through the cracks of society's institutions, but this felt more like falling into the crater of an active volcano. "It's no wonder that depression is the leading cause of suicide," I thought, "when people can't get the help they need." *

The issue, it seemed to me, is that depression is not a "tangible" problem like substance abuse. And since depressives as a rule do not make the headlines with their self-destructive acts—like driving a BMW into a tree while loaded on cocaine—their illness is not taken as seriously.

For a while, I contemplated getting hooked on drugs so that I might receive some decent care and attention. A few months later I read Elizabeth Wurtzel's *Prozac Nation* and discovered another depressive who faced the same dilemma. Wurtzel writes:

> I found myself wishing for a real ailment, found myself longing to be a junkie or a cokehead or something...It seemed to me that if I could get hooked on some drug, anything was possible. I'd make friends. I'd have a real problem. I'd be able to walk into a church basement full of fellow sufferers and have them all say, "Welcome to our nightmare! We understand! Here are our phone numbers, call any time you feel you're slipping because we're here for you."

Meanwhile, there was no one—i.e., no institutional structure— that was there for me. As I paced back and forth, hitting myself furiously while I waited for Joan to arrive home from work, I was left pondering, "Where can I find a therapeutic environment that will nurture me back to health?" Discovering the answer to this question was becoming a matter of life and death.

---

* Many people with mental disorders, especially the poor, end up behind bars. According to the U.S. Bureau of Justice and Statistics, prisons now house more than 280,000 mentally ill inmates (16% of the inmate population). People who are ill need treatment, not incarceration. See Mark Larabee and Michelle Roberts, "Jails, Prisons, Confront Influx of Mentally Ill Patients," *The Oregonian*, October 24, 1999, p. A16.

CHAPTER THREE

TREADING FIRE

"When a man finds that it is his destiny to suffer, he will have to accept his suffering as his single and unique task. No one can relieve him of his suffering or suffer in his place. His unique opportunity lies in the way in which he bears his burden."
Victor Frankl

"War is hell. So is mental illness."
Binford W. Gilbert

The towering door closed behind me with a grave finality. "Are you sure you have to keep it locked?" I asked the orderly. "I voluntarily checked myself in here, so I don't think I'm going to try to escape."

"It's not you we are worried about," he replied. "With all of the addicts on this ward, we can't risk having any more drugs smuggled into the unit. That's why no one is allowed to go outside."

This was not the private facility at Springbrook with its manicured walking paths. With all of my other options exhausted, I had entered Pacific Gateway Hospital, a dual diagnosis psychiatric facility in the Portland area. Unlike Springbrook (and other drug and alcohol treatment centers), Gateway accepted patients who suffered solely from mental disorders. While Springbrook's clientele consisted of doctors, lawyers and other professionals, Gateway ministered to the common folk. Like pilgrims converging on Mecca, they streamed in from all parts of the Pacific Northwest, seeking salvation from the "three D's"—drinking, drugging and depression.

At Gateway, instead of having 72 hours to get better, my managed care provider had granted me seven to ten days (an inadequate time to heal from depression, let alone get clean and sober). It was the best I could muster.

Words of Hope

Only two hours remained before I was to be admitted to the psychiatric ward of Pacific Gateway Hospital. As my partner Joan packed my suitcase, I became increasingly anxious about being taken to an unknown and threatening environment. My friend Kathleen shared with me the following words of hope and encouragement:

1. You are falling apart in order to be put together in a new way. You will come through this because you are loved.

2. As a result of this breakdown, you will emerge a better person.

3. You are strong; you made a decision not to give up in the past, and you will not give up now.

4. All of the good you have done will help you to a better future.

My days at Gateway were spent attending groups, playing backgammon, and being beaten at speed chess by a mercurial manic-depressive who supported his drug habit by hustling chess games on the street. During my stay, my condition declined, not because of the environment (Gateway had an excellent reputation), but because the depressive illness had taken on a life of its own and was metastasizing through me like a psychic cancer. The downward trajectory of my disease was evidenced by the increasing frequency and duration of my anxiety attacks. Without the option of outdoor exercise, I was reduced to pacing the hallways, wearing out both the carpet and my welcome. My sorry plight earned me the sympathy of the hard-core heroin users who housed the ward ("We thought we had problems," they said to themselves, "but this dude is really messed up.")

As the day grew closer to my release, I began to panic. Joan was now working full time, and if I could not create an alternative support system, I would be shipped off to the state hospital at Salem.

Admission Summary: Pacific Gateway Hospital

PATIENT: Bloch, Douglas. This is the first Pacific Gateway hospitalization for this 47-year-old white male.

REASON FOR ADMISSION: The patient is depressed, anxious, and increasingly out of control.

MENTAL STATUS EXAMINATION: Patient is a well-developed, well-nourished adult male appearing stated age. Patient's speech was variable in flow from slow to pressured. Thought content was that he was over-whelmed, hopeless, helpless and out of control, and that he needed help. His mood was markedly anxious with an undercurrent of depression. His affect was mildly labile. Recent memory based on object recall is good. Remote memory based on historical reconstruction is good. Intelligence, based on vocabulary, fund of knowledge and educational achievement is above average to superior. His insight is fair. His judgment is poor. He presents as extremely dependent and hopeless. He denies suicidal or homicidal ideation at this time.

STRENGTHS AND ASSETS: (1) The patient is very intelligent. (2) The patient tends to form a good therapeutic alliance.

ATTENDING DIAGNOSIS: (1) Major depression; (2) Recurrent, severe panic attacks with agoraphobia (patient reports episodes in which he is so anxious he cannot leave the house); (3) Generalized anxiety disorder.

INITIAL TREATMENT PLAN:
PROBLEM LIST (1) Depression; (2) Anxiety.

MEDICATION: I will probably increase the Zoloft. He took 50 mgs. the first time today. May increase the Elavil and may increase the Klonopin.

PLAN OF TREATMENT: Admit the patient to the adult unit. Work with the patient on the issues of stress management and anxiety reduction. Get the patient stabilized on medication. Work with him on issues of self esteem. Get him transitioned to day program.

ESTIMATED LENGTH OF STAY: 5 days.

GOALS, DISCHARGE CRITERIA: (1) The patient will be stable on medications; (2) The patient will be able to manage his affairs outside the hospital.

Signed Dr. ▇▇▇▇▇▇▇▇▇▇▇▇▇▇▇▇▇▇▇▇   10-23-1996

One day, shortly before my release, I noticed a new person in the lunchroom who wasn't from our unit.

"Hi." I reached out my hand. "My name is Douglas."

"My name is Tom Peters," came the reply.

"Are you a patient on the ward?"

"I attend day treatment next door."

"What's that?"

"It's where people go after they leave the hospital. It's pretty good, actually. We attend groups most of the day and come here for a free lunch."

The lunch I couldn't have cared less about. The full-time structure was another matter.

"What are the hours?"

"Nine-thirty till three-thirty, kind of like going to school."

Later that day I approached my psychiatrist, who confirmed that the program was for real.

"How soon can I get in?" I inquired.

'The program is crowded right now, but they may have space for you. I'll introduce you to the director, Mike Terry, tomorrow at lunch."

Two days later, on November 1, 1996, I was discharged from Gateway. I left the hospital's main entrance, made a right turn, walked one block, and found myself at the doorstep of the Sellwood Day Treatment Center.*

Day treatment was a highly structured outpatient program consisting of group and individual therapy that was available to recently hospitalized patients. The center was housed within a historic landmark—the home of Dr. Sellwood, after whom the Sellwood district of Portland is named. The two-story dwelling was constructed in 1906 and expressed the Victorian charm and elegance of the homes built during that era. The cheerful, well-lit rooms and tasteful fur-

---

*Not all cities have such a comprehensive program. If a day treatment center does not exist in your area, you can seek out 12-step groups, depression support groups, or any combination of structures that work. (Mental health support groups can be located by calling your local hospital or by contacting the organizations listed in Appendix C.)

nishings conveyed a sense of home and family. Day treatment was more than a psychiatric clinic; it was a true therapeutic community. Its healing milieu supplied three ingredients that were crucial for my stabilization:

1) **Containment:** Being in a structured environment with defined limits and daily tasks decreased my anxiety.

2) **Contact:** Nurturing connection and support from staff and patients helped me to focus outward and to escape my inner nightmare.

3) **Routine:** A regular, daily rhythm with predictable activities calmed and soothed my nervous system.

The heart of the program was group therapy, which ran from 9:30 a.m. to 3:30 p.m. and was facilitated by members of the treatment team—a psychiatrist, three psychologists, two social workers, a nurse, an art therapist, a movement therapist, and two drug and alcohol counselors. Day treatment provided me with a complete, *uninterrupted* support system which far surpassed the assistance that any single therapist could offer. For the next nine months, this program would play a pivotal role in my survival.

Day Treatment Schedule

9:30 10:30	Living Skills	Managing Emotions	Living Skills	Managing Emotions	Social Skills
10:30 11:30	Coping Skills	Problem Solving	Problem Emotions	Relationships Trauma Survivors	Coping Skills
11:30 12:30	Medical Group Evaluation	Women's Group _ Men's Group	Relationships Group _ Psychotherapy	Mind & Body Group _ Psychotherapy	Communication Skills
12:30 1:30	L	U	N	C	H
1:30 2:30	Movement Therapy	Self-Esteem	Stress Management	Crafts	Self-Esteem
2:30 3:30	Relapse Prevention	Art Therapy	Anger Management	Relapse Prevention	

It was not the content but the *context* of day treatment that I found so healing. The psychological information presented in the groups was fairly elementary—I had learned most of it in my first year of undergraduate studies. It didn't matter. I was not attending the program to add to my intellectual knowledge; I was there because I *needed* the structure and support. I decided to humble myself and to accept the help that was so generously offered.

Asking the Right Question

Shortly after my arrival at day treatment, I was assigned my individual therapist, Pat Ritter. Pat was a registered nurse and a recovering alcoholic who, having been clinically depressed herself, understood mental illness from both sides of the hospital door.

"This is your life," Pat stated matter-of-factly at our first meeting. "For reasons we may not understand, the universe has given you the challenge of major depression right now. You do not get to choose whether you have this mental illness. Your choice lies in how you are going to deal with it." *

"But what about those self-help books that say you can create anything you want if you just apply the right technique?" I asked. I was thinking about all the "can do" motivational self-help tracts I had read (and written) in my quest for self-improvement.

"They may work in other contexts," she replied, "but not in this one. This time you are dealing with a force that is more powerful than your ego."

As Pat spoke, I imagined myself as a sailor who had survived a terrible shipwreck and was lost at sea. I shared my image with Pat.

"What is the task of that sailor?" she asked.

"To try to stay afloat until help comes."

"Precisely! Your job is to create an 'emotional life raft' that will keep you afloat, until the pattern of your illness shifts."

"And how do I do this?"

---

* In his classic book, *Man's Search for Meaning,* Victor Frankl says that while imprisoned in a Nazi concentration camp, he discovered that "everything can be taken from a man but one thing—the ability to *choose* one's attitude in any given set of circumstances."

"In AA we have something called the '24-hour plan.' Instead of promising never to drink again, we focus on keeping sober for the current twenty-four hours. I suggest you adopt a similar strategy."

Pat was right. Whenever I contemplated the prospect of dealing with my pain over the long term, I became overwhelmed. But if I could reduce my life to a single 24-hour segment of time—that was something I could handle. If I could tread water (or, being in hell, tread fire) each day, then perhaps I could survive my ordeal.

A Survival Plan for Living in Hell

"My definition of a man is this:
a being who can get used to anything."
Dostoyevsky

Working together, Pat and I created what I called "my daily survival plan." The central idea was simple—to develop coping strategies that would get me through the day, hour by hour, minute by minute. Because I was fighting a war on two fronts, I had to devise and employ techniques that would deal with *both* the depression and the anxiety. I used my coping strategies to create four categories of support, which I have summarized on the following pages. These categories are: *physical support, mental/emotional support, spiritual support*, and most importantly, *people support*.

Putting together a survival plan did more than help me cope. In designing and carrying out this program, I became "the captain of my ship," an empowering move for someone who felt powerless. As Pat later reflected, "When you made the decision to do more, I saw a glimmer of hope in your eyes."

Here, then, is the plan we created.

A Daily Survival Plan for Responding to Depression/Anxiety

What follows is a brief outline of my daily survival plan. I have rewritten it in the second person so that you can adapt it to your individual needs. Remember, the goal is to identify coping strategies that will keep you safe and get you through each day until the pattern of the depression shifts.

A. People Support

Find a way to structure your daily routine so that you will be around people much of the time. If there is a day treatment program in your area, some form of group therapy, or depression support groups at your local hospital, attend them. Don't be embarrassed about asking for help from family members or friends. You are suffering from an illness, not a personal weakness or defect in character.

B. Physical Support

1. Exercise is one of the best ways to elevate and stabilize mood as well as improve overall physical health. Pick an activity that you might enjoy, even if it is as simple as walking around the block, and engage in it as often as you can (three to four times a week is ideal).
2. Eat a diet that is high in complex carbohydrates and protein, avoiding foods such as simple sugars that can cause emotional ups and downs.
3. Adopt a regular sleep schedule to get your body into a routine.
4. Take your medication as prescribed. Check with your health care professional before making any changes in dosage. Be patient and give the medicine enough time to work.

A Daily Survival Plan for Responding to Depression/Anxiety

C. Mental Support

Monitoring self-talk is an important strategy in helping to stabilize one's mood. Although you may not be able to control the depression and anxiety, you may be able to modify the way you think about your symptoms. You may wish to work with a therapist who specializes in cognitive therapy.* He or she can help you to replace thoughts of catastrophe and doom with affirmations that encourage you to apply present-moment coping strategies. Perhaps the most powerful thought you can hold is "This too, will pass."

D. Spiritual Support

If you believe in God, a Higher Power, or any benevolent spiritual presence, now is the time to make use of your faith. Attending a form of worship with other people can bring both spiritual and social support. If you have a spiritual advisor (rabbi, priest, minister, etc.), talk with that person as often as possible. Put your name on any prayer support list(s) you know of; don't be bashful about asking others to pray for you. The universe longs to help you in your time of need.

Because of the disabling nature of depression, you may not be able to implement all of these strategies. That is okay. Just do the best you can. Do not underestimate the power of intention. Your earnest desire to get well is a powerful force that can draw unexpected help and support to you—even when you are severely limited by a depressive illness.

---

* Please see pg. 181 for information on cognitive and other forms of therapy used to treat depression. A sidebar on cognitive distortions also appears on pg. 165.

People Support

The centerpiece of my survival strategy involved being around people. Interacting with other human beings drew me out of my tormented inner world and gave me something external to focus on. Talking with others was often the only intervention that would calm me down in the midst of a major anxiety attack. Like a screaming infant who is held by his mother, I found human contact tranquilizing and soothing.

My sense of connection with people also gave me a reason not to harm myself. I did not want to afflict my friends and family with the anguish that would result from my self-imposed departure. Kim, a lifeguard at the pool where I swam, agreed with my thinking. "Other people are a good reason to stay alive," she affirmed.

Knowing the curative effect of human caring and connection, I committed myself to attending day treatment. Unfortunately, getting to the clinic was not so simple. Like many people who suffer from depression, my symptoms were most severe in the morning. Oftentimes I would wake at 6:00 a.m., paralyzed by fear and overwhelmed by anxiety. To deal with my immobility, I asked five of my friends if they would each pick a day of the week to call me and roust me out of bed (hearing a caring person's voice on the other end of the telephone line served as a natural tranquilizer). The plan worked beautifully, and on those days when I was totally incapacitated, my friend Christine would drive me to day treatment. Instead of being home pacing the floors and hitting myself, I had a place to go where being around others ensured that I was safe.

In addition to group therapy, the other cornerstone of day treatment was my individual therapy, which took place on Tuesdays and Thursdays. These sessions did not consist of the usual insight-oriented psychotherapy. Being in *survival mode,* my goal was to focus on present-moment coping strategies. For example, I often entered Pat's office in the middle of a full-blown anxiety attack and spent the session pacing the floor while Pat gently coaxed me into taking a Klonopin. In this way, Pat functioned as a cheerleader, encouraging me from the sidelines, even though she could not directly influence the outcome of the game.

Attending day treatment was like going to a regular job—except here the task was to get well. My "co-workers" suffered from a wide range of mental disorders—depression, anxiety, manic-depression, schizophrenia, multiple-personality disorder and PTSD (post-traumatic stress disorder). The patients at day treatment did not fit the stereotype of "crazy people" that I had been taught as a child. These were brave souls who struggled against powerful and deadly brain disorders. They were my comrades in healing, and together, we formed a "brotherhood of pain."

Many of my fellow group members lived on SSI (supplemental security income) or SSD (social security disability) while Medicare paid for their therapy.* (I frequently wondered where the wealthy depressives went for help.) My friends commuted to the clinic on the bus, often traveling many hours over long distances. Some were homeless and were forced to live in whatever transition shelters would accept them. (I, who owned my own home, felt like Bill Gates in comparison.) Suddenly I realized that our celebrity-obsessed culture had it all backwards—that these nameless souls, stigmatized by their poverty and mental illness, were our true heroes—for they possessed what Woody Allen, in the opening lines of the film "Manhattan," rightly called the most important human attribute—courage.

Day treatment was a true life raft that kept me afloat during the most critical period of my illness. The program's only limitation was that it did not provide 24-hour care. Groups ended at 3:30 p.m. on Monday through Thursday, and 2:30 p.m. on Friday. Since Joan and my friends were all working, I needed to find additional support for the rest of the afternoon. The solution came in the form of Terry, a home health aide whom I located through an agency in the Yellow Pages.** Terry was a guardian angel who stayed with me on weekday afternoons and guided me through various mundane tasks

---

* More information about financially surviving a mental illness can be found in Part Two, Section 7.

★ ★The cost of hiring a home health aide can be reasonable, about $10 to $12 an hour.

that kept me focused—i.e., cleaning the house, balancing my check-book, mailing books to my readers, buying vegetable starters for the garden, taking a leisurely hike in Forest Park, and so on.

Weekends were also a challenge because they lacked the structure that day treatment provided. I organized my time as best as I could, asking Joan and my friends to take "shifts" as my caretaker (the task was too big for any one person). Walks in nature alternated with car drives along the Columbia River Highway, games of Scrabble, piecing together jigsaw puzzles and watching movies (when I could focus). Since it is extremely demanding to be around some-one who is emotionally and physically agitated, I will always be grateful to those people who displayed saint-like patience and understanding in the midst of my ordeal.

Support is critical in helping people to cope with all kinds of extreme circumstances. Survivor researcher Julius Siegal emphasizes that communication among prisoners of war provides a lifeline for their survival. And for those who are prisoners of their inner wars, support is equally crucial. In chronicling his own depressive episode, novelist Andrew Solomon wrote:

> Recovery depends enormously on support. The depres-sives I've met who have done the best were cushioned with love. Nothing taught me more about the love of my father and my friends than my own depression.*

Physical Support

The second aspect of my daily survival plan consisted of find-ing ways to nurture my physical body.

1) **Exercise**. Research has shown that regular exercise can im-prove mood in cases of mild to moderate depression. In the midst of my clinical depression, exercise provided a decided, if only tempo-rary reprieve from my emotional torment. For years my favorite physical activity had been swimming; now it became a cornerstone

---

* Andrew Solomon, "Anatomy of Melancholy," *New Yorker,* January 12, 1998. Volume 73, Number 42, pg. 51.

of my survival strategy. My 9:00 a.m. swim helped calm my morning anxiety and prepared me for day treatment. The evening swim elevated my mood and alleviated whatever residual anxiety was still present. When the attacks were particularly bad, I would swim 30 to 40 laps until I collapsed in exhaustion.

On weekends I exercised by taking hikes in the Columbia Gorge, around Mt. Hood, or in Portland's beautiful Forest Park. Although walking in the woods did not eliminate the depression or anxiety, it provided a safe structure in which I could physically burn off a portion of my distress.

2) **Eating and sleeping**. To stabilize my emotions, I ate a diet high in complex carbohydrates and protein (fish, chicken, vegetables, whole grains, pasta, whole wheat breads, potatoes, yogurt, etc.) and avoided foods, such as simple sugars, that produce mood swings. Fortunately, loss of appetite was not one of my symptoms, and so I ate regularly.

Although my prior depressive episodes had been marked by severe insomnia (few things are as debilitating as waking up at 3:00 a.m. and not being able to get back to sleep), this time I was able to rest, thanks to small doses of the antidepressant Elavil as well as the antianxiety drugs Klonopin and Ativan. This allowed me to keep a regular sleep schedule, which helped my body get into a rhythm.

On those nights when I experienced "early morning awakenings" (a classic symptom of depression), I reminded myself that no one ever died of insomnia. If I couldn't fall asleep with 20 minutes, I would get up and read (if I could focus), walk around the block, watch some television, or do some simple housework. Within an hour I was usually back to sleep.

3) **Medication**. While antidepressants did little to alleviate my depression, I learned to use the drug Klonopin to manage my anxiety. Klonopin is an antianxiety medication which is a member of the benzodiazepine family that includes Xanax, Ativan, Valium, Librium, etc. Despite my fears of getting hooked on the drug, I soon realized that the benefits of taking Klonopin (i.e., containing my anxiety) outweighed the risks—depression combined with anxiety

is more likely to result in suicide. Thus, when my anxiety began to escalate, I ingested a half milligram of Klonopin and was guaranteed two to three hours of temporary relief. Although I sometimes felt a bit groggy, being sedated was preferable to jumping off a bridge.

Mental/Emotional Support

Although I could not always control the painful symptoms of depression and anxiety, I could influence the way I thought and felt about those symptoms.

1) **Monitoring self-talk**. Monitoring one's self-talk is an integral strategy of cognitive-behavioral therapy, a talk therapy widely used in treating depression. The Catch 22, of course, was that the part of me that was supposed to do the monitoring—my thinking self—was itself diseased. I felt like a legless man who is told that the only way to save his life is to get up and walk.

Fortunately, before the onset of my illness I had spent eight years writing books and articles on the subject of positive self-talk. With Pat's help, I used a process from my book *Words That Heal* to create specific affirmations that would counter the all-too-frequent thoughts of gloom and doom that dominated my brain. For example, the statement "My depression will never get better" was replaced by the affirmation "Nothing stays the same forever" or "This, too, will pass." (I'll say more about this process in Chapter Five.)

Switching from negative to positive self-talk was a process that occurred once, twice, sometimes ten times a day. Since the depressed brain tends to see life through dark-colored glasses, monitoring my inner dialogue proved to be a constant and unending challenge.

2) **Keeping a mood diary**. One of the survival techniques I used to stay alive in my hell was to keep track of my anxiety and depression on a day-to-day basis. To this end, I created a daily mood scale.

Somehow, the simple act of observing and recording moods gave me a sense of control over them. I also used the mood diary to track my reactions to pharmaceutical drugs and to record daily thoughts and feelings. This ongoing log served as an important

Daily Mood Scale

1-10 Depression Scale	1-10 Anxiety Scale
8-10 despair, suicidal feelings	8-10 out-of-control behavior, hitting, rhyming voices
6-7 feeling really bad, at the edge	6-7 strong agitation, pacing
5 definite malaise, insomnia	5 moderate worry, physical agitation
3-4 depression slightly stronger	3-4 mild fear and worry
1-2 minorly depressed mood	1-2 slight fear and worry
0 absence of symptoms	0 absence of symptoms

progress report, both for myself and for my healthcare providers. It also provided an operational definition of recovery—my psychiatrist defined my getting well as seeing both the depression and anxiety ratings decrease to a score of "2" or below for six consecutive weeks. As my mood scale for the month of January 1997 indicates, however, I was light years from that goal (see following page).

3) **Venting when I need to**. Part of surviving meant being able to express my feelings—especially anger and grief about my plight. With Pat's encouragement, I vented my rage and fury through yelling, pounding a pillow, or painting my feelings in art therapy.

Later I learned that the body's immune system is actually strengthened by expressing feelings—and that *both* positive (joyful) and so-called negative (sad/angry) feelings are *equally therapeutic*. There is something about catharsis—giving full expression to one's deepest feelings of anguish—that is good for us.* Perhaps that is why the Book of Psalms contains as many lamentations as songs of praise.

4) **Being compassionate with myself**. As part of my emotional self-care, it was important to release the toxic feelings of blame, guilt or shame that are so often felt by a person who is depressed. As Pat reassured me, "Depression is an illness, like diabetes or heart

---

* Moyers, Bill, *Healing and the Mind*, Doubleday, New York, 1993, pp. 197-99.

January Mood Diary

Date	D	A	D = Depression; A = Anxiety
Jan 1	6	2	
Jan 2	6	4	Interview at OHSU hospital to see if I should go in.
Jan 3	4	4	
Jan 4	9	6	
Jan 5	9	3	Take Lithium; go on hike and feel worse.
Jan 6	2	4	
Jan 7	9	10	I call Menninger Institute in Kansas to see about long-term stay.
Jan 8	4	2	
Jan 9	4	10	
Jan 10	4	8	Get acupuncture in the morning; it does not last.
Jan 11	10	8	
Jan 12	4	9	
Jan 13	3	10	Major anxiety attack at the pool; take Klonopin.
Jan 14	8	10	
Jan 15	10	8	
Jan 16	10	9	Suicidal feelings. On the verge of hospitalization.
Jan 17	6	8	
Jan 18	5	2	Best day in a month because of support; spend day with Kathleen, Judy and Joan.
Jan 19	8	4	
Jan 20	5	6	
Jan 21	6	10	How long can I take this?
Jan 22	8	8	
Jan 23	8	10	
Jan 24	8	2	Start out anxious. Take Klonopin and go into depression which is just as bad.
Jan 25	2	7	
Jan 26	5	9	Superbowl Sunday. Spend day at LEC for support.
Jan 27	2	5	
Jan 28	5	2	
Jan 29	5	1	
Jan 30	3	1	Best day in three months. Spend time with friends.
Jan 31	1	1	Stayed home from day treatment; opened mail and did finances. Went to look for a kitten to adopt.

disease. It is not caused by a personal weakness or a defect in character. It is not your fault that you have this disorder. "

Once again I turned to the affirmation process. Whenever I started to judge myself for being depressed I would repeat, "It's not my fault that I am unwell. *I am actually a powerful person residing inside a very sick body.* I am taking good care of myself and will continue to do so until I get well."

5) **Focusing on the little things**: One day I asked Pat, "If all I am doing is trying to survive from day to day, how do I find any quality to my life?"

"The quality is in the little things," she replied.

How true! Shortly after Pat's comment, Portland was unexpectedly blessed with a sunny day. As I beheld with awe and wonder the magnificent pinks and red hues of the sunset, I recalled the words of poet Robert Browning—"God's in his heaven; all's right with the world!" The experience was made all the more poignant by its transitory nature; I knew that in a matter of hours my depression would return, and I would be cast back into outer darkness.

In another instance, a friend and I spent an evening listening to the celestial chants of the Taize monks, founders of an intentional spiritual community located in the south of France. I was particularly moved by one refrain:"*Within our darkest night, you kindle the fire that never dies away, that never dies away...*" As my voice merged with the voices of the audience, I was momentarily catapulted into ecstasy. Like a trapeze artist balanced on the high wire, I stood suspended above the abyss of my suicidal thoughts, safe from harm.

Having moments like this was akin to making deposits into an "emotional bank account." When I sank back into my depression I would draw upon my stored memories and affirm that life could still be beautiful, if only for an instant. *

---

* Although I have described the pain of depression as "seemingly unrelenting," there were tiny moments of respite. Every now and then a day or two of relief from the intense pain would offer me a time to relax, recoup, and feel a tiny bit of hope. If the pain were 100 percent continuous, no one would survive a clinical depression.

6) **Adapting to the cyclical nature of the illness.** Another adjustment I had to make was understanding the up and down nature of my depressive illness. There were two levels at which this occurred. First, I observed that days of intense anxiety would alternate with those of immobilizing depression.

Second, like the person with a chronic physical disease such as cancer, I came to learn that periods of progress and recovery were often followed by unwanted setbacks. Such relapses were particularly dangerous, for my accompanying disillusionment led to despair and suicidal thinking. To counteract these thoughts I trained myself to say, "One day, the respites will last. One day, they will turn into a genuine recovery." I also reminded myself of Dougal Robertson's famous counsel from his manual describing how he and his family survived thirty-eight days lost at sea. Robertson wrote, "*Rescue will come as a welcome interruption of the survival voyage.*"

Spiritual Support

The spiritual aspect of my struggle centered around a single word—FAITH. I wanted desperately to believe that my suffering had meaning and purpose, and that one day it would end. The irony was that I had authored a number of spiritual self-help books which provided readers with healing affirmations and spiritual encouragement in the face of fear, doubt and despair. Over the past decade, I had received hundreds of letters and phone calls from people who testified that my words had helped them to overcome a variety of physical and emotional challenges. "Read your own books!" my friends would tell me. I did so from time to time, but whatever comfort I derived from the passages was drowned out by my pain which gave evidence to the conviction that God had truly abandoned me.

Despite my absence of faith, I began to attend church again. My place of worship was the Living Enrichment Center (LEC), a large, nondenominational metaphysical New Thought church located in Wilsonville, Oregon. It taught many principles of the Unity

School of Practical Christianity, whose philosophy I had studied for twenty-five years.* Like day treatment, attending LEC gave structure to my day and provided me with a community of like-minded people where I could hear messages of hope and inspiration that I had once believed.

To help bolster my waning faith, one of the ministers at LEC suggested that I take up an old hobby—gardening. On the day I planted my garden, I was so agitated that three people had to steady me while I sowed the seeds in the fertile soil. Nonetheless, the message I gave the universe was clear: "I expect to be alive in the fall to reap the harvest."

❀ ❀ ❀ ❀

These, then, were the main components of my "daily survival plan." Like a soldier on the battlefield, my primary job was to keep myself alive until the end of the day. Here is an example of how this strategy worked during a typically hellish twenty-four hours.

A Day in the Inferno
"I have developed a new philosophy...I only dread one day at a time."
Charlie Brown

The phone rings once, twice, three times. I reach to pick it up. "Rise and shine!" sings the cheery voice. "It's your friend Christine with your daily wake-up call."

As I emerge from my oblivion, I quickly scan my body for signs of agitation. I feel my left leg starting to twitch, the first sign of an oncoming anxiety attack. I take a few deep breaths and attempt to relax, but it's like trying to maintain my ground in the face of a charging bull.

"I think I'm going to need some help. Could you drive me to day treatment?" I ask feebly.

"Sure," my friend replies. "I'll be right over."

---

* The Unity School of Practical Christianity was founded by Charles and Myrtle Fillmore in 1889. It was formed to teach how the principles of the Old and New Testaments can be practically applied to helping people live fuller, more abundant and joyful lives.

Depression Life-Raft Card

At Pat's suggestion, I wrote down some of my main survival strategies on a three-by-five card and carried it around in my pocket. Reading the card helped me to stay on task and keep me focused in the present, instead of catastrophizing about the future. Today, I still refer to the crumpled card when I feel myself losing my center.

I am surviving one day at a time.
I do this by practicing these self-care and self-nurturing strategies:

- I follow a routine.
- I go to day treatment.
- I do deep breathing.
- I say my affirmations.
- I eat three meals a day.
- I take my daily swim.
- I see my therapist and psychiatrist.
- I take walks around the block.
- I talk on the phone with my friends.
- I socialize as much as I can.
- I go for my weekly massage.
- I take my Klonopin.
- I pray for healing.
- I tell myself "This, too, shall pass."

As Christine hangs up, the agitation becomes so strong that I can no longer lie in bed. I hurriedly get up and begin to pace the floor. It is the start of another day in hell.

Knowing that Christine is on her way helps to calm me a little. Still, my body is shaking as I struggle to dress, so I take half a milligram of Klonopin with some orange juice. Soon, Christine arrives and drives me to the community pool, where she waits in the lobby while I take my morning swim. Because my anxiety is high, I thrash about in the lap lane, barely avoiding a collision with oncoming swimmers. After ten minutes of frenetic activity, I jump into the hot tub. The warm, relaxing waters add to the sedating effects of the Klonopin. I'm glad that Christine is driving.

I arrive at day treatment in time for the 10:30 a.m. goals group. I sit through the meeting in a daze. Sedation is better than agitation. Then in the 11:30 a.m. medication group, the Klonopin wears off, and I start to feel the initial sensations of an anxiety attack. In a few minutes my body becomes so agitated that I start rocking to and fro like an autistic child.

"Christ!" I think to myself. "I was starting to calm down, and now this has to happen. It's futile. I'll never get better." With each new catastrophic thought, I feel myself being dragged into the mire of hopelessness and despair.

Suddenly a voice in my head cries out, "CANCEL! CANCEL!" I realize what my mind is doing and switch gears to repeat my affirmations.

"This attack will not last forever."

"I've been here before and have survived."

"I can get through this."

"I have options. I can take a Klonopin, talk to a staff person, or walk around the block."

Fortunately, we are about to go to lunch, which is served at the hospital next door. Our group marches rank-and-file to the hospital lounge, where I engage in my daily ritual of doing the newspaper crossword puzzle to distract myself from my pain. At 12:30 p.m. the receptionist asks me to stop, and our group files into the lunchroom. Along the way, we pass the barbed-wire courtyard of the psychiatric ward where I once resided. I wave at the patients, some of whom I recognize, knowing that I could rejoin them at any time.

At lunch, the hospital food is atrocious, but the fellowship is healing. I enjoy the one-on-one interactions with a counselor and a fellow patient. At a quarter past the hour we are asked to leave the lunchroom. The next group starts at 1:30 p.m., but with a new anxiety attack coming on, fifteen minutes seems like an eternity. How will I contain myself without losing control? I grab a patient, saying "I can't be alone right now. Please walk with me." And he agrees.

After I ingest a second Klonopin, the afternoon sessions go a bit smoother, and at 3:30 p.m. Christine picks me up and drives me to my weekly massage. My massage therapist lives and works in a houseboat on the shores of the Willamette River. During the session, I am soothed by the gently lapping waves and the singing of the birds. For the next forty-five minutes, I experience a respite from the pain.

All too soon I am awakened from my reverie by the sound of Raeanne's voice, telling me it is time to leave. "No!" I protest. "I want to lie here forever." Moments later, a gentle nudge tells me that I must make room for the next client. I quickly dress and walk along the moorage back to the shore. The colors of the sky are a thousand shades of indigo blue, and the clouds look like elephants; I feel as if I am on a drug—which I am. I don't like the side effects of these antidepressants.

Christine drives me home. After thanking her, I go inside to check my schedule. At 6:00 p.m., I will take my evening lap swim and then have dinner with my friend Ann. What will I do for the next hour? Unstructured time is the enemy; I can't be alone with the anxiety right now. I call the Metro Crisis Line and explain my predicament. Talking to someone gives me a focus and decreases my agitation. Human contact is my salvation.

By 6:00 I am calm enough to drive myself to the community center's swimming pool. As I begin my second lap swim of the day, I feel the Klonopin wearing off. To cope with the anxiety, I synchronize the rhythm of my strokes and my breathing to a 4-4 beat, using my affirmation to fend off despairing thoughts:

"I am peace-ful, I am peace-ful, I am calm."
1 2 3 4,   1 2 3 4,   1 2 3 4.
"I am peace-ful, I am peace-ful, I am calm."
1 2 3 4,   1 2 3 4,   1 2 3 4.

It takes two repetitions of my affirmation to swim one length of the pool; four repetitions equals one lap. As the laps unfold, my nervous system unwinds. My brain releases a few endorphins. I am swimming not for my health, but for my life.

After my swim, I eat dinner with my friend Ann and watch an intriguing episode of "Mystery!" on PBS. Like many people who suffer from depression, I am most anxious and depressed in the morning and feel calmer as the day progresses. On this particular evening, the black cloud lifts and I actually feel normal again. Later, as I drift off to sleep, I pray that my newfound peace will carry over into the morning. "Maybe this is the turning point," I think. "Maybe tomorrow will bring my salvation."

But like Bill Murray's character in the movie *Groundhog Day*, I awake at dawn to find myself in the all-too-familiar anxious and depressed state. It's time to tread fire all over again.

❂ ❂ ❂ ❂

As I have shared in this account, my battle to survive was waged not just day by day, but hour to hour and minute to minute. Like a volatile stock market, my psyche was subject to unpredictable episodes of anxiety and depression which rained down upon me like showers blowing in from the Oregon coast. As each downpour subsided, I was granted momentary relief—until the next front came in. Because I never knew when an anxiety attack would strike, I had to be ready at a moment's notice to readjust my plans (quite a lesson in learning to be flexible!).

Living this way was quite draining. I felt as if I were at the mercy of a strong undertow dragging me out to sea. I would struggle with all my might to swim a few strokes towards shore, only to be pulled back towards the ocean by the overpowering current. By the end of the day I was run down and exhausted, which at least helped me fall asleep. But as the constant battle against the unrelenting black tide began to wear me down, I wondered whether the struggle was really worth it. Soon, my rhyming voices had composed a new verse: "Madness or suicide, it's yours to decide."

"Melancholia," by Albrecht Durer

CHAPTER FOUR

MADNESS OR SUICIDE, IT'S YOURS TO DECIDE

"The pain of depression is quite unimaginable to those who have not suffered it, and it kills in many instances because its anguish can no longer be borne. The prevention of many suicides will continue to be hindered until there is a general awareness of the nature of this pain."
William Styron

*"I am the wound and the knife!...
Victim and hangman alike."*
Charles Baudelaire

P hilosopher Albert Camus once wrote that the only real philosophical question to ask is whether or not to kill yourself. To a person suffering from depression, however, the question of suicide is not academic. The pain of depression is intense, seemingly ever-present, and it feels like it will never end. Being clinically depressed can be compared to having an ongoing nightmare where the only way to end the dream is to annihilate the dreamer. According to the National Institute of Mental Health, 15 percent of those diagnosed with a major depressive disorder who are not treated (or who fail to respond to treatment) will end their lives by suicide (this is 35 times the normal rate).* People with serious illnesses such as cancer and heart disease do not kill themselves in large numbers; depressed people do.

---

*This statistic comes from the National Institute of Mental Health. Suicide in America kills more people (about 32,000 a year) than homicide. Comparing this figure to 43,000 breast cancer deaths per year and 42,000 driving fatalities, one realizes that suicide is a major undiagnosed health problem in this country. Moreover, for every one person who commits suicide, sixteen attempt it, which translates to 500,000 attempts per year, or one every minute.

Many theories exist that attempt to explain the motivation for suicide. Freud postulated a death instinct. Others have suggested that man is endowed with "a drive to destruction." But to anyone who has experienced suicidal pain, the explanation is so simple, so self-evident, that it requires neither psychiatric nor psychological jargon. Death is chosen because suffering is so acute, so agonizing, so intolerable, that there comes a time—depending on the individual's tolerance for pain and the available support—that *ceasing to suffer* becomes the most important thing. This "aggregate pain model" of suicide is supported by the DSM-IV in its diagnostic section on major depression:

> The most serious consequence of a major depressive disorder is attempted or completed suicide. Motivations for suicide may include a desire to give up in the face of *perceived insurmountable obstacles* or an intense wish to end an *excruciatingly painful emotional state* that is perceived by the person *to be without end*. [Emphasis added]

During my dark night, I met a woman who was battling cancer. She wrote a poem about her struggle and her hope for recovery called "The Crawl Through Hell."

> So I crawl. Slowly I crawl. I inch my way through hell.
> Count the days. Each one is less to endure.
> Each day I am closer to the end.
> Back to the world. Back to life.
> Life is the light at the end. The tunnel will end.
> It is long but it has an end.*

To the depressed person, however, there is no light at the end of the tunnel. One does not crawl, because there is no *place* to crawl

---

* Used with permission. Excerpted from "The Crawl Through Hell," by Lynne Massie, published in the book, *The Buttercup Has My Smile*.

The wailing woman in Pablo Picasso's "Guernica"

to. Both ends of the tunnel are sealed off, and a sign on the door reads "No Exit." *

People in life-or-death survival conditions, such as being lost in the wilderness or being held prisoner of war, will dream and plan for the future in order to make their present conditions tolerable. The critically ill heart patient expresses his faith in his upcoming surgery by making a date to play golf six weeks after the operation. The imprisoned soldier dreams of being reunited with his wife and family. But the depressed person sees no viable future. There is nothing to look forward to, no dreams to fulfill, only the never-ending agony of the eternal present. In this context, I saw suicide not as an act of self-destruction, but as an act of self-love.

---

* Other images of hopelessness include: being trapped in a *dense black fog*: falling into a *bottomless abyss*; being locked in a *cold, dark dungeon*; sitting helplessly on a *melting ice floe*.

"No," I replied. "I don't believe it is a sin to commit suicide. I can't see why a loving and merciful God would punish someone for wanting to end his suffering."

"I'm sorry to hear you say that," Pat responded solemnly.

"Why?"

"Studies have shown that people who lack a moral or religious belief that suicide is wrong are more likely to act on the impulse."

Pat's analysis was true. Without a clear moral reason not to kill myself, my resolve to avoid suicide was only as good as the kind of day I was having. When graced with five or six hours without symptoms, I would think, "Maybe I'm in remission," and hope for the best. Too often, however, the respite would give way to a downturn in mood which brought with it the voices of doom—i.e., "Suicidal ideation is a hit across the nation" and "Madness or suicide, it's yours to decide." My choices seemed clear—either spend the rest of my life in hell (I believed I would live out my days in a state mental hospital), or put an end to the pain. Both outcomes were unacceptable, but I could not imagine a third alternative. In my anguish I cried out, "God! Show me another way—or at least give me some hope that another way is possible."

Meetings with Angels

"For we are saved by hope, but a hope that is not seen is not hope: for why would a man hope for that which he sees? But if we hope for what we see not, then do we with patience wait for it."
Romans 8:24-25

When Paul the Apostle wrote "We are saved by hope," he was not speaking in platitudes. Research has shown that the risk of depression is correlated more with *hopelessness* than with the intensity of the depression. It seems that we can endure all sorts of pain and suffering if we are even remotely optimistic that things will get better, or that there is a meaning to our suffering. Conversely, people with lesser degrees of depressive pain can become suicidal if they lose hope for a better future. Hopelessness, not sadness, is the antecedent to suicide.

If a way out of hopelessness did exist, I knew that I could not find it alone. Since my mind was trapped inside an "either-or" thought loop (as depicted by the rhyme "Madness or suicide, it's yours to decide"), it would take another person to lead me out of my mental prison.

The first counselor I approached was the Reverend Mary Manin Morrissey, the spiritual director of the Living Enrichment Center. Having known me from the early days of LEC, Mary took a special interest in my case.

"When you start to think that all is hopeless and that there is no solution except suicide," she said, "remind yourself that you are under the influence of a 'drug' called depression. This chemical imbalance is distorting your view of reality. Thus, you should not consider your feelings of hopelessness to reflect the truth of your situation."

"How do I prevent myself from giving in to the despair?" I asked.

"Try to think of your depression as a bridge instead of an abyss, a transition period instead of an end point. There is a universal law of polarity which says that all states of consciousness eventually *turn into their opposites*—i.e., pleasure becomes pain and pain becomes pleasure. Likewise, your suffering will one day turn into joy."

"That's impossible," I replied. "To me, depression is a bottomless black hole from which there is no escape."

"Then you will need to have the 'soul strength' or 'spiritual endurance' to stay in the pain until it repatterns and transmutes," Mary replied. "There is a Higher Power that is more powerful than any condition, including this depression. Maybe you had this breakdown so you would be forced to turn to God above anything else."

"Do you have any ideas on how to do that?"

"I know that you are a student of the Old and New Testaments," Mary replied. "Throughout the Bible, especially in the Book of Psalms, we hear about God's promises of deliverance. I suggest you read through the psalms and write down the verses that give you comfort or hope. You might even want to post them in your home where you will be sure to see them on a regular basis."

I was glad that Mary had faith in my recovery. In the days that followed, I took her suggestion to heart. I located a number of psalms, as well as inspirational quotations from my book *I Am With You Always,* and placed them in strategic locations in my office, bedroom, and the bathroom.* Looking for additional words of spiritual encouragement, I visited my local bookstore and spoke to the store owner, Lisa, about my ordeal. After listening intently, she walked over to the new arrivals table and pointed to a beautifully decorated book called the *Celtic Tree Oracle.* Lisa explained that the text describes the symbolism of the twenty-five letters of the Celtic alphabet. Each letter was associated with a tree or bush and was linked to a specific aspect of Celtic philosophy and cosmology. **

I have always felt an affinity to the tree kingdom, which I have nurtured through a quarter century of hiking in the forests of the Pacific Northwest. "Perhaps," I thought, "these trees could speak to me now." During the Middle Ages, it was customary for monks to open up the Bible at random, point to a passage, and receive guidance from it. "Why not do the same with this book?" I thought.

With a prayer on my lips I opened the volume and found myself staring at a page with the Celtic letter "Eadha"—which translates as "white poplar." The interpretation reads as follows:

> This tree is concerned with finding the spiritual strength and endurance to face the harsh realities that life presents to us, often over a long, debilitating period of time. It conveys a sense of the ability to endure and conquer. In this way it prevents death and the urge to give way under the impossible odds you must overcome. It is, therefore, of great assistance on the journey towards rebirth.

---

* The quotations I used can be found in Appendix A, "Promises of Deliverance."

** The Celts were an ancient tribal culture that inhabited the British Isles before the time of Christ. The Druids, the wise elders of the Celts, had a very special relationship with the natural world and considered trees to be particularly sacred.

The White Poplar

I was deeply moved by how clearly the reading depicted my predicament, as well by as the hope that it offered.

"This is an auspicious event," Lisa remarked after I showed her the passage. "It indicates that you want to live, and that spirit will help you to survive your ordeal." Lisa then photocopied the image of the poplar (as well as it's interpretation) so that I could carry it around as a symbol of protection. In future weeks and months, I looked at the picture and read the words of encouragement whenever I felt myself slipping.

My next visit was to a spiritual counseling service sponsored by a New Thought church in the Portland area. As I approached the space where the lay ministers were seated, I wondered how they would respond to my situation. If I have one criticism of New Thought spirituality or its psychological counterpart—the power of positive thinking—it is that it focuses exclusively on the good and neglects the dark side of life. And so it came as no surprise when the volunteer approached me with a cheery smile and said, "What shall we affirm today? Prosperity? Health? Happiness? Creative self-expression?"

"Actually, I was thinking of committing suicide," I replied.

With a combination of concern and amusement, I watched the volunteer's face turn white. "I think I should get my supervisor," she said, as she hurried out the door.

When the supervisor arrived, I assured her that this was no joke, that I really was depressed and needed help. Understanding the seriousness of my predicament, she sat down with the volunteer and recited two "positive prayers" which affirmed my capacity for healing and wholeness.

I find no fault with the church practitioner for being overwhelmed. Many friends, and even some psychotherapists, could not handle the intensity of my suicidal pain. Whenever I tried to share my suicidal thoughts, they would either get angry or abruptly change the subject. Only those people who were specifically trained to treat major depression, or who had "been there and back," could deal with my extreme condition.

One such person was a social worker named Judy. Having attempted suicide herself, she knew firsthand what goes on in the mind of a suicidal individual. Judy saw her clients, many of whom were in severe crisis, out of her small Victorian home, nestled in the Columbia River Gorge, twenty-five miles east of Portland. At our first meeting, she got right to the heart of the matter.

"*Suicide is not chosen,*" Judy said emphatically. "*It comes when emotional pain exceeds the resources for coping with the pain.*"

While speaking, Judy showed me a picture of scales to illustrate her point.

"You are not a bad or weak person," she continued. "Neither do you want to die; you just want to end your suffering."

I nodded in agreement.

"Your problem is that the scales are weighed down on the side of the pain. To get the scales back in balance, you can do one of two things: discover a way to reduce your pain, or find a way to increase your coping resources."

I explained that the former option seemed impossible.

"Then let me give you a coping resource that I'm sure you will find lifesaving," Judy said, as she handed me a pamphlet titled "How to Cope with Suicidal Thoughts and Feelings." I read it briefly and felt a mild sense of hope.*

"One more thing," Judy added. "I know you think that killing yourself will end your pain. But according to what I've read, consciousness continues even after death. Some people even believe that we reincarnate and return to earth in order to work out issues that we didn't resolve in this life. Perhaps there is no easy escape."

"What other option are you suggesting?"

"Stick around until you get better."

"Beating Michael Jordan in a one-on-one basketball game would be more likely."

"Crises, including suicidal ones, are time-limited," Judy countered. "Eventually, something's got to give. Provided you don't kill yourself, you will be around to experience the next chapter of your life."

"That's easy for you to say, but you're not in this hell. My intuition is telling me that I'm stuck here forever."

"Cognitively, you cannot help but think 'I am permanently frozen in horrible pain.' This is what depression is—a failure of the imagination. The chemical imbalance in your brain is preventing you from envisioning a positive future. Nevertheless, I want you to at least make room for the *possibility* that some unexpected good might grace your life."

---

* The information from this sheet, as well as other strategies for preventing suicide, can be found on pp. 213-17.

Sensing that I was stuck in unbelief, Judy leaned back in her chair and recounted the following parable.

> According to an ancient tale, a Sufi village was attacked and captured by a group of warriors. The king of the victorious tribe told the vanquished that unless they fulfilled his wish, the entire village would be put to death the following morning. The King's wish was to know the secret of what would make him happy when he was sad, and sad when he was happy.
>
> The village people constructed a large bonfire, and all night long their wise men and women strove to answer the riddle: what could make a person happy when he is sad, and sad when he is happy? Finally, sunrise dawned and the king entered the village. Approaching the wise ones, he asked, "Have you fulfilled my request?" "Yes!" they replied. The king was delighted. "Well, show me your gift." One of the men reached into a pouch and presented the King with a gold ring. The king was perplexed. "I have no need of more gold," he exclaimed. "How can this ring make me happy when I am sad, and sad when I am happy?" The king looked again, and this time he noticed that the ring bore an inscription. It read, *This, Too, Shall Pass.*

"It is an immutable law of the cosmos," Judy continued, "that the only constant in the universe is change. Haven't things happened to you that you never would have predicted?"

I nodded my head as I recalled the many experiences, both good and bad, that life had unexpectedly brought me.

"Since you cannot know your future with absolute certainty, then, allow for the possibility that a healing may be waiting for you around the corner. Pat tells me that you have already created a survival plan for yourself."

"I use it to get through each day."

"Good. Then stick with your strategy. Instead of fretting about the future, simply create the support that you need to stay alive, one day at a time. Please repeat this statement: "I am creating the support that I need to stay alive, one day at a time.""

"*I am creating the support that I need to stay alive, one day at a time,*" I said meekly.

"Good! Now I want you to repeat this affirmation every day. It doesn't matter whether you believe it; keep saying it anyway. I know that you are going to live." *

Judy's heartfelt sincerity and intensity left a deep impression on me. Although I felt hopeless, she seemed so confident. "Maybe she's right," I mused.

❀ ❀ ❀ ❀

Lisa, Mary and Judy were three guardian angels who came to me in my darkest hour. They presented a vision of healing to me that I could not see for myself. Although their faith in my restoration did not remove my physical and psychological pain, it did give me a reason to hang on. And as long as I stayed alive, a miracle was possible.**

---

* In addition to her counsel, Judy gave me her phone number as well as the number of the American Suicide Survival Line (1-888-SUICIDE) and said that I must call **anytime** I was in danger of harming myself. She also gave me a number of Internet sites on suicide prevention that proved to be amazingly helpful (see Appendix C).

** Suicide is not just my personal problem. It is the eighth leading cause of death for all Americans and the third leading cause of death for young people aged 15 to 24. On July 28, 1999, the Surgeon General of the United States officially recognized suicide as a national health crisis and issued "The Surgeon General's Call to Action to Prevent Suicide." To learn more about this important campaign to raise awareness about the causes and prevention of suicide, call the Office of the Surgeon General at 202-690-7694 (or visit the Web site at http://www. surgeongeneral.gov).

Prayer for Going Through a Dark Night of the Soul

This is a combination prayer and affirmation that I composed and read during my depressive episode. I hope that it may be a support to you as well.

1. I accept the fact that I am going through a dark night of the soul. I am dying to the me that I have known.

2. I embrace my pain fully and accept my present condition. I understand that on some level my soul needs this experience.

3. Although I feel all alone, I know that God is with me.

4. I realize that this experience has a purpose and teaching, and I ask spirit to reveal it to me.

5. Although I am in pain, I know that my travail will end, and that love, inspiration and direction will reenter my life.

6. I ask the universe to give me the strength, courage and guidance to see my way to my rebirth.

7. I give thanks for my situation just the way it is.

CHAPTER FIVE

BEARING THE UNBEARABLE PAIN

"The mind is its own place,
and in itself can make a Heav'n of Hell
or a Hell of Heav'n."
John Milton

I n the weeks following my conversation with Judy, the image of scales as a metaphor for suicide haunted and obsessed me. To put the scales (and my life) back in balance, I realized, I must increase my coping resources or find a way to reduce the pain.

"Reduce the pain?" I thought incredulously. "How can I find relief from agony this extreme?" I recalled what William Styron had told his daughter on the eve of his hospitalization—"I would rather have a limb amputated without anesthesia than to be suffering the kind of pain I am feeling at the moment."

It was at this point that an old college friend of mine serendipitously reentered my life. Teresa Keane was a registered nurse who worked at the Oregon Health Sciences University Medical School, where she taught stress reduction to patients with chronic pain. Her classes were based on the groundbreaking work of Jon Kabat Zinn, a meditation teacher featured in Bill Moyers' 1996 PBS documentary, "Healing and the Mind." Kabat Zinn teaches the Buddhist practice of "mindfulness meditation" to patients suffering from intractable physical pain. Through employing his techniques, they learn to alleviate not only their physical discomfort, but their accompanying emotional distress as well.

I met with Teresa in her office at OHSU, where I described the nature of my torment.

"Facing pain is a learned skill," Teresa responded. "When you are in a lot of pain, whether it is a migraine headache or suicidal torment, the pain dominates all of your awareness and becomes all-encompassing. It's hard to remember a time when the distress was absent, and it's hard to believe that it will ever go away. It's as if both past and present are blotted out, and you are left stranded in your present misery."

"At least you understand," I remarked.

"However," Teresa continued, "if you can release your judgment of your pain and just observe it, you will notice a very important fact about the nature of pain—pain comes *in waves!*"

Upon hearing these words, I remembered the grief I felt after my divorce. There were times when I was so overwhelmed by sorrow and loss that I could barely function. After a period, however, the pain and the longing let up, perhaps for a day or two—until the heartache returned and began the cycle all over again—pain turning into relief, which turned into more pain, followed by more relief, etc.

"This is the body-mind's built-in protective mechanism," Teresa explained. "If the pain were truly nonstop, you wouldn't survive. And so you are granted a few gaps in between the intense sensations to stop and catch your breath."

"But it feels like the pain is unrelenting," I protested. "If you were clinically depressed, you would understand."

"The key to reducing your perception of pain," Teresa continued dispassionately, "is to uncouple the sensations in your body *from the thoughts about them.*"

"What does that mean?"

There are two levels of pain that you are feeling," she explained. "The first level is physiological—the raw pain in your body. The second layer (and this is where you have some control) consists of how you interpret your experience. Perhaps you may be thinking, 'This torment is killing me,' or 'This will last forever,' or 'There is nothing I can do about it.' Each of these despairing thoughts creates a *neurochemical reaction* in the brain that creates even more distress. If

Detail from Michelangelo's "Last Judgement"
in the Sistine Chapel

you can learn to detach yourself from these judgments, much of the
pain that arises from them will diminish." *

"How do I do this?"

"Think of your anxiety or depression as a large wave that is
approaching you. As the wave makes contact, see if you can ride the
wave by focusing on *your breath*. Breathe *through* the sensations, breathing in and out while attending to the sound of your breathing. Don't
try to analyze what is happening, just breathe. It's not even about
getting through the day; it's about getting through each breath."

When I had worked as a salesperson in the corporate world, I
learned the skill of breaking large goals into manageable parts. Now
I discovered that one could divide pain into manageable parts. If I
couldn't handle getting through the day, I would try to make it

---

*In a 1997 study, volunteers were given a painful stimulus once, and then a suggestion
that the next stimulus would be either more painful or less so. As measured by PET brain
imaging, the volunteers experienced either greater or lesser pain from the new stimulus in
accordance with the type of suggestion they received. This suggests that the experience of
pain can be modified at the level of perception.

through the next hour; if an hour seemed too long, I set my sights on the next minute or second.

Teresa showed me another powerful technique to use with my self-talk when my pain became intense. Whenever I cried, "My pain is unbearable," Teresa would reply, "Tell yourself the pain is *barely* bearable."

"The pain is barely bearable," I repeated aloud. There was a shift and I felt it.

In another session I screamed, "I can't take it anymore!"

"You can *barely* take it," Teresa responded.

"I can barely take it," I replied.

Mental Illness as a Spiritual Practice

"Emotions are like waves;
Watch them come and go in the vast ocean of existence."
Neem Karoli Baba

Teresa was teaching me the practice of mindfulness, a spiritual practice of living in the present moment. In traditional meditation, when the mind wanders, one gently brings it back to a central focus (the breath, a candle, etc.). I was challenged to do the same, especially when, in response to intense emotional pain, I projected my present condition into the future using catastrophic self-talk that led to suicidal thinking—e.g., "If I have to put up with this suffering for the next 30 years, I might as well end my life now."

"Just return to the here and now," Teresa would say. "Over a period of time you can learn to relate differently to your pain. You can work with the pain and live around the corners of pain and develop your life around it. Eventually the turbulent emotional waters will become calm again. In the meantime, you can find inner stillness and peace right within the most difficult life situations."

"You've got to be kidding," I responded somewhat angrily. "How do you expect me to stay centered when the emotional equivalent of a migraine headache is pounding my skull?"

"Stop fighting the pain and see it as your life," Teresa calmly replied. "It doesn't mean you should *like* your discomfort. But there

Back to the Present

One of the most challenging aspects of practicing mindfulness was having to deal with my catastrophic thoughts and feelings about the future. These would inevitably arise when I suffered an unexpected anxiety attack or was engulfed by particularly bad depression. Self-statements such as "I can't go on like this" or "I won't live the rest of my life in this pain" further escalated my despair and hopelessness and drew me closer to the prospect of suicide.

As a way to keep me safe, Teresa and I devised a simple but powerful three-step technique for responding to catastrophic and despairing self-talk. I have rewritten these steps in a prescriptive fashion so that they can be used by others.

1. **Notice** what is happening. Become aware that your mind is dwelling on thoughts of catastrophe and doom. Identify the catastrophic thought—e.g., "I'll never get better."

2. **Realize** that these thoughts are not about the present but about the future. Since the future has yet to occur, it cannot harm you.

3. **Refocus** onto the present moment through positive self-talk and constructive action. For example, you might replace the statement "I'll never get better" with "What self-care strategy (calling a friend, going for a swim, taking an antianxiety medication, etc.) can I choose *right now* to get me through this period?" Then put the strategy into action.

I cannot recall how many times this simple process allowed me to endure a day, an hour, or a minute of intense pain. In giving me a way to manage my catastrophic (and potentially dangerous) thinking, this technique literally saved my life.

is something transformative that happens when we simply *allow* ourselves to experience our pain without trying to judge, change or resist it in any way. Let me show you."

At that moment, Teresa reached over and pressed a tender point between my right thumb and index finger (I later learned that it was a particularly sensitive acupuncture point).

"Ouch! That hurts," I protested.

"Breathe into the place in your body where you feel the pain," Teresa responded compassionately. "See if you can ride the waves of sensation as you would ride the ocean's waves. As you do this, notice how the experience of your pain begins to change."

I breathed into the soreness and observed that the pain in my hand softened and decreased, until I could hardly feel it.

"Good work," Teresa replied. "Now see if you can do the same with your emotional pain."

On days when my depression and anxiety fell below a "5" on the mood scale, Teresa's technique worked well. As I breathed "into" the pain of depression and stopped resisting it, the pain diminished. But during those all-too-frequent instances when the agony registered close to "10," I simply could not surrender. "Get the hell out of here!" I screamed at the hurt—and then felt guilty because I was not able to detach and "let go."

"This is not about right and wrong," Teresa responded. "It's about *struggle* and *practice*. It's about learning to cope—discovering which options work for you and which ones don't."

❁ ❁ ❁ ❁

Mindfulness meditation did not work all of the time, but it worked enough. The moments of peace it provided, when combined with intense exercise and small doses of the antianxiety drug Klonopin, interrupted the pain cycle sufficiently so as to make my suffering "barely bearable." *

---

* Those who have experienced childhood violence or sexual abuse may find that relaxation techniques such as deep breathing may elicit feelings of anxiety. If this occurs, consider practicing meditation or relaxation under the supervision of a trained therapist who can help you process these feelings.

CHAPTER SIX

OVERCOMING THE STIGMA
OF DEPRESSION

"The last great stigma of the twentieth century
is the stigma of mental illness."
Tipper Gore

"In the school of life, the best students get the hardest problems."
Anonymous

U p until this point, I have been describing the pain of depression as I experienced it on a physiological and emotional level. There existed a second level of distress that, though less primal, was nonetheless debilitating in its own way. This was the *guilt* and *shame* I felt about being depressed.

Despite the fact that such celebrities as Mike Wallace, William Styron, Patty Duke, Tipper Gore and Ted Turner have publicly shared their battles with depression or manic depression, the stigma of mental illness remains. After my first hospitalization, I remember the dilemma I faced in trying to explain my three-day absence to my employer. If I told the truth—that I was being treated for anxiety and depression—I stood a good chance of losing my job. Instead, I reported that I had been treated for insomnia at a sleep clinic.*

"Clinical depression is a medical condition, similar to diabetes or heart disease," my psychiatrist responded when I confessed how I had concealed my hospitalization. "We need to stop making depression a moral issue. Is the person with a disorder of the pancreas or the circulatory system weak-willed, lazy or defective? Of course not. And neither is the individual who suffers from depression."

---

* "60 Minutes" reporter Mike Wallace faced a similar predicament during his first episode of clinical depression. "Because I wanted to keep working," he explained, "I chose to keep my illness a secret."

Unfortunately, a recent survey taken by the National Mental Health Association revealed that 43 percent of Americans still believe that depression is the result of a weak will or a deficit in one's character. Many doctors also subscribe to the "defect in character" theory. Consider the observations of physician A. John Rush:

> Doctors are still reluctant to make the diagnosis [of depression] because they, too, feel like, "Oh you must have done something wrong. How did you get yourself into this pickle?" which sort of means the patient is to blame. It's okay if you have a neurological disease—Parkinson's, Huntington's, urinary incontinence, a busted spine because you got into an auto accident—but once you move up to the higher cortical areas, now you don't have a disease anymore; now you have "trouble coping"; now you have a "bad attitude." *

I have often wondered why it is so scary to be open about our frailties. With the revelation that depression and other forms of mental illness have a biological component, people should no longer feel that their symptoms are caused by personal inadequacies or a lack of willpower. On the contrary, only a *strong* and *courageous* person could bear and ultimately transform so much pain.

I believe that the stigma surrounding mental illness arises from living in a culture where feelings of vulnerability are considered weak and unacceptable. This is especially true for men who are raised with the injunction that "big boys don't cry"—i.e., it is not okay for men to be vulnerable and show their feelings.** This fear of being seen (by themselves and others) as vulnerable and weak, leads many

---

* As quoted in the chapter "Overcoming the Stigma and the Shame," from the book *On the Edge of Darkness: Conversations About Conquering Depression*, by Kathy Cronkite, New York, Doubleday, 1994, pg. 79.

** The price that men pay for being stoic, stuffing their feelings and holding the pain in, is depression. Family therapist Terrence Real says that when men are not in touch with their painful emotions, they may act them out through alcoholism, domestic violence, and other antisocial behavior. An example of this is the recent spate of mass shootings—all done by depressed men or boys.

men to lose touch with their own feelings and to avoid being in situations where strong emotion may be present. For example, the observant reader will note that thus far my entire support system has consisted of women. A good male friend who avoided me during my illness later confided, "When you were depressed, I was afraid to be around you for fear that I might 'catch' your depression." What he meant was that being in my presence might cause him to tap into his own *latent* depression, a proposition that was so uncomfortable, he had to split.

Women also suffer from this bias against feeling. If a woman works in a male-dominated field such as construction, policing, or law, she is forced into the same mold as men. Women attorneys or construction workers who cry are criticized or passed over for promotions, just as men in these professions would be. A woman working in a non-traditional field who feels and expresses her emotions is labeled as unstable, unreliable and weak. One woman police sergeant tells a story of being sent by the men on the force into a domestic violence situation on her first day at work, to see if she was "tough enough to be one of the guys." It was made absolutely clear that she should show no fear or sadness about the attack the batterer had made upon his wife and children.

Politics is another field, traditionally the province of men (now being entered by women), where vulnerability is unacceptable. In 1972, presidential candidate Edmund Muskie was considered unfit to hold office after he allegedly cried in public. Similarly, Thomas Eagleton, the Democratic vice presidential candidate in the 1972 election, was forced to exit the race when it became known that he had received ECT for the treatment of depression. I find it incredible that this bias still exists, given the fact that many great political leaders—Abraham Lincoln, Teddy Roosevelt, Eleanor Roosevelt, Joan of Arc, and Winston Churchill (who called his malady "the black dog")—suffered from depression.

Abraham Lincoln is a particularly intriguing example of someone who achieved greatness in spite of the fact that he experienced

Abraham Lincoln is one of many famous people
who have suffered from depression.

bleak, despairing periods of depression throught his life—no doubt
brought on by the early death of his mother and cold treatment at
the hands of his father. A typical depressive episode is described by
Karl Menninger in his book *The Vital Balance*:

> On his wedding day, all preparations were in order and
> the guests assembled, but Lincoln didn't appear. He was
> found in his room in deep dejection, obsessed with ideas
> of unworthiness, hopelessness and guilt. Prior to his ill-
> ness Lincoln was an honest but undistinguished lawyer
> whose failures were more conspicuous than his successes.
> This was when he was considered well—before his men-
> tal illness made its appearance. What he became and
> achieved after his illness is part of our great national
> heritage.*

---

* K. Menninger, M. Mayman and P. Pruyser, *The Vital Balance: The Life Process in Mental
Health and Illness*, New York, Viking Press, 1967.

In today's political climate, where image, style and sound bites are more important than substance, one wonders if someone like Lincoln, or other introverted American presidents such as Thomas Jefferson, could be elected. Clearly it is time to reassess our evaluation of what makes a leader.*

The Challenge of Being a Nobody

For many people, the stigma of being depressed is compounded by shame and guilt about not being a "productive member of society." The depressed person may become a "nobody" when his disability makes him unable to work or to earn a living. How, then, does an individual measure his self-worth when he or she is not working or producing?

This is the question I asked myself as I struggled to come to terms with not living up to the expectations of my cultural programming. I was the first-born son, raised in an upwardly mobile middle-class Jewish community where competition for entrance into Ivy League schools began in the third grade. Unlike my Catholic friends, who attended a nearby parochial school and were taught to avoid "the seven deadly sins," I learned that there was only one deadly sin—"not living up to one's potential." This potential, of course, was very specifically defined—unless you became a doctor, a lawyer, or ran your father's business, you were considered a failure. There were, of course, exceptions. One could always teach at Harvard, make a fortune on Wall Street or win the Nobel Prize. As long as the gods of Status and Recognition were served, our parents and teachers would be happy.**

Such pressure to produce necessarily takes its toll. I distinctly recall my sadness when, in the middle of my junior year in high school, a good friend of mine suddenly stopped coming to class.

---

* Even "spiritual" people get depressed. The Biblical figures of Moses, Saul, David, Elijah, Jeremiah, Jonah, Paul, and Jesus (in his humanness) experienced depression. David's laments are evidenced throughout the Book of Psalms.

** This reminds me of a joke in which a group of Jewish theologians were asked the controversial question, "When does life begin?" After debating among themselves, they concluded that a fetus is not viable until after it graduates from medical school.

Rumor had it that he had suffered a "nervous breakdown" and was whisked away to a special school in Connecticut. Understanding that other promising minds had likewise succumbed to mental illness was my only consolation as I filed for Social Security disability benefits at the age of forty-eight, while many of my classmates lived in half-million-dollar homes and earned six-figure incomes.

Lacking money, power and prestige (the standards by which I was raised to judge myself), my sense of failure and inadequacy continued to plague me. One day, I was invited to a potluck dinner, where I met an attractive woman who had just been hired as a professor at the prestigious Reed College, after having obtained her Ph.D. from Harvard. After describing her exploits in great detail, she asked the dreaded question—"And what do you do for a living?"

I paused for a moment to contemplate my response. Recalling my father's injunction to always tell the truth, I responded, "I attend day treatment and collect disability income."

The woman looked at me with a mixture of bemusement and pity before making a discrete exit. I felt as if someone had placed a name tag on my shirt—the kind you get when you attend a singles group or a self-help seminar—that read "Worthless." *

❈ ❈ ❈ ❈

This interaction (or lack of it) hammered home the question, "What happens to a person's self-esteem when a lifelong emotional disability such as clinical depression interferes with his ability to be productive in societal terms?" Like the former athlete who is confined to a wheelchair after a paralyzing accident, I had to accept my limitations and find a new way to define my existence. I knew from my spiritual studies that a human being's essential worth and goodness comes from who he is, not what he does. I understood that friends and family were working overtime to keep me alive, not

---

* Not living up to outer expectations can be deadly for some. In Japan, the shame and stress of recent job layoffs have caused suicide rates to reach record numbers. (Stephanie Strom, "In Japan, Mired in Recession, Suicides Soar," *New York Times*, July 15, 1999, pg. A1)

because of my degrees or my bank account, but because they loved me. Moreover, being down in the dumps had its advantages. Like the fallen hero in Bob Dylan's "Like a Rolling Stone," being stripped of my privilege dissolved my arrogance and made me a more humble and compassionate human being.

Still, given my programming, it was an ongoing struggle to validate myself in the absence of external markers. Then one day, one of the group members who knew of my struggle said:

> "Douglas, **who you are** is not a function of how much money you make."
> "Douglas, **who you are** is not a function of how many credentials you have."
> "Douglas, **who you are** is not a function of your vocational identity or occupational title."

My therapist Pat commented, "Sam has done a good job of defining who you are not. Can you find a positive way to describe who you are?

At that moment, I blurted out, "*Who I am is a spiritual being who is on this earth to grow in love and wisdom.*"

From then on, I strove to redefine my identity in non-achievement terms. For example, one day I noticed that I said a few kind words to a fellow patient at day treatment. Instead of taking that act for granted, as I usually might, I focused on it and valued it. Rather than dismissing it as a minor event (compared to doing something "really great"), I saw it as important.

Pat supported this attitudinal shift.

"Your brother may work on the 66th floor of an office building in Manhattan, but your 'work' right now is to heal from this illness, a much harder job than being a vice president of Citibank."

"How do you figure that?" I asked.

"Just managing to stay functional, given your level of pain, is a major achievement. I'm sorry that no one is giving you stock options for your display of courage. But the absence of financial reward does not invalidate the important work you are doing."

until the person actually takes it. In other words, you patients are all a bunch of guinea pigs." This comment was not pejorative—it simply conveyed the reality that finding the best medication can be a long and arduous process.

After much deliberation, the doctor I was seeing decided to start me on Prozac. That evening, I took my first dose, and within thirty minutes of ingesting the 10 milligram green-and-white tablet, my mind and body were consumed by angry and violent thoughts and feelings. I felt as if I wanted to kill my best friend. "What the dickens is going on?" I thought, as I struggled to get to sleep.

The next morning I awoke to find a strange woman in my living room. My housemate explained that she had appeared at 6:00 a.m., seeking refuge from her boyfriend, whom she claimed had threatened her with a kitchen knife. Fearing that my hostile thoughts had invisibly magnetized this disturbing visitation, I called my psychiatrist, who recommended that I discontinue the Prozac.

A few weeks later I decided to give Paxil a try, this time taking it in the morning. By the time I arrived at work, however, I felt as if I had received intravenous shots of double espresso. I felt so agitated that it took all of my effort and willpower to remain in my seat as I answered nonstop customer-service calls for the next six hours. I finished my shift in a state of total exhaustion.

The following day my manager took me aside. "Great work, Bloch!" he said enthusiastically. "You answered 25.67 telephone calls per hour, more than anybody in the bank's call center. What made you so efficient?"

I was going to suggest that the entire customer service department be put on Paxil, but thought better of it.

Finally, I gave Zoloft my best shot, taking it on a lovely summer's day hike in the Columbia Gorge. While it was less jarring to my system than Prozac or Paxil, it was still far too energizing. Great ideas came to me, but they raced by too quickly to be of any use. Not only my thinking, but also my speaking went into overdrive.

My friends complained that I acted like a manic depressive on speed. Three weeks later I decided to bag it.

I later discovered that the phenomenon I experienced is known as "SSRI overstimulation." It seems that certain anxiety-prone individuals may experience a transient excitation, often described as a speedy sensation, when they first take an SSRI drug such as Prozac or Zoloft. In some instances, this reaction can result in a full-blown panic attack!* Later I learned that starting out on minute doses of a medication can decrease the intensity of this stimulation. But given the quantities I was taking at the time, the side effects were simply too agitating for me to continue.

If At First You Don't Succeed

Now it was the winter of 1997 and I was struggling to dig myself out of a major depressive episode. Once again I began my search for the right chemical that would restore order to my deranged biochemistry. At the hospital and the day treatment center I attended, all of the clients were on drugs—usually an average of three to five different types of medication, which were constantly being readjusted and fine-tuned. Sometimes an entire regime would be stopped, and a host of new drugs would be tried. Many patients were periodically readmitted to the hospital so that the new medications could be carefully monitored. In the long run, all of this tinkering offered a tentative peace, and in some instances a marked improvement of mood.

Encouraged by these successes, I decided to give Zoloft another try, but with my anxiety at record highs, it was like pouring gasoline on a wildfire. I then turned to the older tricyclic antidepressants, which for many people are just as effective as the SSRIs, at one-tenth the cost.** Yet aside from Elavil, which sedated me so that I could sleep, they too failed to diminish my symptoms.

---

* Raskin, Valerie, *When Words Are Not Enough,* New York, Broadway Books, 1997, p. 99.

** Erica Goode, "New and Old Antidepressants Are Found Equal," *New York Times,* March 19, 1999, pg. A1.

Finally, it was on to the MAOI inhibitors, Nardil and Parnate, which are hardly used these days because of their dietary restrictions. Once again, I felt nothing except the side effects of a racing heart and some bizarre hallucinations. In total, I experimented with about fifteen antidepressants, including some the newer drugs such as Wellbutrin, Luvox, Serzone and Remeron—all of which failed to produce the expected results.

I specifically remember being jealous of the manic depressives at day treatment because they had a magic bullet—lithium—that miraculously evened out their moods. I found no such biochemical panacea that would heal my symptoms.

Looking for alternatives, I scoured the medical journals, but could only find scientific studies on the efficacy of the antidepressants I had already tried. They gave the encouraging statistic that 80 percent of people with depression could be treated with medication. "But what about the other 20 percent?" I wondered. If approximately 17 million people in the country suffer from depression, then 3.4 million are not helped by drugs.[*]

Only later did I run across two articles in the *New York Times* and *U.S. News and World Report* which showed me that I was not alone. Steven Hyman, director of the National Institute of Mental Health, was quoted as saying, "Given how common depression is, it is a *major public health threat* that 20 percent of people don't get more than a modest benefit from any of our therapies."[**] To deal with this unsolved problem, the NIMH has decided to sponsor its own clinical trial on treatments for "treatment-resistant depression" and will award a multimillion-dollar contract to the research team that offers the best-designed plan for a national study. [***]

---

[*] For those people who do not have success with traditional antidepressants, other options exist. Please refer to pg. 196, "Natural Alternatives to Prozac."

[**] As quoted in Schrof, Joannie M. and Stacey Schultz, "Melancholy Nation: Depression Is on the Rise, Despite Prozac. But New Drugs Could Offer Help," *U.S. News and World Report*, March 8, 1999, Volume 126, Number 9, pg. 57.

[***] Erica Goode, "Some Still Despair in a Prozac Nation: Depression Proves Tenacious for Sufferer and Doctor Alike," *New York Times,* July 29, 1999, pg. D1.

A Disastrous Side Effect

"Biological systems are incredibly complex.
Whenever you intervene, there are unintended consequences."
Gregory Bateson

"People vary greatly in their sensitivity to drugs.
One person's remedy may be another person's overdose."
Dr. Jay S. Cohen, from a report in the journal *Postgraduate Medicine**

The irony of my search for the right antidepressant is that it was a traumatic reaction to a medication that catalyzed my break-down.** Many psychiatrists were incredulous when I told them my story. "You can't get that ill on just 37.5 milligrams of Effexor," they insisted (therapeutic doses range from 150 to 350 milligrams a day). But I knew that what I experienced was real. Five months later, I had the good fortune to meet a Native American herbalist and M.D. who validated my story. "You've had a drug-induced mania," Terrona explained. "It's far more common than the experts are willing to admit."

Intrigued by her comments, I obtained a package insert and read the following contraindications: "Effexor is contraindicated in people known to be hypersensitive to it." What a Catch 22! How does one know if he is hypersensitive to a medication until he takes it?—and then it's too late. The warnings continued, "3% of patients discontinued the drug due to anxiety, nervousness and insomnia." This may seem like a small number—until you discover that you are among that three percent. I called the antidepressant's manufacturer to report my experience. The customer-service representative apologized for my inconvenience and assured me that she would add my report to the company's research findings. Meanwhile, I was left with the challenge of finding my way out of hell.

---

* Jay S. Cohen, "Ways to Minimize Adverse Drug Reactions: Individualized Doses and Common Sense Are Key." *Postgraduate Medicine*, Sept. 1999, v. 106, pg. 163 (7)

** I do not believe that the drug "caused" my depression; rather it significantly magnified the symptoms that were already present.

How Big a Dose? Ask the Patient

Before writing a prescription, doctors should give every patient a questionnaire to determine whether he or she needs the standard dose. Here some sample questions.

1. Are you sensitive to any prescription or nonprescription drugs?
2. How are you affected by alcohol?
3. Do some drugs make you tired or sleepy: cold or allergy remedies or antihistamines? Tranquilizers or anticonvulsants? Motion-sickness remedies or antinausea agents?
4. Do some drugs give you energy or cause anxiety or insomnia: coffee, tea, chocolate, other caffeine-like substances? Appetite suppressants (prescription or nonprescription)? Cold or allergy remedies or decongestants?
5. Have you ever had a reaction to epinephrine (adrenaline chloride, often injected by dentists along with pain-numbing medication)?
6. Have you every had any side effects from any other prescription or non-prescription drugs (like impaired memory or coordination, blurred vision, headaches, indigestion, diarrhea, constipation, dizziness, palpitations, rashes, swelling, ringing in the ears, other reactions)?
7. Overall, how would you describe yourself with regard to medication: Very sensitive? Not particularly sensitive? Very tolerant—i.e., you usually require high doses?

---

* Excerpted from Denise Grady, "Too Much of a Good Thing? Doctor Challenges Drug Manual," *New York Times*, October 12, 1999, pg. D1.

It is not my intention here to put down Effexor or any antidepressant. Research shows and experience demonstrates that the vast majority of people are helped by these medications. Hence, I would recommend that anyone who is suffering from clinical depression try them under medical supervision.

On the other hand, there is a downside to psychiatric drugs. These are very *powerful* psychoactive substances, that when given to an overly sensitive individual, can wreak havoc on the very brain chemistry they are intended to heal. Hence, anyone who is thinking of going on medication should locate a well-trained pharmacologist who is up to date on the latest research and can carefully monitor the drug's known and unknown side effects.

In addition, the informed consumer should always read the package insert to learn about potential contraindications (ask your pharmacist for a free insert). Although the toxic reaction I experienced was extreme, I do not believe it is unique. Such overreactions can best be prevented by starting with a *very low* dose of the medication, and then adjusting upwards. In addition, I have found that it is preferable to begin a new medication during the day. At night my defenses are down and my unconscious is open, making me more vulnerable to adverse reactions. I suspect that this may be true of a percentage of other people who suffer from depression and are prone to anxiety.

The Treatment of Last Resort

After it became clear that the drugs I tried had proved unsuccessful, I asked my psychiatrist for an explanation.

"You have a case of treatment-resistant depression," he said. (This is also known as refractory depression.)

"What does that mean?"

"It is a type of depression that is not helped by our available medications."

"If antidepressants don't work, is there another way to heal?"

"I would try ECT or prayer."

ECT (electroconvulsive therapy), commonly known as electric shock therapy, is the treatment of last resort for clinical depression. In ECT, the brain is stimulated with a strong electrical current which induces a kind of epileptic seizure. In a manner that is not clearly understood, this seizure rearranges the brain's chemistry, resulting in an elevation of mood.

Like many people, I was put off by the gruesome reputation of ECT (as popularized in the movie "One Flew Over the Cuckoo's Nest")—until I saw it heal my mother of a life-threatening depression. My partner Joan's aunt, who suffers from manic depression, was also stabilized by ECT, as were a number of patients at day treatment. I thought to myself, "If electricity can jump-start a stalled heart, why can't the same current be used to heal a sick brain?"

Intrigued, I consulted a number of medical journals and learned that ECT is very effective in certain types of major depression and mania.* Nonetheless, I was terrified at the prospect of having my brain zapped with a lightning bolt and then waking up with a blistering headache and not remembering what I had for breakfast. (One of the significant side effects of ECT is short-term memory loss, especially for events that occur around the time of the treatments.) Thus, I was in no way disappointed when the doctor who evaluated me for ECT said that because of my nervous system's hypersensitivity, he was reluctant to try the procedure.**

I returned to Dr. Stark with my findings.

"Medication doesn't seem to work, and I'm not considered a good candidate for ECT," I moaned.

"That leaves prayer," he replied.

---

* A more detailed description of how ECT works is found in Part Two, pg. 189, "Electroconvulsive Therapy, Beneficial or Barbaric?"

** I did not know it at the time, but there exists a "milder" version of ECT. In a procedure called RTMS (Rapid Transcranial Magnetic Stimulation) a powerful magnet is used to induce an electric current in the brain. See Part Two, pg. 195, for more information on this new treatment.

CHAPTER EIGHT

GOD IS MY ANTIDEPRESSANT

"Scientific prayer or spiritual treatment is really the lifting of your consciousness above the level where you have met your problem. If only you can rise high enough in thought, the problem will then solve itself."
Emmet Fox, "What Is Scientific Prayer?"

"Ask and you shall receive. Seek and ye shall find. Knock and the door shall be opened. For everyone who asks receives, and he who seeks finds, and to him who knocks, it shall be opened."
Matthew 7:7-8

Actually, I already was following Dr. Stark's advice. For the past four months, I had been placing weekly prayer requests in the prayer boxes at the Living Enrichment Center. Adele, one of the prayer volunteers, had taken a personal interest in my case and was writing back to me once a week. Concerned about the gravity of my condition, Adele contacted the Reverend Eddy Brame, head of pastoral counseling at LEC, and told her of my predicament. Shortly afterwards, I received a call from Eddy.

"When one of our congregants was dying of cancer," Eddy explained, "we decided to bring all of her support—her family, friends, minister, physicians, and social worker—together in one room. Their combined prayers created a powerful healing energy that allowed Carol to live far longer than anyone expected. I think that the same principle might work for you.

"Mary, myself, and members of the prayer ministry would like to schedule a meeting with you on Monday, July 14 at 4:00 p.m. in Mary's office. Can you attend and bring members of your personal support team?"

"Praying Hands" by Albrecht Durer

The invitation could not have come at a better time. By the early summer of 1997, I was truly desperate. My depressive episode was now in its tenth month, and during the prior ninety days my anxiety and depression had reached all-time highs—eclipsing the dark days of November and December. In pursuit of relief, I had tried every conventional and alternative treatment I could find, including:

- Sitting at the feet of, and being blessed by, two Tibetan monks who were disciples of the Dalai Lama.
- Receiving a soul retrieval, a shamanic healing, and a series of acupuncture treatments.
- Ingesting Chinese herbs, homeopathic remedies, megadoses of vitamins and a panoply of antidepressants.

Despite my concerted efforts at finding a traditional and/or alternative cure, I still remained trapped in the black hole of depression. "What have I got to lose?" I thought. I told Eddy that I would accept her invitation. I now had three weeks to prepare for what I believed was my last hope for survival.

Answered Prayers

Here is one of the many letters I received from the LEC prayer ministry in response to my weekly prayer requests.

Dear Douglas,   April 20, 1997

Thank you for trusting your prayer request to the Living Enrichment Center Prayer Ministry. We are praying with you and for you, knowing and accepting that God's grace is guiding you towards a complete healing from depression and anxiety. We see you making the best choices and with God's loving guidance, moving into health, joy, and vitality.

On a separate page we have enclosed an affirmation that can support you in knowing the truth. As we put our focus on God and the Divine qualities of wholeness, balance, creativity, peace and oneness, we know that transformation occurs. As you repeat your affirmation, know that there are many others supporting you in prayer.

Blessings,

Adele

Affirmation
My body is a holy temple, infused with Divine intelligence.
Every organ, cell and tissue is bathed in the revitalizing power of spirit.
The power to experience miracles is in me now.
I open my mind to the healing love of God.

The "God Meetings"

"We do not come to grace; grace comes to us."
M. Scott Peck, *The Road Less Traveled*

As the time of the meeting with the LEC ministers drew nearer, I suggested to my partner Joan that we spend a day in retreat at a Trappist monastery located in the small town of Lafayette, Oregon, twenty miles southwest of Portland. Thomas Merton had been one of my spiritual mentors and I hoped that spending time in his order might be a source of inspiration to me. It was one of those glorious Oregon summer days that almost compensates for the other nine months of interminable rain. We arrived at the monastery at midday, and spent the afternoon hiking the lovely grounds. Afterwards, I wandered into the library, where I stumbled upon an audio tape by ayurvedic physician Deepak Chopra, whose books on holistic health and spirituality were all the rage in the United States. In his talk, Chopra asserted that the brain had its own "internal pharmacy," as evidenced by its ability to manufacture painkilling endorphins.

"There really is such a thing as healing from within," I thought. "If only I could find a way to access my body's natural healing system." I walked to the chapel next door, got down on my knees, and prayed for such a healing.

The following day, Monday, July 14, did not begin auspiciously. I woke up in my normal agitated state and barely made it to day treatment for the morning groups. After lunch, I returned home, where I met Joan and my friend Stuart. At 3:00 p.m. we drove out to LEC, just avoiding Portland's daily rush hour traffic madness.

The Reverend Mary Morrissey's spacious office was located on LEC's ninety-five-acre campus on the second floor of the main building. Pictures of Jesus, Buddha and other spiritual teachers adorned the walls, complemented by a large magnolia tree which bloomed outside a picture window. Mary had arranged the chairs and couches in a circular pattern around a glass coffee table, at the center of which sat an angelic figurine. Ten other individuals were present besides Stuart, Joan and myself—six staff people from LEC (including three ministers), a minister friend from a local Unity church, the leader of my men's group, my therapist, Pat, and Judy, the social worker. I was deeply moved that twelve people had taken time out of their busy schedules to support me.

Mary facilitated the meeting in a straightforward fashion. She began by leading us in an affirmative prayer, taken from the writings of New Thought writer Jack Addington:*

> *There is no power in conditions;*
> *There is no power in situations;*
> *There is only power in God;*
> *Almighty God within me right now.*
> *There is no person, place, thing, condition or circumstance*
> *that can interfere with the perfect right action*
> *of God Almighty within me right now.*
> *I am pure spirit, living in a spiritual world.*
> *All things are possible to God through me.*

Mary then asked the participants to introduce themselves, re-count how they had met me, and describe their thoughts on the ultimate outcome of my ordeal. As people shared their perceptions, a common theme emerged—everyone affirmed that I could be healed of my affliction. Although I disagreed with their prognosis, I was moved by the unanimity of their faith.

When my turn arrived, I briefly recounted the history of my depressive episode as well as my present feelings of hopelessness and despair. Normally, I would have stopped there, but the previous day Mary had given an inspired sermon on "the mental equivalent."

---

* Throughout this and subsequent chapters, I will be using the term "God" to de-scribe a Higher Power or creative intelligence that infuses the universe. If the traditional concept of God seems alien to you, you may wish to think of such ideas as the vastness of the human spirit, an intelligent order in nature, the life force, creative inspiration, or quali-ties such as goodness, truth, love, beauty, peace, justice, etc. The words we use are less important than the universal reality they describe.

This is an ancient metaphysical principle which states that before something can manifest in the outer world, there must first exist an idea or "mental equivalent" of it in the world of thought. I complimented Mary on her talk and said that I wished to create a mental equivalent of *what wellness would look and feel like for me* The group embraced my idea, and so I asked each participant to join with me in affirming my picture of wholeness over the next thirty days. I promised to write out my vision and send it to the members by the end of the week. The plan was that every day (preferably at 9:00 a.m.) each person would read my vision statement while picturing me as whole and well. The meeting ended with a prayer of thanksgiving.

The Rebirth Statement

I left the group feeling nurtured by the loving attention I had received, but without any sense that a healing had taken place. If anything, things seemed to get worse, as my anxiety rose above a "5" for the next two days. Then, on Thursday morning, July 17 (my thirteenth wedding anniversary), I awoke with a clarity and a peace that I had not experienced in five months. The normal symptoms of intense agitation and feelings of hopelessness were totally absent. I felt as if a dark cloud had lifted.

I could scarcely believe it. "Is this a miracle or a mirage?" I asked myself. I had experienced other remissions, but they had normally lasted only two or three days (the longest I had gone without symptoms was ten days in February). Grateful for what little peace I did have, I spent the afternoon walking with a friend through the holy grounds of the Grotto, a local Catholic shrine dedicated to the Virgin Mary.

The next day I faxed my rebirth statement to the ministers at LEC and to the rest of my support team. The opening lines read:

> With help from God, I am reborn to a new life. I have learned the lessons that the anxiety and depression came to teach and thus have fully and freely released these symptoms from my body/mind. They are replaced by inner peace, emotional stability, vitality, wholeness, wellness and joy. My brain chemistry is stabilized and in perfect balance. I am healed and made whole.

The remainder of Friday passed without symptoms. That evening, I recorded in my mood diary that my anxiety and depression had dropped below a "2." (This was my psychiatrist's definition of remission.) In my journal I wrote, "I actually feel good. There is no pain to bear, no suffering to endure." A person who has not lived with chronic, debilitating anxiety and depression cannot fully appreciate what it feels like to be liberated from one's anguish. For me it was as if a ten-month migraine headache had suddenly ceased.

On Saturday, July 19, I hiked to Multnomah Falls with a friend and watched the full moon rise over Mt. Hood. "I haven't seen you this well in five months," Kathleen joyfully observed. Sunday morning I attended church and spoke with Mary Morrissey about my remission. Referring to the Monday support group, Mary exclaimed, "That was a 'God meeting!'"

"What do you mean?" I asked.

"I could feel the presence of spirit fill the room with love and peace." *

"So what do you think is happening?"

"I sense that you are having a spiritual healing."

For the next twenty-one days, I continued to experience a life without anxiety and depression. Then, exactly four weeks after the God meeting, I experienced a relapse, brought on by a recurrence of

---

* The other people I spoke with at LEC said that they too had sensed a Light and a lightness of being in the room that day.

cellulitis—a severe infection of the soft tissue in my lower leg—and an unexpected separation from a close friend (once again, loss triggered a depressive episode). For a brief time, the old symptoms returned and I was back in the inferno as my depression and anxiety levels skyrocketed to "8" and above. Fortunately, a second support meeting had been scheduled for August 26, just two weeks away. Because I believed that the "injection of Light" from the first meeting had catalyzed my remission, I had faith that my symptoms would end as soon as I met with my support team. Although I was in great pain, I was no longer hopeless about my recovery.

At the second God meeting, people commented that I had clearly improved (there were now fourteen people besides myself who attended). Members of the group remarked that even with the relapse, I seemed more vital, less agitated, and more lighthearted. I read my rebirth statement aloud and received helpful feedback on how to make it stronger and more definite. By the next day, my mood had once again lifted. My rebirth statement was taking form.

Subsequently, Mary scheduled our God meetings once a month in order that I might receive regular "injections" of spiritual energy.* With each new dose of Light, I became stronger and more stable. By the conclusion of the third God meeting in September, my mood swings had ceased. I no longer contemplated suicide. My sense of humor returned. I was able to concentrate and to spend long periods of time by myself. I no longer needed shifts of people to monitor and keep track of me. In short, my depression and anxiety had healed without drugs or other conventional medical treatment (see graph on the facing page).

Three additional God meetings were held at LEC in October, November and December. At the October meeting, the group supported me in disposing of the tranquilizers I had saved for a future suicide attempt. The male members accompanied me to the men's room, where we emptied several hundred tablets into a large

---

*This is similar to what occurs in conventional treatment for major depression, where patients who have been treated with electroconvulsive therapy receive monthly "maintenance" doses of ECT to prevent relapse.

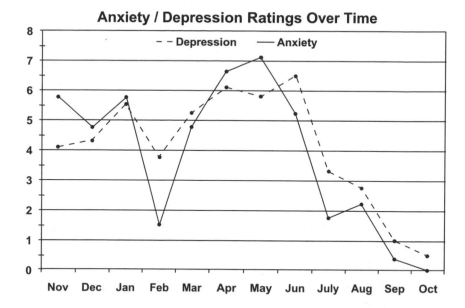

Anxiety / Depression Ratings Over Time

ceramic container. Then, each of us blessed the pills and dropped them, one handful at a time, into the toilet bowl. After a prayer of thanksgiving, we flushed them into oblivion.

At the November gathering, the group and I created another potent ritual. I burned the suicide note I had written the previous year, but not before photocopying it. On the back of the duplicate copy I wrote the following:

> "The words on this sheet were written at the depth of my depression. I am keeping a record of them so that if I ever experience this state again, I can remind myself that no matter how bad things look or feel, there is always a reason for hope. I now let go of the despair expressed in this note and replace it with thoughts of hope and optimism. I turn the page on the past and begin a new chapter of my life."

Each group member added his or her words of affirmation and encouragement to make the blessing complete.

From Despair to Gratitude

No matter how hopeless things seem or feel, each new day brings the opportunity for a new beginning. To reinforce this attitude, I made a photocopy of the suicide note I had written in 1996 and then inscribed a new set of affirmative statements at the bottom of the sheet. I have replicated here both the note and a letter I wrote to myself which contains the new beliefs.

> To my friends and family,   Nov. 12, 1996
>   I know that this is wrong, but I can no longer endure the pain of living with this mental illness. Further hospitalizations will not help, as my condition is too deep seated and advanced to uproot.
>   On some deeper level, I know that my work on the planet is finished and that it is time to move on.
>
>   Douglas

A reminder to myself,   11-20-97

The words on this sheet were written at the depth of my depression. I am keeping a record of them so that if I ever experience this state again, I can remind myself that no matter how bad things look or feel, there is always a reason for hope.

I now let go of the despair expressed in this note and replace it with thoughts of hope and optimism. I turn the page on the past and begin a new chapter of my life.

During this three-month period, I continued to submit my weekly requests for healing, which were prayed over by the LEC prayer team and the entire ministerial staff. By the year's end, my support team felt that I was stable enough to continue the God meetings without the help of the church. My first reaction to the prospect of losing the church's support was that of fear. Fortunately, my therapist Pat assured me that I was well enough to make it on my own. The God meetings have since continued in my home as "Master Mind groups" in which group members both *give* and *receive* spiritual support (I will say more about this process in the next chapter).

Because my healing was not caused by a physical substance, it is difficult to substantiate what occurred. No one photographed or recorded the doses of spiritual light I received. I possess no X-rays depicting that a cancerous tumor had shrunk. Neither did I throw away my crutches or "take up my bed and walk." And yet it was clear that something miraculous had taken place.

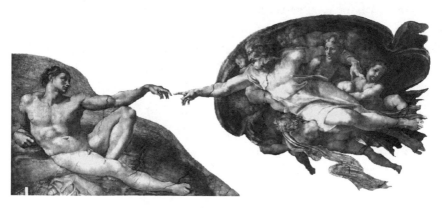

Michelangelo's "The Creation of Adam"

There is a story in the Gospel of John in which the disciples, after seeing a man who was blind from birth, asked Jesus, "Rabbi, who sinned, this man or his parents that he was born blind?" Jesus answered, "Neither this man nor his parents sinned, but that the works of God should be revealed in him." Likewise, on some level, I believe I was stricken with depression so that spirit could work a miracle in and through me—and that others could witness it.

The Power of Prayer

At the height of my illness, Mary Morrissey had said, "There is a power within you that is greater than any condition you may face. If you ask that Higher Power for its assistance, help is available."

The healing power of prayer was not a new idea to me. The spiritual tradition of Unity and other New Thought metaphysical schools teach what is called "affirmative prayer"—a process of building and affirming an inward consciousness of what one desires. When this inner picture manifests in the external world, it is called a "demonstration." I had demonstrated many things in my life—a new car, a lovely home, a book contract (even a pair of tickets to a sold-out Grateful Dead concert)—but never a healing of this magnitude. Fortunately, I was graced with a group of dedicated people who collectively held a vision of my wellness.

It is my belief that the key "ingredient" in my healing was the presence of *group energy*. I had met and prayed with Mary Morrissey many times; I had prayed with other ministers and members of the prayer team, as well as with my therapist—and still I continued to decline. It wasn't until someone said, "***Let's put all of your support people together in one room***" that the healing power of prayer became fully activated. The *combined* prayers and positive thoughts of the group members set up a spiritual energy field through which Divine Love moved and healed my body and soul.*

Given the fact that many cases of depression have been known to resolve on their own, some doctors have suggested that I might have recovered without any spiritual intervention. Nonetheless, I choose to believe that my healing was a Divine blessing. During my illness, a good friend had given me a book about the apparition of the Virgin Mary at Lourdes and the subsequent healings that had followed. I knew that a similar miracle was occurring in my life when, on the drive home from the second God meeting, Joan, Stuart

---

* In the gospel of Matthew, Jesus tells his disciples, "Where two or three are gathered together in my name [i.e., my nature], there am I [Divine consciousness] in the midst of them." In the Jewish religion, the power of group consciousness is the rationale for a minyan—a minimum of ten Jews that is required for a communal religious service.

and I witnessed four magnificent rainbows illuminating the Oregon afternoon sky. Referring to Noah's encounter with the rainbow after the Flood, and God's promise of reconciliation, Stuart exclaimed, "This is just like living in the Bible!" And so it was.

The Power of Support

It was not only God who healed me; it was people. One cannot overcome an illness like major depression (or any dark night of the soul experience) by oneself. The weight of the agony is too immense, even for the strongest-willed individual, to bear alone.

During my illness, two people close to me, a previous therapist and a fellow student of metaphysics, committed suicide in the midst of similar bouts of depression. The cause of their tragedies, I believe, lies in the words of Spanish philosopher Miguel de Unamuno, who said, "Isolation is the worst possible counsel." My friends had retreated into environments in which they were cut off from family, friends and therapeutic assistance. Fortunately, many people in the Portland area extended themselves to me—the staff and patients at day treatment, my partner Joan, countless friends, and the prayer ministry of LEC. Without them I would not have survived.

In a recent special aired on National Public Radio, Mike Wallace, William Styron and Art Buchwald spoke candidly about their depressions and about the lifeline of support that developed among them during their episodes. (All three were living on Martha's Vineyard at the time of their ordeals.) In his acknowledgment of Art Buchwald's support, Styron said:

> I have to give Art credit. He was the Virgil to our Dante. Because he'd been there [in hell] before, like Virgil. And he really charted the depths, and so it was very, very useful to have Art on the phone, because we needed it. Because this is a new experience for everyone, and it's totally—it's totally terrifying. And you need someone who has been there to give you parameters and an understanding of where you're going.

In my depressive state, I did not have a Buchwald—a brother or sister survivor who had been to hell and back—who could assure me of my future deliverance.* What I did have, however, was a committed group of individuals who "kept the high watch" by holding a vision of my healing until it came to pass. And so I learned the lesson that is granted to survivors of emotional and physical trauma: when Divine love heals us, it most often comes through the healing love of other people.

❂   ❂   ❂   ❂

As I read over the description of my recovery, I feel moved to add an important postscript. Just because spiritual intervention was a catalyst for my recovery, it doesn't mean that this is the path for everyone. For some people, healing may come from finding the right medication or nutritional supplement; for others, it may be through falling in love or pursuing a passion. Since the majority of people who are treated for depression eventually get better (i.e., most depressions are episodic), if you can endure the pain and set a strong intention to get well, you will likely be graced by some healing modality that works for you. (The key is to hang on until the pattern of the illness shifts.)

In addition, many people have observed that I attracted a particularly large support network of committed people. While this is true, I believe that support is available to anyone who earnestly seeks it. Potential resources include family; friends; co-workers; mental health professionals; one's church, synagogue, or other place of worship; 12-step meetings; 24-hour crisis lines; and telephone prayer lines (listed in Appendix C).

Even with the many resources that are available, some people feel too ashamed, shy or anxious to reach out for help. If asking for assistance seems hard, please reconsider calling *someone*, even if it is a crisis line. Reaching out *will* make a real difference in your recovery. I promise.

---

* For a cassette copy of the radio program *A Conversation with Mike Wallace, Art Buchwald and William Styron*, call the Dana Alliance for Brain Initiatives at (800) 65-BRAIN.

CHAPTER NINE

LIVING IN RECOVERY

"God, grant me the serenity to accept the things I cannot change,
the courage to change the things I can,
and the wisdom to know the difference."
Rheinhold Niebuhr (the Serenity Prayer)

One year has passed since the initial God meeting. During that time my challenge has shifted from getting out of hell to *staying* out. Although remaining well is easier than getting well, relapse is an ever-present danger. Surviving an episode of depression is not like having the measles—you do not develop an immunity to the disease. Although the symptoms of depression can be controlled, the underlying predisposition does not go away. While it is true that some individuals experience just one major depressive episode in a lifetime, half of those who have been severely depressed are at risk to become depressed again.

There are, however, advantages to having lived through a major depression. With the experience of the disease under a person's belt, he or she can recognize depression's various warning signs and engage in thoughts and behaviors that will stave off another descent—a kind of building up of the psychological immune system. In the recovery movement this process is called "relapse prevention."

I believe that the concept of relapse prevention can be applied to recovery from depression as well as from addictions. For me, relapse prevention consists of two important stages:
1) engaging in positive, healthy behaviors that promote recovery.
2) avoiding negative thoughts and behaviors that can trigger a depressive episode.

A helpful way to visualize relapse prevention is to take a piece of paper and draw a horizontal line across the middle. Write "+10" at the top of the paper, then below it write "+9," "+8," ..."+1," until you come to the horizontal line which represents zero. Then, below the horizontal line write "-1," "-2," etc., ending with "-10" at the bottom. Any behaviors or attitudes that promote recovery are posted above the horizontal line; those that may lead to relapse are posted below. A "-10" signifies actual relapse. In the case of the alcoholic or addict, behaviors listed below the line would include going to bars, dropping out of recovery programs, and ultimately drinking or using drugs ("-10"). For myself, a "-10" means reexperiencing extreme anxiety (pacing, hitting myself), depression, suicidal thinking, and ultimately hospitalization.

The goal of relapse prevention is to stay in the positive zone, above the line. During my year of recovery, I have made a powerful discovery—that the *same attitudes and behaviors* that I developed in order to survive my depressive episode are ideally suited for maintaining my recovery. I have turned these coping strategies into a five-part wellness plan that I call my "brain maintenance" program.

As I did with my personal survival strategies, I have organized this treatment plan into four areas—physical, mental/emotional, spiritual, and social/people support. In addition, I have added a fifth category—lifestyle habits. (A diagram on the facing page provides a visual overview of the program which is described in detail on pp. 155-178.)

I would now like to share some of the highlights of my personal brain-maintenance regimen.

Physical Self-Care

Staying emotionally well means taking care of one's body. To this end, I continue to engage in my daily exercise routines. During my depressive episode, I swam twice a day. Now I alternate swimming with stationary bicycle riding, weight resistance training and long walks in the forest.

I have also maintained my balanced diet—avoiding sugar and caffeine, as well as buying foods that are free of herbicides, pesticides, hormones and antibiotics. In addition, I drink lots of water—at least two quarts a day—as I feel better when I am sufficiently hydrated.

Healing From Depression:
A Brain Maintenance Program

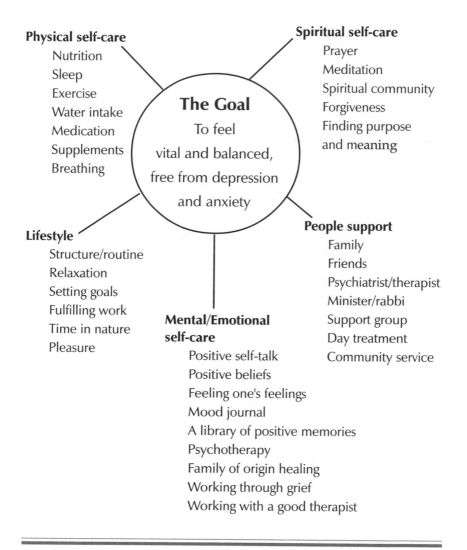

Physical self-care
Nutrition
Sleep
Exercise
Water intake
Medication
Supplements
Breathing

The Goal
To feel
vital and balanced,
free from depression
and anxiety

Spiritual self-care
Prayer
Meditation
Spiritual community
Forgiveness
Finding purpose
and meaning

Lifestyle
Structure/routine
Relaxation
Setting goals
Fulfilling work
Time in nature
Pleasure

Mental/Emotional self-care
Positive self-talk
Positive beliefs
Feeling one's feelings
Mood journal
A library of positive memories
Psychotherapy
Family of origin healing
Working through grief
Working with a good therapist

People support
Family
Friends
Psychiatrist/therapist
Minister/rabbi
Support group
Day treatment
Community service

As part of my nutritional program, I take a good multivitamin and multi-mineral supplement with special emphasis on the anti-oxidants—Vitamins A, C and E. To balance my brain chemistry, I take the natural antidepressant St. John's Wort (300 milligrams three times a day) as well as the amino acid tyrosine. (Tyrosine is the precursor to norepinephrine and dopamine, brain neurotransmitters which are thought to be insufficient in those who are depressed.)

Finally, I make it a priority to get adequate rest (studies show that most Americans are sleep-deprived) and to maintain a regular sleep schedule. During times when stress or worry triggers insomnia, a small dose of the antidepressant Elavil (25 mg. before bed) helps me to sleep until my body can right its course and return to its normal sleep cycle.

Mental/Emotional Self-Care

To keep my depression and anxiety at manageable levels, I have learned to develop positive habits of thinking and feeling. These include:

- Using positive self-talk, especially when I am feeling worried or fearful.
- Reading my rebirth statement once a day, to myself and others.
- Continuing to see my therapist on a regular basis.
- Forgiving myself for my mistakes (as much as I am able to).
- Practicing self-acceptance.
- Affirming that I am not flawed or defective—I am a normal person dealing with a medical condition called depression.
- Making peace with the depression. This means that instead of trying to "conquer" or "defeat" depression, I seek to *adapt to it* and to *accept it* as part of my life. Just as the diabetic learns to live with his illness, I accept the limitations of having this disorder, and adjust my lifestyle accordingly.
- Keeping track of my daily moods.

1-10 Mood Scale

9-10 pure joy
7-8 happiness
6 contentment
5 okay, but something missing
4 malaise/mild depression
3 moderate depression
0-2 clinical depression

When I was struggling to survive, I found that rating my moods gave me a feeling of control in the midst of an out-of-control life. Once the depression lifted, I continued to record my daily mood levels. Then, one day two months into my recovery, I noticed that I actually felt some joy. Having returned to the land of the living, I realized that I needed a new method of evaluating my moods, one that would measure *levels of pleasure* as well as those of pain. With this in mind, I created a revised mood scale (see above), which I now use in place of my original 1 to 10 anxiety and depression scale. Please feel free to adapt it to your own use. At the present time, my mood fluctuates between 4.5 and 6.5, which is fine. After one has endured the fires of hell, neutrality is quite acceptable.*

People Support

Throughout my narrative, I have emphasized that my ability to reach out for support was an essential survival skill. This coping strategy is equally important in my quest to stay out of the dark house. Fortunately, many of the same support people who were with me during my illness—my partner, Joan, my close friends, and my therapist, Pat (as well as my cats Gabriel and Athena)—continue to grace my life.

---

* In the book *Girl, Interrupted*, Susanna Kaysen defines her newfound mental health as "having my misery transformed into common unhappiness."

Excerpt from February 1998 Mood Diary

February 19:   **Depression 0   Anxiety 0   Joy 5**

I took on a new student whom I really like. I haven't taught math in a decade, but I was able to follow the text pretty well. I still remember the formula for the quadratic equation. I am now seeing ten students a week. What a blessing to be able to be productive again.

February 20:   **Depression 0   Anxiety 0   Joy 4**

Today I felt the inspiration to tell the story of my depression. I came up with a title for an article. Perhaps this is what Rev. Michael Moran meant when he said that I had this illness so that I could write about it.

February 21:   **Depression 1   Anxiety 0   Joy 6**

I attended a talk at LEC about survivors of trauma. The speaker said that heroic survivors have two things in common. First, they integrate the traumatic episode into their identity and make it a defining experience of their life. Second, they talk or write about it in a way that is inspiring to others. I am still working on #1 and perhaps beginning #2.

February 22:   **Depression 0   Anxiety 0   Joy 7**

Tonight, my friends and I created a re-birthday party to celebrate my 49th birthday. We drank champagne and listened to live music. Connie led a powerful rite of passage ritual for me. I feel grateful to have come out of the dark house. After seven years of struggle, perhaps I am ready for a new beginning.

Of course, the crucial support that led to my recovery came through the monthly God meetings at the Living Enrichment Center. Ideally, my replacement of choice for the LEC group would have been a 12-step group—i.e., "Depressives Anonymous." I have often imagined myself attending a "DA" group and introducing myself by saying, "I'm Douglas and I'm a melancholic." Unfortunately, no one has initiated a "Depressives Anonymous" movement (a fact I find it quite remarkable, given that 17 million people in America suffer from depression).

In the absence of Depressives Anonymous, I now meet regularly with my Master Mind team—a group of people who convene in an atmosphere of trust and harmony for the purpose of providing mutual support and encouragement. The term "Master Mind" was first coined by Napoleon Hill in his classic book, *Think and Grow Rich*. Hill discovered that successful businesspeople did not succeed on their own, but depended on a "brain trust" whom they consulted before making important decisions. Hill called this process "the principle of the Master Mind." He writes:

> The human mind is a form of energy. When two or more minds cooperate in harmony, they form a great "bank" of energy plus a third, invisible force which can be likened to a Master Mind. The Master Mind is yours to use as you desire. It is the master way to use organized and directed knowledge as a road to lifelong power.

Years later, Unity minister Jack Boland integrated Hill's idea with the recovery model and made the term Master Mind synonymous with one's Higher Power. (Boland was a recovering alcoholic who brilliantly synthesized the principles of the twelve steps and New Thought spirituality).

Today, Master Mind meetings perform the same function as the "brain trusts" of Hill's time. In a Master Mind meeting, each member is encouraged to surrender to the Master Mind any problem areas, challenges, needs for healing, and heartfelt goals. When such requests are fully and properly made, spirit provides answers and solutions in the most amazing way.

The members of my current Master Mind team all emerged from the original LEC "God group." Since then, it has been rewarding to watch the transformation of a situation where people who were focused solely on supporting me now receive encouragement and assistance from me and other peers. (See Appendix B for more information on the Master Mind process.)

Spiritual Self-Care

Even more than the loving people who supported me, it was the spiritual power which **worked through them** that brought about my healing. Each day I depend on that presence to maintain my wholeness.

To this end, Joan and I continue to attend services at the Living Enrichment Center. As part of my spiritual service work, I now volunteer with the prayer ministry, answering the letters of those who write in with prayer requests.

In addition, I set aside some time each day in which I make contact with my Higher Power. I have constructed a modest altar in one corner my bedroom where I spend fifteen to twenty minutes each morning meditating, writing my goals for the day, and reading selected inspirational literature.

To conclude my time of prayer and meditation, I recite aloud my "Dedication and Covenant with God." It is based on the covenant written by Charles and Myrtle Fillmore, co-founders of Unity, in which they devote their lives to serve spirit in return for spirit's promise to meet all of their needs.

My version of their covenant reads:

I, Douglas Bloch, hereby dedicate myself, my time, my talents, my money, all I have and all I expect to have, to the Spirit of Truth, and through it to various forms of spiritual and artistic service.

It being understood and agreed that the said Spirit of Truth shall render unto me an equivalent for this dedication, in peace of mind, health of body, joyful service, love, life, creativity, community and an abundant supply of all things necessary to meet my every need, without making any of these things the object of my existence.

In the presence of the Conscious Mind of the living spirit. Amen.

I find that reading this covenant is a way of affirming my trust that the goodness of life will sustain and maintain me.*

Lifestyle

In my recovery program, I created the category of "lifestyle" to encompass a number of "brain maintenance" habits and daily living routines that help me to maintain my emotional serenity. Some of these include:

- Spending time in nature (living in Oregon gives me ample opportunity to seek refuge in the mountains, on the coast, or at the Columbia River Gorge).
- Getting plenty of exposure to natural light.
- Finding time to relax and just be.
- Incorporating sufficient amounts of structure and routine into my life.

This last point is crucial. Without adequate structure and a regular routine, I can become excessively involuted and self-absorbed. (I suspect this is true for many people prone to depression.) This is why I awaken, exercise, eat, see students, write, and socialize at approximately the same time each day. Having a stable routine gives me something to look forward to. It calms my anxiety as well as any tranquilizer—and without the side effects.

Work/employment is another way to add structure to one's life. I have always been attracted to the Buddhist concept of "right livelihood"—being involved in work that contributes to society and provides a sense of purpose and meaning. Perhaps that is why I have been drawn back to working with young people.

---

* The Fillmores' idea for the covenant was based on Matthew 6:34, "Seek ye first the Kingdom of God and its righteousness, and all these things shall be added unto you."

Knowing When You're Slipping
"The most powerful thing that any human being can do
is to get out of a bad mood."
The Tibetan Book of Living and Dying

In addition to choosing positive healthy behaviors, the success of my relapse prevention plan depends on my identifying those stressors, attitudes and behaviors that can trigger another breakdown. During my depressive episode, my primary adversary was my deranged biochemistry. Now I must watch out for self-defeating thoughts and their resulting behaviors—what Alcoholics Anonymous calls "stinking thinking." Here are examples of thoughts and behaviors that can get me into trouble.

I am more likely to relapse into depression and anxiety when:
- I don't keep regular sleep hours.
- I overcommit and take on too many projects.
- I don't allow myself to relax.
- I worry about things that I cannot control.
- I dwell on thoughts of despair and hopelessness.
- I catastrophize about the future.
- I compare myself to others.
- I put myself down for not having "achieved" more.
- I feel ashamed about my past.
- I blame others for my misfortunes.
- I criticize myself.
- I forget what I do have to be grateful for.
- I fight against the tendency to depression and see it as the enemy.
- I watch too many television shows and videos.

When I become aware that I am engaging in self-defeating thoughts or actions, I acknowledge my error in thinking and gently redirect myself to a positive thought or behavior. Even when my mood dips for no apparent reason (perhaps because of some biochemical imbalance), I remind myself that feelings of despair, no matter how strongly felt, do not always accurately reflect the reality of my situation. For example, when I wrote my suicide note, I was certain that I had nothing left to live for. (I was clearly mistaken.) My perception of the future was distorted by my illness. Now when I start to feel bleak, I know not to take my pessimism too seriously.

Staying centered is not always easy. During the first few months of my recovery, I became oversensitized to every fluctuation of mood. I felt like the AIDS survivor who may think about relapse whenever he detects a drop in his white blood cell count. Over time, I have become more skilled at managing such catastrophic thinking. When I notice myself responding to a descent in mood with thoughts of doom and gloom, I tell myself, "Douglas, I know you are scared right now. Instead of giving in to your fears, try focusing on something positive" (e.g., calling Pat or a friend, going for a swim, etc.). Each time I follow this wise counsel, my mood eventually passes.

Relax, God's in charge.

Learning to HALT

In my quest for "emotional sobriety," I have borrowed another principle from the recovery movement—the acronym HALT, which stands for *hungry, angry, lonely* and *tired*. Whenever a person is in one of these states, he or she is more likely to reach for booze or drugs, or as in my case, fall into a depressive state. When I notice that I am feeling one of the symptoms of HALT, I take steps to correct the situation.

• If I am *tired*, I take a nap.

• If I am *hungry*, I fix myself a balanced meal or snack, one that includes a healthy serving of protein, as well as proportionate amounts of carbohydrates and fat.

• If I am *lonely*, I reach out to my support system—family, friends, therapist, spiritual community at LEC, and members of my Master Mind team.

• If I am *angry*, I try to adopt an attitude of acceptance and forgiveness.

Dealing with my anger has been especially tricky. Because of the ways in which depression has wreaked havoc on my life, I sometimes feel a certain bitterness towards all of the people and circumstances that have contributed to its occurrence. For example, when I was twelve years old, a psychiatrist told my parents that I needed counseling. They did not pursue it. During my twenties and thirties I saw a number of doctors, none of whom diagnosed my problem as "clinical depression." I also hold myself accountable, believing that I "should" have been able to determine what was wrong with me, given my undergraduate and graduate studies in psychology.

But no matter how much I want to rage against myself and the world, I come back to the same realization—I was doing the best I could. Because society lacked the heightened awareness about depression that we have today, I did not receive the proper information that would have led to my diagnosis and treatment. Now that I finally understand the nature of clinical depression, I am taking better care of myself, and hopefully will avoid further relapses.

Another way that I shift out of the blame game is to give thanks. Putting on an "attitude of gratitude" moves my perspective from resentment to that of abundance. As I turn my attention to what *is* working in my life—my marriage, my friendships, my health and work—I feel more at peace about my condition, and even see it as a valuable teacher.

Overall, I am pleased with my progress. Despite occasional visits to the dark house, I am beginning to have more faith in my newfound serenity. Now that I am reconciled with my partner Joan and have rediscovered my passion for mentoring young people, I am hoping that I can lead a stable and productive life. While my greatest fear is that I will relapse into mental illness, my greatest strength is remembering that I am not a passive victim of the disease. As a good friend and ally told me, *Douglas, you can draw in the energy of love and create a state of grace wherever and whenever you choose. Wherever you are, you can attract to yourself the healing power of the Divine.*

As in recovering from alcoholism, healing from depression is not a one-time event, but an ongoing process. It is a way of life that must be recommitted to every day. And as each evening draws to a close, I thank my Higher Power that I have maintained my serenity and equilibrium for another twenty-four hours.

This is how I practice recovery—one day at a time.

God, grant me the **Serenity** to accept the things I cannot change,

the **Courage** to change the things I can,

and the **Wisdom** to know the difference.

Grant me **Patience** with the changes that take time,

an **Appreciation** of all that I have,

Tolerance of those with different struggles,

and the **Strength** to get up and try again.

— One Day at a Time —

Dante and Beatrice experience the beatific vision in the conclusion of "Paradisio," from Dante's *Divine Comedy*. The poet wrote, "A light there is in the beyond which makes the creator visible to the creature, who only in beholding him finds peace." The artist is Gustave Dore.

CHAPTER TEN

AFTER THE PAIN, THE JOY

"No one is as capable of gratitude
as one who has emerged from the kingdom of night."
Elie Wiesel

"Enlightenment begins on the other side of despair."
Jean Paul Sartre

T here is an ancient spiritual truth which states that "every adversity contains within it the seed of an equivalent or greater good." Like the lotus flower that blooms in the depths of the mud, something redeeming can emerge from even the most horrendous situation. This was certainly true of my experience of major depression. When I awoke from the nightmare, I found that the illness had left unexpected gifts in its wake. The black cloud of depression had a silver lining.

The first of these blessings was compassion. As a result of my ordeal, my empathy has deepened—for all who suffer, and especially for those who are afflicted with mental illness. Having gained a greater understanding of the frailties of human existence, I am less likely to judge others. Before my episode, I might have said about a person with a neurosis, "How could he stay in that dysfunctional marriage?" or "Hasn't he cured his addiction yet?" Now, when I meet a person who is in pain, I release my judgment and say silently, "Friend, I know what it is like to be at the mercy of your demons. I bless you, and pray that you will find your way home."

On the eve of my second hospitalization, Joan had remarked, "Think of your stay in the hospital as a training ground for learning how to cope." In many respects, my *entire illness* was a lesson in learning how to manage intense pain. Thus, a second gift of the depression has been the development of emotional coping skills that I now use to create stability and serenity in my daily life.

In addition, I have gained a new perspective about the meaning of distress. Whenever I start to get irritated because something is not working out as planned, I say to myself, "What's the big deal? I almost died. I almost committed suicide." What was once a crisis, I now regard as an inconvenience. I am reminded of the saying, "Don't sweat the small stuff." After you have stood at brink of the abyss and faced death, everything is small stuff.*

Yet another blessing I have received has been the reconciliation of my marriage. My divorce in 1996 initiated an overwhelming reaction of grief and loneliness which created the depression that ultimately led to my breakdown. During my illness, my ex-wife Joan became a major support in my healing—accompanying me to LEC's Sunday services and driving me to the monthly God meetings. Our commitment to my recovery and to our spirituality rekindled the love that drew us back together.

Finally, my reconciliation with Joan was part of a bigger picture. Having my own "near death" experience made me realize what I truly valued in life—the love of my wife, friends and family. (I didn't want to lose them or see them lose me.)

Breaking Down to Break Through
"The depth of darkness to which you can descend and still live is an exact measure of the height to which you can aspire to reach."
Laurens van der Post

In 1977, Czech physical chemist Ilya Prigogine won the Nobel Prize for his theory of dissipative structures. Prigogine showed that "open systems" (those systems having a continuous interchange with the environment) occasionally experience periods of instability. When this imbalance exceeds a certain limit, the system breaks down and

---

* Martha Manning, who wrote about her own hellish experience with clinical depression in the book *Undercurrents*, says: "My baseline for awful will never be the same."

"Job and His Family Restored to Prosperity," by William Blake

enters a state of "creative chaos." Yet, out of chaos and disorganiza-
tion, a new and higher order spontaneously emerges. This phenomenon—known as spontaneous transformation—has been recognized
as the basis of physical evolution.

I believe that what holds true on the physical plane is valid on
the psychological plane as well. Hence, so-called "nervous break-
downs" can be seen as rites of passage into a more mature spiritual
consciousness. In other words, we are always moving towards ex-
panded levels of awareness, even when our world seems to be falling
apart. As survivor researcher Julius Siegal describes it:

> In a remarkable number of cases, those who have suffered
> and prevail find that after their ordeal they begin to oper-
> ate at a higher level than ever before … The terrible ex-
> periences of our lives, despite the pain they bring, may
> become our redemption.

Although I would never want to trivialize the suffering that depression brings, I do feel changed for the better by my healing experience in ways that would not have occurred had I undergone a lesser ordeal. On the other had, not everything has improved. In the last three months of my episode, I gained thirty pounds (one of the side effects of Elavil). In addition, my metabolism has slowed down, and I sleep more than I used to. Yet, the infirmities of my physical body have been amply compensated by a heightened spirituality and peace of mind.

What Goes Down Must Come Up

Ten years ago, I wrote the following in my book of affirmations, *Words That Heal*:

> *What goes down must come up.*
> *There can be no death without rebirth.*
> *Every ending is followed by a beginning.*
> *The experience of hell is a precursor to the glory of heaven.*

These words are no longer an intellectual supposition. Having learned their truth firsthand, I have a personal message for anyone who is going through a "dark night of the soul" experience:

> *If you are on the edge of the abyss, don't jump.*
> *If you are going through hell, don't stop.*
> *As long as you are breathing, there is hope.*
> *As long as day follows night, there is hope.*
> *Nothing stays the same forever.*
> *Set an intention to heal,*
> *reach out for support, and you will be helped.*

I realize that not everyone can develop the spiritual endurance to hold on—and there is no shame in that. But for those whose will to live is greater than their suffering, there exists the eternal promise of resurrection and rebirth. Like the mythical Phoenix, we who are consumed by fire will rise again from the ashes.*

I began this book with a quotation from Teddy Roosevelt, a courageous soul who experienced numerous episodes of depression during his life. His words, *"It is not having been in the dark house, but having left it, that counts,"* form a credo for all souls who have been to hell and back.

Because depression tends to recur, there is a possibility that I might one day revisit Roosevelt's "dark house." If that occurs, I hope to put this survivor's guide to good use. But for now, I would rather join with the psalmist in singing the 126th Psalm, in which David gives thanks to God for the deliverance of his people:

> The Lord has done great things for us, whereof we are glad.
> Those who sow in tears shall reap in joy.
> He who continually goes forth weeping,
> Shall doubtless come again with rejoicing,
> Bringing his sheaves with him.

---

* Phoenix was the Greek name for the mythological bird that was sacred to the Sun-god in ancient Egypt. An eagle-like bird with red and gold plumage, the Phoenix had a 500-year life span, at the end of which the bird built its own funeral pyre on which it was burned to ashes. Yet, out of the ashes a new Phoenix arose. Symbolic of the rising and setting of the sun, the Phoenix later appeared in medieval Christian writings as a symbol of death and resurrection.

"The Invisible Helper," by Mary Hanscom

FOOTPRINTS IN THE SAND

"You have survived the winter because you are, and were, and always will be, very much loved. And long, long before you felt my warmth surrounding you, you were being freed and formed from within in ways so deep and profound, that you could not possibly know what was happening."
Mary Fahy, *The Tree That Survived the Winter*

I t is a fact of nature that even on the most overcast of days, though its rays are hidden, the sun is still shining. In a similar manner, I believe that God's Light continues to bless us even in our darkest moments. As I reflect back over the period of my illness, I can see that a benevolent, unseen force was protecting me. This "amazing grace" guided me to the day treatment clinic, to my therapist Pat, to those people who steered me away from suicide, and ultimately to the healing at LEC.

Nowhere is the principle of Divine protection more beautifully illustrated than in the anonymous essay, "Footprints in the Sand." I first encountered this inspirational passage in Ann Landers' newspaper column a year before my illness. Soon, I began to see the text inscribed on parchment and plaques that were sold in various souvenir shops. One day, in the depths of my depression, I bought a copy for myself. Afterwards, I read the words often and found them to be a source of solace and hope. I present them here for those readers who have yet to encounter their inspiring message.

Footprints in the Sand

One night a man had a dream. He dreamed he was walking along the beach with the Lord. Across the sky flashed scenes from his life. For each scene he noticed two sets of footprints in the sand; one belonging to him and the other to the Lord.

When the last scene of his life flashed before him, he looked back at the footprints in the sand. He noticed that many times along the path of his life there was only one set of footprints. He also noticed that it happened at the very lowest and saddest times in his life.

This really bothered him and he questioned the Lord about it. "Lord, you said that once I decided to follow you, you'd walk with me all the way. But I have noticed that during the most troublesome times in my life, there is only one set of footprints. I don't understand why when I needed you most you would leave me."

The Lord replied, "My precious, precious child, I love you and I would never leave you. During your times of trial and suffering, when you saw only one set of footprints, it was then that I carried you."

"God Answers Job Out of the Whirlwhind," by William Blake

Chronology of Events

The following is a brief summary of the events that led up to and took place during my episode of major depression.

December 1990. Serious cracks in my six-year marriage begin to appear.

April 1991. I enter group therapy to deal with my marital crisis and to work on family of origin issues.

September 1993. After much deliberation, Joan and I decide to separate.

April 1994. The book that I am writing under contract for a New York publisher is unexpectedly turned down after I submit it. I am now without a creative focus or a love focus. I begin to develop insomnia.

December 1994. I am stricken with the first of a series of chronic bacterial infections in my lower right leg. Intravenous antibiotic therapy is required to vanquish the cellulitis.

September 1995. I file for divorce.

November 1995 and February 1996. Two additional attacks of cellulitis occur.

February 28, 1996. My divorce with Joan is finalized.

March 1. I am laid up with another bout of cellulitis. My mood blackens.

April 1-7. A trip to the Grand Canyon temporarily lifts my spirits.

June through August. I try a number of antidepressants in an attempt to heal my melancholy, none of which help.

August 10. I take the antidepressant Zoloft before bedtime and spend the next two days feeling extremely agitated.

September 4. I take the antidepressant Effexor before bedtime and wake up at three in the morning in a state of major agitation and panic. It takes two hours to get back to sleep. I finally wake up at noon, and experience a black depression for the rest of the day.

September 7. I awaken with out-of-control agitation and panic. Joan drives me to a psychiatric ward in a local hospital. My major depressive episode officially begins.

September 10. I am discharged from the hospital with a diagnosis of "agitated depression."

September 11. Joan moves in with me and becomes my part-time caretaker.

September 12–October 22. My general mood takes a slow, downward direction. I begin to experience daily anxiety attacks which can only be contained through long walks in the woods.

October 21. Joan begins work at a full-time job.

October 23. I admit myself to Pacific Gateway Hospital.

October 31. I am discharged from Pacific Gateway.

November 1. I begin attending the day treatment program at the Pacific Counseling Center.

November 12. I attempt to commit suicide by taking an overdose of tranquilizers, but I am serendipitously interrupted.

November 15. Sedated on the antianxiety drug Klonopin, I rear-end a pickup truck during rush-hour traffic.

December 4–13. A temporary lifting of symptoms is followed by a return to the inferno.

January 2, 1997. I consider admitting myself to the hospital as suicidal feelings return.

February 13. I begin to submit prayer requests to the prayer ministry at the Living Enrichment Center.

February 21–28. I experience a week of unexplained calm and peace.

March 1. The old symptoms return with a vengeance.

April 20. I hire a home health aide to be my companion on weekday afternoons.

May 13. I plant a small vegetable garden.

May 25. After months of agonizing, I decide not to go to the Menninger Psychiatric Clinic in Topeka, Kansas.

June 19. The Reverend Eddy Brame of the Living Enrichment Center asks me to attend a support meeting to be held on my behalf with the ministerial staff of LEC. This proves to be the turning point in my illness.

July 14. A two-hour meeting to support my healing is held in the Reverend Mary Morrissey's office and facilitated by Mary. Twelve people attend. I decide to create a vision statement depicting what wellness would look like for me. The group agrees to affirm this vision with me on a daily basis.

July 17. I wake up free of symptoms. This remission will continue for three and a half weeks.

July 20. Mary confirms that "the holy spirit" was present at our meeting. I spend the day relaxing at the Oregon Coast.

August 11. I experience a relapse and spend two weeks back in the dark house.

August 26. The second "God meeting" takes place. Sixteen people are present. I share my rebirth statement with the group and receive helpful feedback.

August 27. My symptoms once again go into remission. I stop attending day treatment.

September 21. I begin to feel the return of some anxiety, but it is less severe than it had been.

September 25. The third "God meeting" takes place. Eddy Brame is now the main facilitator.

September 26. My symptoms disappear again, this time apparently for good.

October 19. I am able to focus again. I begin to tutor mathematics to high school and college students.

October 23. The fourth "God meeting" occurs, at which I dispose of the medication I had saved up for a possible suicide attempt. This is the one-year anniversary of my being admitted to Pacific Gateway.

October 26. As a symbol of my rebirth, I begin to remodel my home.

November 20. The fifth "God meeting" takes place.

November 25. The symptoms of anxiety and depression have been absent for eight weeks. This means that my major depressive episode is now officially "in remission."

December 10. My inner guidance tells me I am supposed to write an article about my experience.

December 18. The final "God meeting" is held at LEC.

January 15, 1998. The first Master Mind meeting is held in my house. Six members of the God group and I participate. Subsequent meetings will be held biweekly.

February 22, 1998. On my forty-ninth birthday, a party is held at my house to celebrate my emergence from the dark night of the soul. Many of my friends and the LEC support people attend. My article has turned into the beginning of a book.

PART TWO

HEALING FROM DEPRESSION:
A GUIDE FOR PATIENTS, CAREGIVERS, FAMILIES
AND FRIENDS

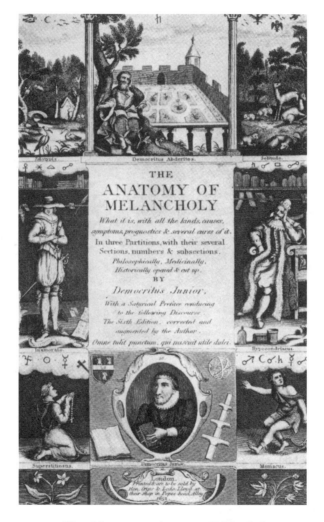

The title page to *Anatomy of Melancholy*
by Robert Burton, first published in 1621

HEALING FROM DEPRESSION:
A GUIDE FOR PATIENTS, CAREGIVERS,
FAMILIES AND FRIENDS

Despite the fact that public awareness and understanding of depression have dramatically increased over the past decade, many aspects of the illness remain in the shadows. Partly due to the stigma that still surrounds mental illness, the majority of people suffering from depression remain undiagnosed and untreated.

To educate the reader about depression and other mood disorders, I have created the following "mini-self-help manual." Like any reference, it is meant to be referred to as needed. Use the content summary listed below to locate specific topics that may be of interest.

If you wish to explore these matters in greater depth, please refer to Appendix C and the Recommended Reading section for the names of *books, Internet sites* and *organizations* that offer help and guidance on the subjects of mood disorders and mental and spiritual healing.

Part Two Contents

WHAT IS CLINICAL DEPRESSION, AND HOW DO I KNOW IF I HAVE IT?

"Depression is an illness. I am sick. I need to be here not because I'm defective, not because I am a moral leper, not because I've fallen from grace or turned my back on God, but for one simple reason: I am sick."
Tracy Thompson, *The Beast*

A depressive illness is a "whole body" disorder, involving one's physiology, biochemistry, mood, thoughts and behavior. It affects the way you eat and sleep, the way you think and feel about yourself, others and the world. Clinical depression is not a passing blue mood or a sign of personal weakness. Subtle changes in the brain's chemistry can create a terrible malaise in the body-mind-spirit that can affect every dimension of your being.

Depression is called the "common cold" of mental illness, not because its symptoms are mild but because the disease is so widespread across cultures. It is the most diagnosed mental health disorder in the United States, among the most debilitating, and the most lethal (15 percent of all untreated clinical depressions result in suicide). According to an estimate in the *Journal of Clinical Psychiatry*, each year depression accounts for a $43.7 billion burden on the American economy, as measured in medical costs, lost productivity in the workplace and at home, and lost contributions of wage earners who die from depression-related suicide. The disorder does not discriminate among its victims—it affects all age groups, all economic groups, and all gender and ethnic categories. While the average age of onset was once a person's mid-thirties, it is now moving towards adolescence and even early childhood. At any given moment, somewhere between 15 and 20 million Americans are suffering from depressive disorders, and about one in five will develop the illness at some point during their lifetimes.

Although depression has become the malaise of our times, it has plagued humankind since antiquity. King Saul of the Bible (who needed David's music to soothe his despondency) was a classic depressive. The Greeks were the first to understand the biological nature of depression and gave it the name "melancholia" (from the roots "melaina chole," meaning "black bile). In the 17th century, English scholar Robert Burton wrote the definitive work of the era on the subject—*The Anatomy of Melancholy.*

Though depression is a serious illness, it is *highly treatable,* as it normally responds to a combination of antidepressants and psychotherapy. Unfortunately, the majority of people with depression do not seek treatment because the symptoms are unrecognized, misdiagnosed, or so disabling that the person cannot reach out for help, or because the individual is deterred by the stigma surrounding mental illness. The promise of highly effective treatment for *sufferers* makes it essential for family members or friends to strongly encourage the depressed individual to seek appropriate treatment.

The Symptoms of Depression

Depression is a complex disorder and its symptoms express themselves on many levels. Depression creates physical problems, behavioral problems, distorted thinking, changes in emotional well being, troubled relationships and spiritual emptiness. While it is also true that some of these symptoms can contribute to the onset of milder depressions, in order to understand the more serious and enduring forms of depression, the text here will focus on how endogenous or biochemical depression can be identified.

The symptoms of major depression can be divided into three categories:

1) disturbances of emotion and mood.

2) changes in the "housekeeping" functions of the brain—those that regulate sleep, appetite, energy and sexual function.

3) disturbances of thinking and concentration.

The most common symptoms of clinical depression include:
- chronically sad or empty mood.
- loss of interest or pleasure in ordinary pleasurable activities, including sex.
- decreased energy, fatigue, feeling slowed down, slowed movement, slurred speech.
- sleep disturbances (insomnia, early morning waking, or oversleeping).
- eating disturbances (loss of appetite, significant weight loss or weight gain).
- difficulty concentrating, impaired memory, difficulty in making decisions.
- agitated actions (pacing, hand-wringing, etc.)
- feelings of guilt, worthlessness or helplessness.
- feelings of hopelessness and despair.
- thoughts and/or talk of death and suicide.
- irritability or excessive crying.
- social withdrawal or isolation.
- chronic aches and pains that don't respond to treatment.
- suicide attempts.
- increase in addictive behavior.

In the workplace, depression can be recognized by the following symptoms:
- morale problems/lack of cooperation.
- difficulty concentrating.
- safety problems, accidents, listlessness.
- absenteeism.
- frequent complaints of being tired all the time.
- complaints of unexplained aches and pains.
- alcohol or drug abuse.
- blaming others.
- increased complaints about a spouse or significant others.

For those who are at home, these symptoms may appear:
• a lack of interest in daily self-care routines.
• less attention paid to children (dependents).
• not wanting to go out of the house.
• not finding any meaning to one's day.
• increased addictive behavior kept a secret.
• feeling overwhelmed by ordinary tasks.
• feelings of guilt and worthlessness.*

In order to best apply this cluster of symptoms to your own situation, think of your symptoms in terms of three words—*number, duration* and *intensity.*

1) **Number.** The symptoms of depression are "additive"—that is, the greater the number of symptoms you have, the more likely you are to be clinically depressed. According to the Diagnostic and Statistical Manual of Mental Disorders (DSM IV), five or more of these symptoms should be present for a person or someone close to that person to consider him or herself "clinically depressed."

2) **Duration.** The longer you have been down in the dumps, the more likely it is that you are clinically depressed. According to the DSM IV, the five or more symptoms must exist for at least *two weeks* for a diagnosis of major depression to be made. (In the case of dysthymia or chronic low-grade depression, symptoms must be present for *two years* or more.)

3) **Intensity.** Many of us can feel emotional pain and still cope with our daily existence. Some experiences of depression are within the normal course of living. The pain of major depression can be so great, however, that its intensity (along with the number and duration of symptoms) can significantly impair one's ability to cope.

Getting proper help for depression begins with proper diagnosis. Of the 17 million people who suffer from depressive illnesses, over two thirds (about 12 million) receive no treatment whatsoever.

---

* Much of the information about the symptoms of depression was provided by the Depression Awareness Recognition and Treatment program (D/ART) of the National Institute of Mental Health. Call (800) 421-4211 for free literature, or visit their Web site (www.nimh.nih.gov).

The minority who do seek help typically consult a number of doctors over many years before the proper diagnosis is made. The questionnaire that follows may help you to determine if you suffer from depression.

Self-Rating Scale for Depression

Have either of the following symptoms been present nearly every day *for at least two weeks?*

A. Have you been sad, blue, or "down in the dumps?"

B. Have you lost interest or pleasure in all or almost all the things you usually do (work, hobbies, interpersonal relationships)?

If either A or B is true, continue. If not, you probably do not have a depressive illness. Now continue by answering the following statements.

Have any of the following symptoms been present nearly every day *for at least two weeks?*

1.	A poor appetite or overeating?	No	Yes
2.	Insomnia—trouble falling asleep, or nighttime awakenings?	No	Yes
3.	Oversleeping (going to bed a lot earlier than usual, staying in bed later than usual, taking long naps)?	No	Yes
4.	Do you have low energy, chronic fatigue or do you feel slowed down?	No	Yes
5.	Are you less active or talkative than usual?	No	Yes
6.	Do you feel restless or agitated?	No	Yes
7.	Do you avoid the company of other people more than you used to?	No	Yes
8.	Have you lost interest or enjoyment in pleasurable activities, including sex?	No	Yes
9.	Do you fail to experience pleasure when positive things occur—such as being praised, being given presents, etc.?	No	Yes

10. Do you have feelings of inadequacy or decreased feelings of self-esteem, or are you overly or increasingly self-critical?	No	Yes
11. Are you less efficient or do you accomplish less at school, work or home?	No	Yes
12. Do you feel less able to cope with the routine responsibilities of daily life?	No	Yes
13. Do you find that your concentration is poor and that you have difficulty making decisions (even trivial ones)?	No	Yes
14. Do you think and/or talk of death and suicide?	No	Yes
15. Have you at any time in the past been acting unusually happy for more than two weeks?	No	Yes

If A or B is true and if you answered yes to five or more of the above questions, you may have a major depressive illness. If you answered yes to #15, you may consider whether major depression is but one phase of a bipolar disorder.*

For the diagnosis to be complete, however, you should have a complete physical exam and blood workup to rule out other medical problems such as anemia, reactive hypoglycemia and low thyroid, all of which cause symptoms which may mimic those of major depression. Specifically, you will want a test of the thyroid function called the TSH (thyroid stimulating hormone) stimulation test as well as the TRH (thyrotropin releasing hormone) stimulation test. (The TRH test is complicated to perform and is thus rarely ordered by doctors; however, it can pick up on thyroid disorders that the TSH test cannot.) It is also important to speak with a mental health professional to rule out the possibility that you are responding to a temporary life upset instead of a biological depression.

---

* Adapted from Donald Klein and Paul Wender, *Understanding Depression*, New York, Oxford University Press, 1993, pp. 13-15.

THE MANY FACES OF DEPRESSION

*"My creative powers have been reduced to a restless indolence.
I cannot be idle, yet I cannot seem to do anything either. I have no
imagination, no more feeling for nature, and reading has become repugnant
to me. When we are robbed of ourselves, we are robbed of everything!"*
Goethe

Getting proper help for depression begins with a proper diagnosis. This is easier said than done, since depression, like the mythological Hydra, is a many-headed beast. There are many types of depressive disorders, each of which contains a multitude of symptom patterns and representations.

What follows is a broad overview of the most common depressive disorders as listed in the Diagnostic and Statistical Manual of Mental Disorders (DSM-IV). For those who have not studied psychology or psychiatry, I hope that this synopsis provides you with an understanding of the brain imbalances that may affect you or your loved ones.

Major Depression
(also known as clinical depression)

This is the mood disorder from which I suffered. Its symptoms are described in Chapter One of my narrative and in the previous section. Along with manic-depressive illness, clinical depression is the most serious of the mood disorders and can result in suicide when left untreated.

Dysthymia

"Good morning, Eeyore," said Pooh.
"Good morning, Pooh Bear," said Eeyore gloomily. "If it is a
good morning," he said, "Which I doubt," said he.
A.A. Milne, *The House at Pooh Corner*

In addition to major depression, there exists another type of depressive illness—dysthymia—that is far less severe, though crippling in its own way. Dysthymia consists of long-term chronic symptoms that do not disable, but keep one from feeling really good or from functioning at full steam. Physically, it is akin to having a chronic low-grade infection—you never develop a full-blown illness, but always feel a little run down.

Although dysthymia implies having an inborn tendency to experience a depressed mood, it may also be caused by childhood trauma, adjustment problems during adolescence, difficult life transitions, the trauma of personal losses, unresolved life problems, and chronic stress. Any combination of these factors can lead to a enduring case of the blues.

Some of the most prominent symptoms of dysthymia are:

- depressed mood for most of the day, for more days than not, for at least two years.
- difficulties in sleeping.
- difficulty in experiencing pleasure.
- a hopeless or pessimistic outlook.
- low energy or fatigue.
- low self-esteem.
- difficulty in concentrating or making decisions.
- persistent physical symptoms (such as headaches, digestive disorders or chronic pain) that do not respond to treatment.

A dysthymic disorder is characterized not by episodes of illness but by the steady presence of symptoms (see diagram on next page).

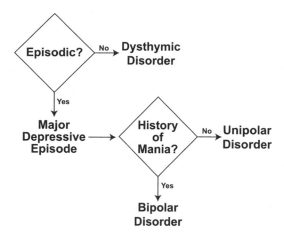

Because dysthymia does not incapacitate like major depression, as a rule, dysthymic people do well in psychotherapy (medication can also be used). During stressful times, a person with dysthymia may be catapulted into a major depressive episode, called "double depression."

Dysthymic disorder is a common ailment, affecting about 3-5 percent of the general population. Unfortunately, because dysthymia is not as severe as clinical depression, the condition is often undiagnosed or dismissed as a case of psychosomatic illness. ("Your symptoms are all in your head," is the all-too-common response from doctors.) Perhaps the most famous dysthymic is Eeyore, the despondent and downcast donkey in A.A. Milne's *Winnie the Pooh*. If you identify with Eeyore (or feel down in the dumps most of the time), it is important that you consult a qualified mental health professional who can make a correct diagnosis. In addition, you can use the wellness strategies described in the "Brain Maintenance" program on pp. 155-178 to improve your mood.

Having a dysthymic temperament also brings with it positive traits. Dysthymic individuals can be serious, profound, deep, prudent, dependable, industrious, patient and responsible.

Manic–Depressive Illness
(Bipolar disorder)
"Terror drove me from place to place. My breath failed me as I pictured my brain paralyzed. Ah, Clara, no one knows the suffering, the sickness, the despair of this illness, except those so crushed."
Composer Robert Schumann, speaking of his manic depression

Although manic-depressive illness (which affects two to three million people) is less common than major depression, it maintains a high profile because of the many creative artists who have suffered from it. Examples include Edgar Allen Poe, Tennessee Williams, Ezra Pound, Virginia Woolfe, Vincent Van Gogh, Alfred Tennyson, Cole Porter and Robert Schumann. In recent times, celebrities such as Abbie Hoffman, columnist Art Buchwald, actress Patty Duke, actress Margot Kidder, and CNN's Ted Turner have been similarly afflicted.

Manic depression has two distinct sides—the *depressive* state and the *manic* state. Mania is a seemingly heavenly state of mind in which all the world is beautiful and everything seems possible. Here are some of the most common characteristics of mania:

- optimism
- euphoria
- little need for sleep
- little need for food
- irritability
- inflated self concept
- grandiose schemes
- unrealistic thinking
- poor judgment
- loss of inhibition
- delusional thinking
- nothing can go wrong
- outbursts of anger
- impulsivity
- spending large amounts of money
- socially inappropriate behavior
- heightened sense of awareness
- flight of ideas
- racing thoughts
- pressured speech
- tremendous energy
- enhanced creativity
- hyperactivity
- feeling that nothing can go wrong
- increased sexual activity
- alcohol and drug abuse

As Kay Redfield Jamison, a psychologist who is diagnosed with manic depression, writes in her memoir *An Unquiet Mind*:

> When you're high it's tremendous. The ideas and feelings
> are fast and frequent like shooting stars and you follow
> them until you find better and brighter ones. Shyness goes.
> The right words and gestures are suddenly there, the power
> to captivate others is a felt certainty. Feelings of ease,
> intensity, power, well-being, financial omnipotence and
> euphoria pervade one's marrow.

Upon hearing this description of mania, people often respond, "If this is a disease, where do I sign up for it?" The problem with mania, however, is that due to the impulsivity and poor judgment that it brings, an episode can wreak havoc on family, friends, the community and the law. Moreover, when the high inevitably wears off, the individual comes crashing down into a state of total darkness and despair. As Jamison describes:

> A floridly psychotic mania was followed, inevitably, by a
> long and lacerating black, suicidal depression. Everything
> —every thought, word and movement—was an effort.
> Everything that once was sparkling now was flat. I seemed
> to myself to be dull, boring, inadequate, thick brained,
> unlit, unresponsive, chill skinned, bloodless, and sparrow
> drab. I doubted, completely, my ability to do anything
> well. It seemed as though my mind had slowed down and
> burned out to the point of being totally useless.

A well-known myth that perfectly describes the manic depressive's fall from grace is the myth of Icarus. Icarus, son of the Greek inventor Daedalus (who built the labyrinth), was given wings of wax by his father. Enamored of his new found ability to fly to great heights, Icarus ignored his father's warning and in a moment of ecstasy flew too close to the sun. The heat of the sun melted the wax which held his wings together, and Icarus crashed into the sea.

The alternation of mania and depression illuminates a second aspect of manic depression—its cyclic nature. Periods of creativity, productivity and high energy alternate with times of fatigue and apparent indifference. Mania leads to depression, which leads to mania which becomes depression, etc. This extreme flip-flop of mood between peaks and valleys is extremely dangerous, as shown by the fact that 20 to 25 percent of untreated manic depressives (including many of the artists listed earlier) commit suicide.

Fortunately, manic depression is highly treatable, due to the discovery of lithium, a simple salt that in 1949 was accidentally found to have a mood-stabilizing effect on bipolar individuals. The downside of lithium treatment is that therapeutic levels of lithium are dangerously close to toxic levels. Lithium poisoning affects the brain and can cause coma and death. Thus, in the initial stages of treatment, lithium concentration in the blood must be frequently monitored. After the lithium blood level stabilizes, levels can be checked every six months.

The side effects of lithium can include hand tremors, excessive thirst, excessive urination, weakness, fatigue, memory problems, diarrhea, and possible interference with kidney function. Lithium is often ineffective in treating bipolar patients who are rapid cyclers—those who experience four or more manic-depressive cycles per year. For these and other patients who fail to stabilize on lithium, the drugs Depakote and Tegretol (originally anti-seizure medications) are also available. For some doctors, Depakote is now the drug of choice, rather than lithium, because its long-term side effects are considered safer.

In addition to taking medication, bipolar individuals can employ a number of preventive strategies to decrease the likelihood of having a full-blown manic attack.

1) Recognize the early warning signs of mania—e.g., insomnia, surges of energy, making lots of plans, grandiose thinking, speeded-up thinking, overcommitment, excessive euphoria, spending too much money, etc. Let friends and family know of these symptoms so that they can also become alerted to the start of a manic episode.

2) Create a stable lifestyle in which you keep regular sleep hours. Studies show that intervals between manic episodes are considerably longer in those people who live in stable environments. In addition, eat a diet that is high in complex carbohydrates and protein, avoiding foods such as simple sugars that can cause ups and downs. Alcohol and caffeine should also be avoided.

3) Use planning and scheduling to stay focused and grounded. Make a list of things to do and stick to it.

4) Try to engage in a daily meditative activity which focuses and calms the mind. If you are too restless for sitting meditation, go for a leisurely walk, taking long, deep breaths along the way.

5) Refrain from taking on too many projects or becoming over-stimulated. If you feel an excess of energy starting to overtake you, channel it into productive physical activities such as doing the dishes, mopping the floor, cleaning out the basement, weeding a garden, etc.

6) Psychotherapy and support groups can help you to explore the emotional aspects of the illness, as well as provide support during times of stress.

7) If you feel that things are getting out of hand, call your doctor or therapist. This is especially true if you start losing sleep, as sleep deprivation is one of the major contributors to mania.

8) Ask a good friend or family member to track your activity level. Sometimes a manic episode can "sneak up on you," and an objective person may be able to spot it before it gets out of hand.

Books, organizations and support groups for manic depression are listed in the Resources for Wellness section at the back of the book.

Cyclothymia

Cyclothymia is a milder form of manic depression, characterized by hypomania (a mild form of mania) alternating with mild bouts of depression. The symptoms are similar to those of bipolar illness but less severe. Many cyclothymic disorder patients have difficulty succeeding in their work or social lives since their unpredictable moods and irritability create a great deal of stress, making it difficult to maintain stable personal or professional relationships. Cyclothymic persons may have a history of multiple geographic moves and alcohol or substance abuse. Nevertheless, when their creative energy is focused towards a worthwhile goal, they may become high achievers in art, business, government, etc. (The cycles of cyclothymia are far shorter than in manic depression.) The ability to work long hours with a minimum of sleep when they are hypomanic often leads to periods of great productivity.

If you identify with the diagnosis of cyclothymia, you may use the wellness strategies described for manic depression, as well as those in the "Brain Maintenance" program (pp. 155-178) to elevate and stabilize your mood. If your highs and lows begin to intensify, seek treatment with a psychiatrist or mental health professional.

Postpartum Depression

In the period that follows giving birth to a child, many women experience some type of emotional disturbance or mental dysfunction. A large percentage of these "baby blues" are characterized by grief, tearfulness, irritability and clinging dependence. These feelings, which may last several days, have been ascribed to the woman's rapid change in hormonal levels, the stress of childbirth, and her awareness of the increased responsibility that motherhood brings.

In some cases, however, the baby blues may take on a life of their own, lasting weeks, months and even years. When this occurs, the woman suffers from *postpartum depression*—a syndrome very much like a major depressive disorder. This depression may also be accompanied by anxiety and panic. In extreme cases, symptoms may include psychotic features and delusions, especially concerning the newborn infant. There may be suicidal ideation and obsessive thoughts of violence to the child.

It is estimated that approximately 400,000 women in the United States experience postpartum depression, usually six to eight weeks after giving birth. Postpartum depression is a treatable illness that responds to the following modalities:

- recognizing and accepting the disorder.
- breaking negative thought patterns.
- creating support systems.
- reducing stressors in one's life.
- exercise and right diet.
- medication (antidepressants and antianxiety drugs).
- psychotherapy.

A good introduction to this often undiagnosed disorder is contained in the book *This Isn't What I Expected* by Karen Kleiman, M.S.W. and Valerie Raskin, M.D. You might also want to visit the web site of the organization Depression After Delivery (http://www.behavenet.com/dadinc).

Seasonal Affective Disorder (SAD)

There's a certain Slant of light,
Winter Afternoons—
That oppresses, like the Heft
Of Cathedral Tunes—
Heavenly Hurt, it gives us.
Emily Dickinson

Patients with Seasonal Affective Disorder tend to experience depressive symptoms during a particular time of the year, most commonly fall or winter. They often begin in October or November and remit in April or May. The symptoms of SAD, also known as "winter depression," are listed below.

- altered sleep patterns, with overall increased amount of sleep.
- difficulty in getting out of bed in the morning and getting going.
- increased lethargy and fatigue.
- apathy, sadness and/or irritability.
- increased appetite, carbohydrate craving and weight gain.
- decreased physical activity.

Researchers believe that Seasonal Affective Disorder is caused by winter's reduction in daylight hours which desynchronizes the body clock and disturbs the circadian rhythms. Winter depression is usually treated by morning exposure to bright artificial light (see pg. 273 for addresses of light box companies). By providing appropriately timed light exposure, the body's circadian rhythms become resynchronized and the symptoms of SAD resolve.

In addition, it is important for the person with SAD to get as much natural light as possible. Here are some suggestions:

- Light up your homes as much as you need to. Use white wallpaper and light-colored carpet instead of dark paneling and dark carpet.
- Choose to live in dwellings with large windows.
- Allow light to shine through doors and windows when temperatures are moderate. Trim hedges around windows to let more light in.
- Exercise outdoors.
- Set up reading or work spaces near a window.
- Ask to sit near a window in restaurants, classrooms or at your workplace.
- Arrange a winter vacation in a warm, sunny climate.
- Put off large undertakings until the summer.

Although the most common form of recurrent seasonal depressions in northern countries is the winter SAD, researchers at the National Institute of Mental Health have uncovered a type of summer depression that occurs during June, July and August. Summer SAD tends to occur more in the southern states such as Florida, as well as in Japan and China. Summer depressives frequently ascribe their symptoms to the severe heat of summer, although in some instances the depressions may be triggered by intense light.

For further information or support about SAD, contact your doctor or visit the Web site of the Society for Light Treatment and Biological Rhythms (http://www.websciences.org/sltbr). Norman Rosenthal's seminal book *Winter Blues* is also a good resource.

Situational Depression

Unlike clinical depression, which is rooted in a biochemical imbalance in the brain and nervous system, situational depression (formerly known as exogenous or reactive depression) is often the result of an identifiable stressful life situation:

- the death of a spouse, parent or child.
- a divorce.
- the loss of a job.
- a financial or health setback.
- a change of residence.
- an accident or being the victim of violence.
- chronic sexual dysfunction.

In circumstances such as these, it would be unusual not to be sad or depressed. Symptoms of situational depression may include insomnia, anxiety, mood swings, and a host of somatic (body-centered) complaints.

Although less debilitating over the long term than clinical depression, situational depression can be extremely painful—as evidenced by the person whose loneliness brought on by a recent divorce becomes intensified over the Christmas holidays. Thus, it is very important to reach out and seek help. Here are some steps you can take:

1) Seek help that is appropriate to the type of challenge you are facing. For example, if you have experienced a personal loss, enter into bereavement counseling and/or join a bereavement support group. If your challenge is monetary or work-related, locate a financial or vocational counselor. If you are experiencing postpartum depression, medical treatment is most likely indicated.

2) Use some of the strategies listed in my survival plan in Chapter Three of the narrative as well those described in the "Brain Maintenance" program. Providing for your physical, emotional and spiritual needs will help you to remain balanced during this challenging period. If you feel that you need to take medication as a temporary support, then consult your physician or therapist.

3) Tell yourself, "This too will pass." Fortunately, your depression is likely to lift when circumstances change back to normal. Realize, however, that you may need to be patient with the process. It may take years to fully grieve a divorce or other major loss.

Existential Depression

A specific kind of situational depression is known as existential depression, brought on by a *crisis of meaning* or *purpose* in one's life. Any significant transition, especially a change of roles in family or work, can trigger this crisis in meaning. A well-known account of existential depression occurred in the life of the famous Russian novelist Leo Tolstoi. In mid-life, while enjoying health, wealth, and great literary fame, Tolstoi fell into a deep despair as he asked himself, "Is this all there is?" Out of his quest for something more, Tolstoi underwent a religious conversion and formulated a philosophy of nonviolence, renunciation of wealth, self-improvement through physical work, and nonparticipation in institutions that created social injustice. Tolstoi's ideas had a profound influence on many social reformers, including Mahatma Gandhi and Martin Luther King, Jr.

The importance of dealing with existential issues should not be underestimated. A number of clinicians have reported that depression (as well as Chronic Fatigue Syndrome) has a strong connection with a person's lack of success in finding his passion—i.e., not being involved in work/activities that feed the core self. After all, Sigmund Freud defined mental health as "the ability to work and to love." If either of these two essential needs is missing, even a person with normal brain chemistry is going to feel out of kilter.

Mood Disorders Due to a Medical Condition

Clinical depression commonly co-occurs with general medical illnesses, though it frequently goes undetected and untreated. While the rate of major depression in the community is estimated to be between 2-4 percent, among primary care patients it is between 5-10 percent. For inpatients, the rate increases to between 10-14 percent.

Treating the co-occurring depressive symptoms can improve the outcome of the medical illness while reducing the emotional and physical pain and disability suffered by the patient. Here are some medical conditions that have been implicated as triggering depressive symptoms:

- endocrine conditions (hypothyroidism, etc.).
- neurological disorders such as brain tumors.
- encephalitis.
- epilepsy.
- cerebrovascular diseases that cause structural damage to the brain.
- viral and bacterial infections.
- inflammatory conditions such as rheumatoid arthritis and lupus.
- vitamin deficiencies (especially vitamin B12, vitamin C, folic acid and niacin).
- heart disease.
- stroke.
- diabetes.
- kidney disease.
- multiple sclerosis.
- cancer.

Anyone who suffers from one of these disorders should treat the underlying illness medically and pursue psychotherapy or counseling if depression accompanies the physical illness.

Medication-Induced Depression

Many people do not realize that a number of common prescription drugs have side effects that can induce depression. Thirty years ago, my mother went into a long-term depression as a result of a reaction to the drug Resperine, a high blood pressure medication. Similarly, my own depression was accelerated by my reaction to large doses of antibiotics given for a leg infection. Prescription drugs with depressive side effects include:

- cardiac drugs and hypertensives
- sedatives, steroids
- stimulants
- antibiotics
- antifungal drugs
- analgesics

It may be worthwhile to consult the Physician's Desk Reference (PDR) or books such as *Worst Pills, Best Pills* (by Wolfe, Sasich, and Hope) to learn if depression is a potential side effect of a medication you are taking. In addition, taking recreational drugs or being exposed to toxic chemicals in the environment may also have an adverse effect on mood.

Usually, stopping the intake of the offending substance will eliminate the symptoms (as happened in my mother's episode). If depressive symptoms caused by the substance linger, then psychological treatment may be necessary.

Substance-Induced Mood Disorder

If you're depressed, you're more likely to use alcohol and other drugs to medicate your feelings. And if you use alcohol and other drugs, you are more likely to develop depression. Thus alcohol and drug abuse can be both the cause *and* result of clinical depression.

When you are both depressed and dependent on alcohol or drugs, you are given a "dual diagnosis." A dual diagnosis simply means that you suffer from *both* a psychiatric disorder (it may a bipolar disorder or depression) *and* chemical dependency. Having a dual diagnosis complicates the healing process, since it means that you have to overcome two major illnesses in order to get well. Fortunately, many outpatient and resident treatment centers specialize in treating individuals with dual diagnoses. These centers are usually covered by insurance and are able to offer long-term treatment. Check with your local hospital or mental health clinic to learn who offers dual diagnosis treatment in your area.

THE ROOTS OF DEPRESSION

"I am not a mechanism, an assembly of various sections.
And it is not because the mechanism is working wrongly, that I am ill.
I am ill because of wounds to the soul, to the deep emotional self
and wounds to the soul take a long, long time, only time can help
and patience, and a certain difficult repentance,
long, difficult repentance, realization of life's mistake,
and the freeing oneself from the endless repetition of the mistake
which mankind at large has chosen to sanctify."
D.H. Lawrence, from the poem "Healing"

There is a famous parable from India about six blind men who encounter an elephant.* The first man runs into the elephant's side and says, "An elephant is like a wall."

The second man has his hand stabbed by the tusk and cries, "An elephant is like a spear."

The third man grabs the elephant's trunk and says, "I have met a snake."

The fourth man bumps against the leg and declares, "You're all wrong. An elephant is like a tree."

The fifth man puts his hand on the elephant's ear and says, "I have discovered a fan."

Finally, the sixth man brushes against the elephant's tail and declares it to be a rope.

On and on for many years, the blind men continue to argue over which one had understood the "true nature" of the elephant.

In recent years, a similar debate has ensued over the true cause of depression. Yet like the elephant, depression is too large and mysterious to be grasped by any one point of view. Depression is a

---

* From the poem "The Blind Men and the Elephant" by John Godfrey Saxe.

complex, multifaceted, multidimensional disorder. Just as there is no single cause of cancer, neither is there a single cause of depression. Depression, like the trunk of a tree, has many roots.

What follows are some of the general and specific factors that contribute to the onset of depression.

Genetics and biology

It is now well accepted that there exists a biochemical component of depression. This is supported by the fact that depression exhibits a host of physical symptoms, such as changes in sleep and eating patterns, diurnal variations in mood, impaired ability to concentrate, physical agitation, and decreased sexual drive. These "housekeeping" functions are controlled by the hypothalamus, the amygdala and the hippocampus, which are located in the "emotional brain," also known as the limbic system.

In addition, depression tends to run in families, suggesting a role for genetic factors. If there is an inherited condition which predisposes some individuals to depression, it is likely to manifest as an imbalance in brain/body chemistry, as is the case in other genetic disorders. In this respect, inheriting a depressive or melancholic temperament may be just as physical as being born with clubfoot.*

Childhood trauma and other psychological factors

Not only do changes in biochemistry affect our psychological states, but changes in our psychology (reactions to trauma, personal loss, rejection) can also alter the biochemistry of the brain and nervous system—sometimes permanently. For example, English psychiatrist John Bowlby observed that premature separation of an infant from its mother can create definite and marked changes in the nervous system, especially if the emotions associated with the trauma are never fully grieved and resolved. Hence, in *Darkness Visible*,

---

* Interestingly, if one identical twin is ill with depression, there is a 30% chance that the other will suffer from it, but for fraternal twins the risk is still 15-25%. This supports the theory that both environmental and genetic/biological factors contribute to depression.

William Styron concluded that his melancholy was rooted in the unexpressed mourning over the death of his mother at age eleven.

Two experiments confirm the interdependence of body, mind and emotions. Researchers at the State University of New York at Stony Brook used the model of "learned helplessness" to create disturbances in the brain chemistries of laboratory rats. Then, when the experimenters taught the rats a way to escape their electric shocks by pressing a lever, the rats' depression subsided and the beta receptor sites in the brain returned to normal. *

A second inquiry conducted by researchers at Eli Lilly measured neurotransmitters in damselfish who were kept in tanks and separated from their natural predators by a glass wall. Since the damselfish could not detect the invisible wall, they thought they were about to be eaten. Over time, the experimenters detected a clear *decrease* in the levels of serotonin in the fishes' brains, ostensibly caused by the animals' fear and anxiety. **

Environmental factors

Environmental factors such as poor nutrition, hormonal imbalances, toxins in the environment, brain injuries, stress, substance abuse, and adverse reactions to medication can lead to depressive states. People become depressed when losing a job, a partner, or after contracting a serious illness.

One kind of external stressor that until recently has been ignored is the presence of viral and bacterial infections. Scientists now believe that bacteria and viruses which frequently invade our body may also unleash a host of major mental and emotional illnesses. For example, streptococcal bacteria—those that cause strep throat—also attack the basal ganglia in the brain, and have been implicated in obsessive-compulsive disorder, anorexia nervosa and Tourette's syndrome. Other pathogens, such as T Pallidum (the syphilis-causing

---

* Demitri and Janice Papolos, *Overcoming Depression*, New York, HarperPerennial, 1992, pp. 88-9.

** Thompson, Tracy, *The Beast: A Reckoning with Depression,* GP Putnam and Sons, New York, 1995, pp. 89-90.

bacteria) and the human immunodeficiency virus have been known to cause anxiety, delirium, psychoses, and suicidal impulses.*

Sociological factors

Finally, depression has a sociological aspect. Many changes in modern society—such as the breakdown of traditional communities, the dissolution of extended families, the widening gap between rich and poor, and our disconnection from the natural world—may play a part in the rising rates of depression worldwide. Isolation as a contributing risk factor for depression is suggested by a British study showing that single parents were more likely to become depressed than married ones.

What makes depression so complex is that all these factors—genetic, biological, psychological, and environmental—are intertwined and constantly affecting one another. As the tale of the blind men and the elephant reminds us, it is sometimes difficult to see the big picture. In addition, specific causal factors may lead one patient's depression to be biologically based, while another's may be caused primarily by stressors in the environment.

Because depression is so multifaceted, it makes sense that its treatment should likewise be multidimensional. In the following pages, we will explore some of the many approaches that have been successfully used to treat depression.

---

* Harriet Washington, "Infection Connection," *Psychology Today*, July/August 1999, pg. 43 (5).

Staying Free from Depression:
Your Personal "Brain Maintenance" Program

*"To optimize the function of the healing system, you must do everything
in your power to improve physical health, mental/emotional health, and
spiritual health... One of the disappointments of my professional life is
meeting so few teachers who see the whole picture of health,
who understand the importance of working on all fronts."*
Andrew Weil, M.D., *Eight Weeks to Optimal Health*

S urviving a depressive episode does not mean that life is suddenly beautiful. For the person who suffers from dysthymia
(low-grade chronic depression), recovery from major depression can simply mean a return to the gray zone. Yet no matter the
severity of your melancholy, there is much you can do to increase
the likelihood that you will continue to stay and feel well.

Since depression is a complex disorder with multiple causes, it
makes sense to treat it on a variety of levels. A good analogy is the
way we approach heart disease. If you went to a cardiologist and
wanted to know how to prevent a heart attack (or to recover from
one), he or she might prescribe a cholesterol-lowering medication
and tell you to eat a low-fat diet, exercise three to four times a week,
and cut down on the stress in your life.

What follows is also a holistic program for the *prevention* and
treatment of depression. I have developed it:

- from my own experience (both during and after my depressive episode).
- from talking with others who are successfully managing their
  depression and anxiety.
- from researching the medical and psychiatric literature.

Healing from Depression:
A Brain Maintenance Program

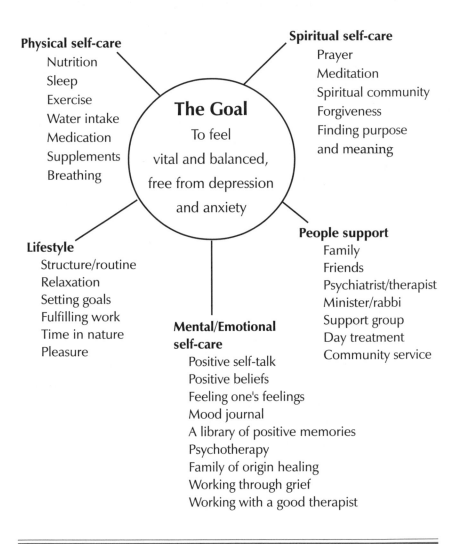

Physical self-care
Nutrition
Sleep
Exercise
Water intake
Medication
Supplements
Breathing

Spiritual self-care
Prayer
Meditation
Spiritual community
Forgiveness
Finding purpose
and meaning

The Goal
To feel
vital and balanced,
free from depression
and anxiety

Lifestyle
Structure/routine
Relaxation
Setting goals
Fulfilling work
Time in nature
Pleasure

People support
Family
Friends
Psychiatrist/therapist
Minister/rabbi
Support group
Day treatment
Community service

**Mental/Emotional
self-care**
Positive self-talk
Positive beliefs
Feeling one's feelings
Mood journal
A library of positive memories
Psychotherapy
Family of origin healing
Working through grief
Working with a good therapist

This "brain maintenance" program is meant to serve:

1) Those individuals who have experienced one or more episodes of major depression and wish to stay well. (Although there is no guarantee that this program will keep depression at bay, it can strengthen your "psychological immune system" and therefore enhance your resistance to the illness.)

2) Those individuals who suffer from dysthymia (low-grade chronic depression) and desire to elevate their mood, as well as prevent a major depression.

3) Those people who are experiencing a major depressive episode and wish to use these strategies as an adjunct to medication and/or psychotherapy. (You may also want to re-read Chapters Two through Four in the personal narrative to see how someone else in extreme distress coped.)

As I did with my personal survival strategies, I have organized this treatment plan into four areas—physical self-care, mental/emotional self-care, spiritual self-care, and people support. In addition, I have added a fifth category—lifestyle habits. The diagram on the facing page gives a visual overview of the program.

As you read through the material, think of my recommendations as guidelines, not hard-and-fast prescriptions. Each person's healing journey is unique. It is up to each individual to sift through the available treatment options and discover what works.

Now, let's begin.

Physical Self-Care

"I have long suspected that the increase in clinical depression in our society is linked to the increased consumption of sugar."
Candace Pert, Ph.D., from the foreword to *Potatoes Not Prozac*

Our body is a temple for the living spirit. If we are to experience wholeness and vitality, it is important that we take care of and honor our body's needs. Being in good health will enhance your ability to do the remaining steps of this program.

Diet and nutrition

Good nutrition supports the optimal functioning of your brain and body. To insure that you are meeting your nutritional needs, eat a balanced diet of healthy foods. Eating as much organic produce as possible will help to minimize the intake of chemicals and preservatives which can cause problems in sensitive individuals.

Another part of nutritional self-care is cutting back on the sweets. Studies have shown that too much sugar can foster anxiety as well as depression. Reducing intake of sugar may also bolster your immune system, reduce allergies and cut the risk of diabetes and reactive hypoglycemia.

Because sugar finds its way into so many foods in the Western diet, I would like to take a moment to describe what happens when the body consumes a high amount of refined sugar. The body, registering abnormally high levels of blood sugar, over-releases insulin in an attempt to lower those levels. Then when too much insulin is released, blood sugar levels drop below normal, resulting in weakness, shakiness, fatigue, hunger, agitation, and sometimes depression. Now that your blood sugar is too low, you seek out a "sugar fix" to relieve your distress. This of course sets up the classic "vicious cycle." The way out of this manic-depressive eating style is to choose proteins and complex carbohydrates—grains, legumes, seeds, nuts and vegetables—over simple sugars. (For an in-depth discussion of sugar's deleterious effects on the body, refer to William Dufty's classic book *Sugar Blues,* listed in the Recommended Reading section.)

Finally, there seems to be a loose connection between depression and food sensitivities. Although no one has proven that allergies can cause depression, it seems reasonable to assume that allergies can aggravate a depressive condition since both conditions are known to involve similar biochemical imbalances (low norepinephrine and high acetylcholine levels). Common food allergens include dairy products, wheat, and corn. If you think you have food allergies, consult a doctor who specializes in allergies or environmental medicine.

Vitamin and mineral supplementation

In addition to eating a balanced diet, you might want to take a good multi-vitamin and multi-mineral supplement with special emphasis on the antioxidants—vitamins A, C and E. The entire vitamin B complex is known to maintain and promote normal mental functioning, so it may be helpful to take a good B complex tablet. Calcium and magnesium, which help to calm the nervous system, are especially helpful to anxiety-prone individuals. Deficiencies of the B vitamins, as well as of magnesium, manganese, zinc and iron, can be a factor in depression.

For information on other supplements that may be helpful in treating of depression, please turn to "Natural Alternatives to Prozac" in Section 5, pg. 196.

Exercise

Exercise—any activity that promotes endurance, flexibility or strengthening—is a natural antidepressant. Aerobic exercise in particular improves circulation, brings increased blood flow and oxygen to the brain, and releases endorphins, the body's natural pain-killing chemicals. Studies have shown that exercise works as well as pharmaceuticals in healing mild to moderate depression. The only "side effects" of aerobic exercise are a stronger cardiovascular system and better overall health. As little as three hours a week can reduce the level of depression.* Even if you have no history of mood disorders, regular exercise can profoundly improve the quality of your physical, mental and emotional well being. Researchers like Candace Pert have shown that "molecules of emotion" are located not just in the brain, but throughout the body.

Our bodies were made to move—movement is a direct expression of our life energy. Whether it is a daily walk in the park, a water aerobics or yoga class, or dancing to your favorite music, get into motion. Start with small steps and remind yourself that you don't have to be perfect. At the pool where I swim, I see many

---

* *Behavioral Medicine Journal*, 1985; v. 291, pg. 109.

disabled, elderly and overweight people taking part in water exercise classes. Thus, even if you have a physical disability or carry extra pounds, it is usually possible to engage in some form of movement.

Abdominal breathing

One of the most powerful ways to impact the emotions and the involuntary nervous system is through the breath. In Sanskrit, the word for breath is *prana*, which also means "life" or "spirit." Most people in our society breathe rapidly and shallowly, using only the upper part of their chests. This is especially true for depressed individuals, whose life force is at a low point.

Abdominal breathing (also called diaphragmatic breathing) involves using your entire chest *and* abdominal cavity to breathe. Some of the benefits of abdominal breathing include:

- increased oxygen to the brain, lungs, bloodstream and musculature.
- stimulation of the parasympathetic nervous system, which produces "the relaxation response."
- a greater integration of mind and body.
- a decrease in anxiety. A few minutes of abdominal breathing can help decrease racing thoughts, slow down the mind and bring a person back into his or her body.
- a greater feeling of aliveness and wellness.

To practice abdominal breathing, wear loose fitting clothes and sit in a comfortable chair. Have your head, neck and trunk straight. Place one hand on your abdomen right below your rib cage. Inhale slowly and deeply into the bottom of your lungs; in other words, send the air down as low as you can. As your abdomen fills with air, you should observe your hand rising while your chest expands only slightly.*

After you have breathed in as much as you can, pause for a moment, and then exhale slowly through your nose or mouth. As

---

* Bourne, Edmund J., *The Anxiety and Phobia Workbook*, Oakland, New Harbinger Publications, 1995, pp. 69-71.

you breathe out, notice your hand moving back towards your body as the abdomen deflates. Feel yourself letting go and becoming limp, like a rag doll, as you exhale fully.

I first learned about abdominal breathing in a yoga class many years ago. You can also learn diaphragmatic breathing techniques in any stress reduction clinic, biofeedback center, pain clinic, or from any individual who has practiced yoga.

Sleep hygiene

Part of staying physically balanced means developing regular sleep patterns that give you adequate amounts of rest. (Studies show that most Americans are sleep-deprived.) Try to develop a sleep schedule—a regular time of going to sleep and arising—and stick to it. Sleep irregularities are among the early warning signs of *both* mania and depression. These symptoms include:

- trouble falling asleep.
- trouble staying asleep.
- early morning awakenings (followed by ruminations).
- sleeping too much.

Sleep medication can be useful in trying to break a pattern of sleeplessness, but it is only designed for short-term use. Behavioral changes, such as those listed in the book *No More Sleepless Nights* by Peter Hauri, can be extremely effective. In addition, you may wish to be evaluated at a sleep clinic to rule out the possibility of physical problems such as sleep apnea. (Sleep apnea is a temporary suspension of breathing that occurs repeatedly during sleep and often affects overweight people or those who have an obstruction in their breathing tract.)

Water intake

To maintain healthy body functioning, it is important to drink adequate amounts of fluids, at least two quarts a day. Your body is composed of 70 percent water. Water is essential to proper metabolism, circulation and elimination. It flushes out toxins and restores chemical balance to cells, tissues and organs. Many people report a direct improvement in mood once they increase their fluid intake.

Given the condition of city water, you may want to purchase a water filter for your kitchen or buy bottled water. It is especially important to drink plenty of water if you are cutting back on caloric intake or exercising more. Also remember that water weight gain is not the same as fat weight gain, and is only temporary—the body "learns" to retain water during periods of dehydration and will "unlearn" this process when you are sufficiently hydrated. If water retention doesn't abate in a few days, consult your doctor— it may be that the medications you are taking, or salt intake are the main culprits.

Medication

If antidepressant medication is part of your treatment plan, it is important to take it as prescribed. Medication is not a miracle cure or a replacement for psychotherapy. What medication can do is to create an inner stability ("take the edge off," as a friend described it) that will allow you to make use of therapy. Some people need to take antidepressants on a long-term basis, while others are able stop the medication after their depression lifts. Consult your medication prescriber to determine the plan that is right for you.

If you need to take antidepressants regularly to remain well, do not think of this as a personal weakness. The diabetic takes insulin, the hypertensive takes blood pressure pills, the nearsighted person wears glasses—and the person suffering from depression takes antidepressant medication when the body requires a little outside assistance to remain in balance. On the other hand, abrupt cessation of medication or sustained "drug holidays" are known to be factors in precipitating relapses of depression, making the later episodes more difficult to treat.

Mental/Emotional Self-Care

"Given the present tools available to help those with mood disorders, the evidence is overwhelming that judicious pharmacological intervention plus a program of self-education—which is the core of psychotherapy—is the best approach to treatment and prevention."
Edward Whybrow, *A Mood Apart*

The new science of psychoneuroimmunology clearly documents the impact of the mind and emotions on the nervous system and immune functioning. Developing positive habits of thinking and feeling is an essential part of the success of your "Brain Maintenance" program.

Monitor your self-talk

Each of us participates in a silent, internal conversation known as "self-talk." This self-talk consists of two inner voices that are in constant dialogue. The first voice, known as the "yes" voice, gives us positive and supportive messages about ourselves and the world. The opposing "no" voice engages in negative, fearful self-talk. The "no" voice is the voice of doubt, worry, anxiety, limitation, shame, and self-blame.

You may have become so used to this internal chatter that you hardly even notice it. Nonetheless, which voice you listen to has a powerful impact on the way you feel. If you find yourself thinking thoughts of pessimism or despair—listening to the "no" voice— start by identifying and labeling these negative thoughts. (Refer to the sidebar on cognitive distortions on pg. 165). Then, systematically replace them with messages of hope and encouragement. You may wish to create a set of positive affirmations that you can repeat regularly. Avoid comparing yourself to other people or being overly critical of yourself. Have compassion for yourself and your situation.

Words and beliefs have the power to change body chemistry. (Think of how the words "I love you" make you feel.) Examine your beliefs about yourself, the world and the future, and determine if any of them need to changing. Examples of irrational and self-defeating beliefs include "It is important for everyone to like me all the time," "I must be perfect in all that I do," "I shouldn't have to suffer," and "It is my fault that I am depressed." Since upsetting feelings come from upsetting ideas, if you question and challenge the beliefs behind your uncomfortable feelings, you can become more and more free of negative emotions.

In addition, develop what psychologist Martin Seligman calls "learned optimism," a way of looking at life in which good events are seen as permanent and all-encompassing, and bad events are seen as temporary and situationally specific. Seligman has demonstrated that this kind of attitudinal mindset—creating empowering interpretations for both successes and setbacks—can heal anxiety and depression as well as enhance school achievement, job performance, and health and longevity.[*]

Stay in touch with all of your feelings

To remain emotionally healthy, it is necessary to feel *the full range* of all of your emotions, even the so-called "negative" ones of sadness, fear and anger. Entering individual or group therapy can provide a safe place where you can learn to identify your feelings and express previously repressed emotions.

Psychologists have observed that it is not the feelings per se, but the suppression of those feelings that can lead to depression and other illnesses. Although the phrase "depression is anger turned inward" may have been overstated, in a number of instances depressed individuals who discharge their anger experience a lifting of their mood.[**] Moreover, a new study has shown that writing about traumatic experiences can improve the health of patients with chronic illness such as asthma and rheumatoid arthritis. [***]

---

[*] Seligman, Martin, *Learned Optimism*, New York, Alfred A. Knopf, 1990.

[**] Flach, Kenneth, *The Secret Strength of Depression,* Philadelphia, J. Lippincott and Co., 1974.

[***] Goode, Erica, "Can an Essay a Day Keep Arthritis or Asthma at Bay?" *New York Times,* April 14, 1999, pg. A19.

Common Cognitive Distortions

Painful feelings are often the result of distorted, negative thinking. Here are some common "cognitive distortions" that accompany a depressive episode.

1. **All-or-nothing thinking**. Seeing things in black-and-white categories—e.g., "If I don't do something perfectly, I'm a failure."

2. **Mental filter**. Picking out a single negative detail and dwelling on it exclusively.

3. **Disqualifying the positive**. Rejecting anything positive that happens, insisting that it doesn't count.

4. **Magnification or minimization**. Exaggerating the importance of some things (such as your faults) and minimizing others (such as your desirable qualities).

5. **Jumping to conclusions**. Making a negative interpretation, even though there are no definite facts that support the conclusion.

a) Mind reading. Arbitrarily concluding that someone else is reacting negatively to you without checking it out.

b) Fortune telling. Being convinced that things will turn out badly.

6. **Emotional reasoning**, Assuming that negative emotions reflect the way things really are—i.e., "I feel it, therefore it must be true."

7. **Should statements**. Using these on yourself produces guilt. Directing them towards others creates anger and resentment.

8. **Labeling and mislabeling**. This is an extreme form of overgeneralization. Instead of saying, "I made a mistake," you say, "I'm a loser." Mislabeling can be directed at others as well—e.g., "He's a jerk."

9. **Personalization**. Seeing yourself as the cause of some negative external event which you are not responsible for.

In cognitive therapy, one identifies the cognitive distortions that are contributing to the depressed mood and replaces them with more realistic and rational thoughts. And when the thinking changes, the feelings often follow.

Mood Chart   (use this chart to track your daily moods)

My mood for most of each day in the month of _____

	1	2	3	4	5	6	7	8	9	10	11	12	13	14
Above the Clouds														
Great														
Good														
Fair														
Not-So-Good														
In the Gutter														

Big Deal of the Day:

15	16	17	18	19	20	21	22	23	24	25	26	27	28	29	30	31

Some people have a problem of feeling too intensely (i.e., being flooded with anxiety or experiencing uncontrollable anger). In therapy, they can learn to express their feelings responsibly (assertively) or to regulate the intensity of their feelings so they do not overwhelm themselves or others.

Keep a mood journal

A mood journal provides a way for you to monitor your moods and emotions on a daily basis, as well as the external and internal events that accompany them (see chart on previous two pages). Tracking subtle shifts in your moods can alert you to the early signs of a depressive downturn, and thus allow you to take action to prevent another episode.

Create a library of positive memories

This is a wonderful, self-empowering technique. Make a list of the ten happiest moments of your life. Go back in time and relive them, using your five senses to recreate, in exquisite detail, those joyful experiences. Then, when you are feeling a bit low or need some inspiration, you can call up those pleasant memories. Because the brain cannot differentiate between a real or imagined experience, its neurochemicals will take on the same configuration as they did when the original events occurred. This deceptively simple, yet powerful exercise can enhance your mood regardless of the external circumstances.

Work on your unfinished family of origin issues (when appropriate)

Unhealed trauma from the past (abandonment, neglect, abuse, etc.) can be an underlying cause of overt or covert depression. One of the most common forms of unfinished business is unexpressed grief. In his famous paper *Mourning and Melancholia*, Freud postulated that depression was caused by incomplete mourning. Elizabeth Kubler-Ross identified the five stages of *death/grieving* as denial, anger, bargaining, depression and acceptance. When we do not fully grieve a serious loss, we can get stuck in the depression phase. Hence, the incidence of depression in people who have experienced a significant loss in childhood—e.g., the death of a parent—is much higher than in those who have not. Therapy can help you to more fully resolve any incomplete grief you may be carrying, so that a more complete healing may occur.

Find a good therapist

The work of emotional healing requires that we find an ally. There are many types of guides to choose from—psychiatrists, psychologists, social workers, pastoral counselors, licensed professional counselors, drug and alcohol counselors, etc. Locating the right therapist means finding the right fit, just as in a marriage or business partnership. Take the time you need and trust your instincts. The person you work with will be an indispensable part of your healing journey. *

It is also okay to take time with a therapist before you decide if you want to continue with that person. At the very least you should feel safe, respected and understood by your counselor. The therapist should also be willing to explain his or her therapeutic philosophy and why he or she is using specific techniques.

Expect ups and downs

The road to recovery is an upward path, but it is not always smooth and steady. Often we take two steps forward, then one step backward. Be patient with yourself and with the healing process. As poet Jack Kerouac said, "Walking on water wasn't built in a day."

---

* For approaches to therapy, see Section 5, "Seeking Professional Help: A Guide to Options," pg. 181.

People Support

*"Anything that promotes a sense of isolation often leads
to illness and suffering. Anything that promotes a sense of
love and intimacy, connection and community, is healing."*
Dean Ornish, *Love and Survival*

Throughout this book I have emphasized that an essential survival tool for overcoming clinical depression is the ability to reach out for support. Having healthy relationships not only helps to alleviate depression, but also helps to prevent its recurrence. Isolation, on the other hand, makes one more vulnerable to mental and physical illness.

In a groundbreaking study at Stanford University, psychiatrist David Siegel found that women with breast cancer who attended an emotional support group lived twice as long as women in a control group who received no support. In addition, cardiologist Dean Ornish has discovered that intimacy has a pronounced effect on both preventing and healing cardiac disease.

Building a good support network takes time and the process is unique to each person. It means surrounding yourself with people who can validate what you are going though and who can unconditionally accept you. Some of the members of a support system may include:

* **family** and close **friends**.
* an **ally** such as a counselor, psychologist, psychiatrist, rabbi, minister, priest, 12 step sponsor or friend in whom you can confide.
* **group support**. Here is where you can gain (and give) help and encouragement from (and to) others who are going through experiences like yours. In a support group, you learn that you are not alone in your suffering, and that there are others who truly understand your pain. To find a depression or anxiety support group in your area, call your local mental health clinic, hospital, the National Alliance for the Mentally Ill (800-950-NAMI) or the Depressive and Related Affective Disorder Association (410-955-4647).

Other types of group support you may wish to seek out include a 12-step group (the 12 steps work beautifully when applied to depression—see Part Two, Section 6), a women's group, a men's group, group therapy, a self-help group that focuses on any issue you are dealing with, or a Master Mind group. (To learn about Master Mind groups, please refer to Appendix B.)

In addition to the support of human beings, I want to mention the support of animals, especially **domestic pets**. The unconditional love that we give to and receive from our animal friends can be as healing as human love. (This is why pets are increasingly brought to hospital wards and nursing homes.) A loving relationship with a cherished pet provides bonding and intimacy that can strengthen one's psychological immune system and help keep depression at bay.*

Spiritual Self-Care

"A counselor helps you work through the depression.
A spiritual advisor helps you find God in the depression."
sister Rea McDonnell, author of *God Is With the Broken-Hearted*

"At the hospital I was separated from alcohol for the last time. There I
humbly offered myself to God as I understood Him, to do with me
as He would. I placed myself unreservedly under his care and protection.
I have not had a drink since."
Bill W., founder of Alcoholics Anonymous

Mental health researchers have defined a phenomenon known as "religious coping"—a reliance on a spiritual belief or activity to help manage emotional stress or physical discomfort.** It was this type of spiritual coping that drew me to the Living Enrichment Center and to my ultimate healing. Here are some aspects of spiritual self-care that can be used to promote emotional serenity.

---

* Without knowing it, I took this advice when I adopted a neglected stray cat in the middle of my recent depressive episode. As Gabriel got better, so did I.

** Pargament, Maton and Hess, *Religion and Prevention in Mental Health*, New York, Haworth Press, 1992, pg. 107.

Prayer and meditation

The eleventh step of the 12 steps suggests that we "seek through prayer and meditation to improve our contact with our Higher Power." (It is helpful to think of prayer as talking to God, and of meditation as letting God talk to you.)

If you believe in prayer, take regular time to pray, both by yourself and with other people. Meditation involves stilling the mind so that we can hear the "still small voice" of God within and be open to spiritual guidance. There are many forms of meditation available— TM (transcendental meditation), Zen centers, the books of Buddhist priest Thich Nhet Hahn, or the simple form of meditation described in Herbert Benson's work, *The Relaxation Response*. Since many people in the modern world are so mentally active, a walking meditation (consciously focusing on each step) is an excellent way to calm the mind while burning off nervous energy. Spending time in nature is also a fine way to commune with one's spiritual source.

Spiritual community

Whatever your spiritual path, worshipping with others in spiritual community is a powerful way to deepen one's faith. All spiritual traditions have emphasized joining with others as a way to gain assistance in strengthening one's spiritual life. One of the Buddha's main teachings was to "seek the sangha"—i.e., a community of like-minded believers. Similarly, one of the greatest spiritual movements of the 20th century—Alcoholics Anonymous—has made community fellowship the foundation of its healing work. Moreover, as I discovered, the power of prayer can be enhanced in a group setting.

Forgiveness

The word "resentment" comes from the Latin root "resentir," meaning "to feel over and over again." Resentment keeps our energy bound up in the past, unavailable for full expression in the present. Holding grudges also prevents us from experiencing joy, our natural antidepressant. Since we are often hardest on ourselves, self-forgiveness is a key aspect of the forgiveness process.

Purpose and meaning

During his concentration camp experience, physician Victor Frankl discovered that a prisoner's survival depended on his ability to find meaning in his experience. Some prisoners found meaning in wanting to bear witness to the suffering they had observed; others desired to live for the sake of a spouse or a child; still others longed to complete an unfinished work.

After the war, Frankl realized that the need for meaning was not just applicable to prisoners of war; it was a universal human need. In his role as a psychiatrist, Frankl found that many types of mental illness—including depression—improved when a person found a worthwhile purpose upon which to base his life. Knowing that life has purpose and meaning can give us the courage to live life to the fullest, even during those times that are unavoidably painful.

Service

All spiritual traditions stress service as a part of one's spiritual path. A fundamental symptom of depression (and unhappiness in general) is self-absorption. Service allows us to transcend our suffering by shifting our focus away from ourselves. As author Tracy Thompson writes in regard to her own recovery, "Help others. Be of service. Only in this way will you find your way out of the prison of self." In this vein, an article in *Psychology Today* reports that volunteer work leads to a phenomenon called "helper's high"—a physiological change in the body that produces physical and emotional well being, as well as relief from stress-related disorders.*

The amount of service that you perform does not have to be large. If you are feeling limited in your capacity to give, start with some form of service that requires a low level of commitment—such as nurturing a pet or a plant. Extending yourself even a little bit will be good for the recipient and good for you.

---

* Luk, Alan, "Helper's High," *Psychology Today*, October 1988, Volume 22, #10, pp. 39, 42.

Leading a Healthy Lifestyle
"Those who do not find some time every day for health
must one day sacrifice a lot of time for illness."
Father Sebastian Kneipp

Here are some lifestyle habits that can help you to maintain balance and stability in your emotional life:

1) Find ways to create **structure/routine** in your daily activities. Optimal amounts of structure seem to decrease anxiety and help stabilize emotions.

2) Find ways to connect to the **natural world**. Whether it's watching a moonrise over a mountain peak, a sunset over the ocean, or simply taking a leisurely walk in your city park, spending time in nature can elicit a healing connection to Mother Earth. There is scientific evidence which shows that contact with nature—even if it is just a view of trees from a window—can improve coping ability and mental functioning in people who are ill or under stress. As John Muir, father of the wilderness movement, said, "Climb the mountains. Get their glad tidings. Let the winds and the storms blow their energy into you, and watch your cares drop off like autumn leaves."

3) Part of connecting to nature means getting enough exposure to **natural light.** Many spiritual paths teach that God and light are one and the same. For those people who are light-sensitive, inadequate exposure to light can create depressive syndromes such as Seasonal Affective Disorder (SAD). If you live in a dark climate and suffer from SAD, use full-spectrum lights or halogen lamps to enhance your exposure to light. An hour of exposure to outdoor light in the early morning can also make a difference. Some people find that lighting candles on a dark winter's day brings warmth and coziness to the environment. (See Appendix C for how to obtain light boxes for seasonal depression.)

4) Strive for **balance**. If you have a tendency to be manic as well as depressed, endeavor to keep yourself on an even keel. Remember, what goes up must come down. Balance also means taking

The Prayer of Saint Francis of Assisi

This is one of my favorite prayers and is a perfect expression of the principle of selfless service, a way of giving that comes back to us tenfold.

Lord, make me an instrument of Your peace.

Where there is hatred, let me sow love.

Where there is injury, pardon.

Where there is doubt, faith.

Where there is despair, hope.

Where there is darkness, light.

Where there is sadness, joy.

O, Divine Master, grant that I

may not so much seek

To be consoled as to console.

To be understood as to understand.

To be loved as to love.

For it is in giving that we receive.

It is in pardoning that we are pardoned.

And it is in dying that we are born to eternal life.

enough time to rest and regenerate so that you do not overextend yourself with too many projects or commitments. Because our culture puts so much emphasis on doing, it is important to schedule in periods of time to **relax and just "be."** You may wish to meditate, walk, listen to your favorite music, or engage in a hobby where you can relax in a focused way. In addition, finding a creative outlet such as music, painting, gardening, photography, writing, or woodworking can bring a sense of purpose and meaning to your life.

5) **Avoid using drugs and alcohol** as a means of alleviating discomfort. As I have stated throughout this book, depression and alcoholism/addiction are related and may even be aspects of the same disorder. While it can be tempting to use alcohol to relax or get to sleep (or to use caffeine to focus), you run the risk of develop-

ing a new problem—chemical dependency. Apply the tools described in this section—e.g., deep breathing, exercise, massage, self-talk, 12-step groups, prescribed medication, etc.—as an alternative.

6) When asked for his definition of mental health, Sigmund Freud replied, "The ability to work and to love." **Employment** is therapeutic for a variety of reasons; it draws us outside of ourselves, brings us into contact with other people, and gives us a sense of identity and independence. As one middle-aged woman recently testified at a mental health conference, "The most important factor in my recovery was being able to return to work!" Conversely, I have seen depression brought on by a person's lack of employment, or being involved in work that does not express a genuine passion.

The need for fulfilling work was confirmed by writer/researcher Betty Friedan in her book, *The Fountain of Age*. Friedan discovered that people aged gracefully when they had close personal relations and were involved in a series of creative projects that gave full expression to their abilities and talents.

7) Closely related to work is the process of **goal setting.** Goal setting gives you the means to take that imagined future and bring it into the present. In setting goals, we define what we want, and then develop a concrete plan by which we can manifest that good. Goals should be realistic and attainable by small, incremental steps. Having a positive vision of the future gives life purpose and meaning—a powerful antidote to depression. In addition, achieving small goals, especially after a period of depression, can help you to believe in yourself and your ability to change.

8) Try to find small ways to experience **joy** or **pleasure**. Create a "Play/Pleasure Inventory Chart." Write down those activities that are enjoyable and sprinkle your life with them—e.g., eating a good meal, working in the garden, nurturing a pet, spending time with friends, etc. Think of things that are fun, used to be fun, or might be fun. You can then schedule times for these activities into your weekly routine.

One type of pleasurable experience that is also good for the body is therapeutic massage. Massage relaxes the muscles, promotes lymph drainage and stimulates the immune system. Human touch is profoundly healing for body, mind and spirit.

While many people are "touch hungry," those folks who have experienced physical violence or sexual abuse may need to be "desensitized" to their negative conditioning around touch before they feel safe and open to its healing benefits. If you think this may be true for you, consult with your therapist or someone who specializes in treating survivors of physical/sexual trauma.

9) Begin and end each day with an **uplifting thought or word.** You may choose a prayer, an affirmation or a statement of thanksgiving. There are a host of daily affirmation books and collections of inspirational stories that you can refer to. This simple ritual of focusing on and affirming the good helps to create an optimistic attitude which strengthens the immune system and the body's ability to cope with stress.

As you may have surmised, there is nothing new or radical in what I have suggested. The plan is a simple common sense approach to living a healthy and balanced life. But simple does not mean easy. Developing and sticking to good habits requires persistence, discipline and diligence (ask anyone who has quit smoking). But the dedication is worth it. Having spent too many days in the dark house, I do not wish to return; and I am confident that neither do you.

There is one final point that I would like to emphasize. No matter how many episodes of depression you have experienced, **you are not your illness.** The label "depression" does not define *who* you are but *how* you are suffering. If you start to believe that having depression makes you inherently defective, remind yourself that *you are a normal person responding to an abnormal condition.* Your spiritual essence transcends depression and cannot be touched by it or any illness. As the great 20th century visionary Pierre Teilhard de Chardin put it, "We are not human beings having a spiritual experience. We are spiritual beings having a human experience."

Above all, try to be at peace with your condition. Some people have diabetes, others heart disease; you get to deal with depression. By applying the strategies described in this section, and by drawing upon other resources in this book, you can take small steps to improve the quality of your life. Remember, life is not always about fairness, but about how gracefully we learn the teachings of our unique path. Best wishes on your transformational journey.

SEEKING PROFESSIONAL HELP:
A GUIDE TO OPTIONS

I n the previous section, I outlined some "self-help" strategies that individuals can use to strengthen their psychological immune systems. There are times, however, when despite a person's best efforts, the depression does not change or becomes a chronic and debilitating disorder. If you are not sure whether you are clinically depressed, you may want to check the Self-Rating Scale for Depression which appears on page 135. Then, ask yourself this question: "Are my moods or symptoms beginning to interfere with the way that I cope with daily life?" If the answer is "yes," or even "maybe," it is time to reach out for assistance. Ideally, the time to get help is before things *really* get bad.

There are a number of qualified health care professionals who offer care and treatment for depression. They include:
- psychiatrists.
- clinical psychologists.
- clinical social workers.
- psychiatric nurse practitioners.
- family practice physicians and internists.
- marriage and family counselors.
- pastoral counselors.
- clergy.
- drug and alcohol counselors.

Although only psychiatrists, physicians and nurse practitioners can prescribe medication, members of the other groups offer psychotherapy and often "refer out" for the medication component. Thus, you may end up seeing a medical doctor for your medication and another professional for therapy.

The relationship between doctor and patient, or therapist and client, plays a critical role in the healing process. Your relationship with your mental health care provider will be as important as any treatment you choose. Consequently, it is important that you feel comfortable with him or her. In this respect, it is a good idea to interview several therapists before you make a final decision about the person who will be your guide and advocate.

Obtaining the proper referral is an important initial first step in your healing. There are several ways to do this.

1) **Word of mouth.** Ask people you know (family, coworkers, friends, a family physician or internist) if they know of anyone who has been helpful to them or others.
2) **State licensing boards.** You can call and ask for referrals. Feel free to ask about a practitioner's credentials, how long he or she has been in practice, and his or her experience in treating major depression.
3) **Associations of helping professionals.** You can contact these organizations for referrals to mental health professionals in your area. Here are some phone numbers to start with. Additional information is provided in Appendix C.
    - American Psychiatric Association: (202) 682-6220
    - American Psychological Association: (202) 336-5800
    - National Association of Social Workers: (800) 638-8799
    - American Association for Marriage and Family Therapy: (202) 452-0109
    - American Association of Pastoral Counselors: (703) 385-6967
    - American Society of Clinical Hypnosis: (312) 645-9810

To assist you in getting started with assessing your treatment options, the following pages provide an overview of the standard treatment modalities for clinical depression—psychotherapy, medication, and electroconvulsive therapy (ECT). In addition, I have included a number of alternative medical approaches such as diet, exercise, magnetic therapy, and the supplementation with herbs, vitamins, minerals, and amino acids.

Let's begin our discussion of treatment options with the major psychotherapies that are used to treat depression.

Psychological Therapies

"Genes are not destiny. Attachment in infancy, the attention we receive, and what we learn from others will forever be important in shaping who we are."
Edward Whybrow, *A Mood Apart*

If you seek counseling for depression, you will most likely be treated with one or more of the three following forms of psycho-therapy:
- the psychodynamic approach.
- the cognitive-behavioral approach.
- the interpersonal approach.

What follows is a very brief introduction to each therapy.

The **psychodynamic approach** was pioneered by early psychiatrists such as Freud, Jung and Adler. This system relates the development and maintenance of depressive symptoms to unresolved conflicts and losses rooted in childhood. The psychodynamic approach can involve long-term therapy (more than a year), with the emphasis placed on the individual's gaining insight into the nature of his or her problems, working through conflicts, and finding new ways to look at relations with others. The therapist-patient relationship is a key part of the treatment because of the client's tendency to transfer unresolved feelings about a parent or authority figure onto the therapist (a process called "transference"). Since Freud believed that many depressions were caused by unexpressed mourning, the patient may also be encouraged to grieve his or her early losses, including deaths and the emotional unavailability of primary caregivers.

More recently, the psychodynamic approach has been broadened to include women's issues, the social factors that contribute to mental health problems, and an interpersonal focus on the client's primary relationships.

In **cognitive-behavioral therapy**, patients are taught new ways of thinking and behaving to replace faulty beliefs about themselves, the world, and the future. Specific focus is placed on identifying erroneous assumptions, expectations and conclusions ("this will never end"), and letting go of self-destructive thoughts ("I'm worthless; no one can love me because I am depressed"). The behavioral aspect of therapy teaches constructive behaviors—such as learning to relax, to set goals, and to be assertive—that will help in overcoming feelings of helplessness and powerlessness. The cognitive approach may involve short-term therapy aimed at resolving current problems, or it may explore entrenched, unrecognized belief systems and emotional habits learned in childhood that contribute to current depressive symptoms.

Finally, cognitive behavioral therapy also seeks to reduce emotional distress by using a wide variety of strategies to induce physiological changes in the brain and nervous system. Such strategies include meditation, visualization, progressive muscle relaxation, biofeedback, and stress reduction techniques.

Interpersonal therapy looks at the role of interpersonal relationships (or lack of them) in contributing to depression. The depressed person is taught new skills for interacting with people and developing healthy, functional relationships. In many cases, the task is to rebuild impaired or absent social bonds or to heal family or work conflicts. Improving interpersonal communication skills is a central focus of the therapy.

A fourth therapeutic approach, more popular in Europe than in the United States, consists of the existential psychotherapies, the most noted of which is **logotherapy**, created by psychiatrist Victor Frankl. While a prisoner of the Nazi concentration camps, Frankl observed that those people who found a meaning to their suffering and to their lives were more likely to survive their ordeals. Logotherapy focuses on helping the client to deal with the existential problems of human existence—discovering the meaning and purpose of life and finding worthwhile ideals to live for.

Each of these approaches has proven valuable in treating various levels of depression. The technique (or techniques) you choose should depend on your temperament, your level of functioning, the severity of the depression, and the therapist's training and background. Research has shown that any of these therapies can be beneficial if used by a competent professional. Moreover, in today's therapy office, it is not unusual for therapists to be familiar with several psychological theories and to combine eclectic technical approaches tailor-made for each individual's needs.

The important thing is to try some type of therapy with a professional trained in the assessment and treatment of depression. Studies show that psychotherapy and medication are more effective in treating depression than medication alone, especially in the long-term maintenance of mental health.

Antidepressant Therapy

In the past three decades, antidepressants have become the treatment of choice for people with major depression. Before World War II, these drugs did not exist. In the 1950s two drugs, one an antipsychotic and the other a tuberculosis medication, were accidentally found to elevate the moods of depressed individuals. Since then, a host of new substances has been synthesized, specifically for the treatment of depression. Most recently, medications have been developed that specifically target the particular neural pathways of depression, with less generalized neural impact, and therefore far fewer side effects.

Current theory links the biochemical causes of mood disorders to a deficiency of three of the brain's neurotransmitters—serotonin, norepinephrine and dopamine. Antidepressants don't actually create more serotonin, norepinephrine and dopamine. Instead, they are believed to limit the reabsorption of these chemicals into the brain's nerve cells, thereby increasing the amounts of neurotransmitters available in the space (synapse) between the sending and receiving cells. This in turn causes a better neural transmission from cell to cell, resulting in an elevation of mood.

There are three groups of antidepressants. The first and oldest group is the **tricyclics;** examples include Imipramine (Tofranil) and Amitriptyline (Elavil). Like the other antidepressants, tricyclics take two to four weeks to begin working, and six to eight weeks to achieve full effectiveness. Their side effects may include dry mouth, blurred vision, sexual dysfunction, fatigue, weight gain, constipation, and abnormalities in the cardiovascular system. Such discomforts can often deter a person from staying on the medication long enough for the beneficial effects to begin to be felt.

The second group of antidepressants is called **monoamine oxidase (MAO) inhibitors**, or MAOIs for short (examples are Nardil and Parnate). Monoamine oxidase is an enzyme that breaks down neurotransmitters. Hence, by inhibiting the production of MAO, these drugs increase the amount of neurotransmitters retained in the synapses. Unfortunately, the MAOIs have cumbersome dietary restrictions. They cannot be taken with foods that contain the amino acid tyrosine—such as aged cheese, beer, wine, chocolate and liver.

The third and most recently developed class of antidepressants is known as the SSRIs—**selective serotonin reuptake inhibitors**. This group, which includes Prozac, Zoloft, Celexa and Paxil, is as effective as the tricyclics in treating depression, but generally has fewer and milder side effects. Nonetheless, the SSRIs may be highly agitating for some patients (producing anxiety and insomnia), who thus may require additional sleeping medications.

Finally, there exists a class of "atypical" antidepressants that includes Serzone, Effexor and Wellbutrin.

No one class of antidepressant is better than any other. It cannot be overstated that different medications work for different people, depending on the complex interaction between an individual's biochemistry and the drug's pharmacology. This is why finding the right medication is often a matter of trial and error and good medical follow-through.

Antidepressants do not get you "high"; neither are they addictive. They work by reestablishing the right proportion of neurotransmitters in your brain so that nerve impulses can be effectively communicated from cell to cell.

In the start-up period of taking antidepressants there may be a trade-off. While waiting for the medication to take effect, you may have to endure side effects which may (or may not) be temporary, before you know if the antidepressant will work for you. Moreover, it may take several trials on different drugs before the right one is found. For those persons who find relief from the hell of depression, enduring the side effects may well be worth the discovery of a medication that lifts one's mood. Moreover, in many instances the side effects are temporary and drop out with continued usage.

It is also important to note that in a small minority of cases, some people experience a recurrence of depression while still on medication, a phenomenon known as "Prozac poop-out." When this occurs, relief may be attained by changing medications or dosages under careful medical supervision.

In addition to taking antidepressants, you may want to practice many of the "brain maintenance" strategies that I discussed in the previous chapter. I recommend that you approach depression from a "holistic perspective" since it may take weeks or months to find the best antidepressant—and not everyone is helped by medication. Hence, it is good to cover your bases and work on *all fronts simultaneously*, as this will provide the best chance for overall success.

How long should medication be taken?

The short answer is "as long as you need it." This will depend on how well your body can rebalance its biochemistry on its own. Some people have only one major episode and never need treatment again (just as some individuals suffer just one heart attack or one bout with cancer).

Others heal from depression, go off medication and continue to feel well until a later date, when the depression returns. This usually requires going back on medication and/or engaging in other forms of treatment until the episode passes.

Finally, some folks discover that as soon as they stop medication, their symptoms return. These people usually need to take antidepressant medication on a long-term basis in order to correct underlying biochemical imbalances. As I mentioned earlier, if you need to stay on medication to remain well, try not to think of this as a personal weakness. If your body requires assistance to remain in balance, it is no different than having any other illness that requires medication (e.g., insulin for diabetes, antihypertensive drugs for high blood pressure, cholesterol-lowering drugs for heart disease).

Unfortunately, studies show that 70 percent of patients prematurely discontinue their medication—or discontinue their medication abruptly rather than gradually. Such premature or abrupt cessation is associated with a 77 percent increase in the rate of relapse or recurrence of the depressive episode. The moral of the story is do not make any changes in your medication regimen without telling your physician.*

Knowing your medication

To increase the likelihood that a medication will work well, patients and families must actively participate with the doctor prescribing it. Questions you should ask include:

- What is the name of the medication and what is it supposed to do?
- When and how often do I take it, and when do I stop taking it, if at all?
- What, if any, food, drinks, other medications or activities should I avoid while taking the prescribed medication?
- What are the potential side effects, and what should I do if they occur?
- What written information is available about the medication?

To help you identify and research your medication, I have created a sidebar that lists the most commonly prescribed drugs for

---

* "Adherence to Treatment to Prevent Depression Relapse," *American Family Physician*, April 1, 1999, v59 i7, pg. 1929.

depression, bipolar disorder, and anxiety by their generic (chemical) names and trade (brand) names. If your medication's trade name does not appear, look it up by its generic name, or ask your doctor or pharmacist for more information.

Alphabetical Listing of Medications by Trade Name

Antidepressant medications

Trade name	Chemical or generic name
Adapin	doxepin
Anafranil	clomipramine
Asendin	amoxapine
Aventyl	nortriptyline
Desyrel	trazodone
Effexor	venlafaxine
Elavil	amitriptyline
Ludiomil	maprotiline
Luvox	fluvoxamine
Marplan	isocarboxazid
Nardil	phenelzine
Norpramin	desipramine
Pamelor	nortriptyline
Parnate	tranylcypromine
Paxil	paroxetine
Pertofrane	desipramine
Prozac	fluoxetine
Serzone	nefazodone
Sinequan	doxepin
Surmontil	trimipramine
Tofranil	imipramine
Vivactil	protriptyline
Wellbutrin	bupropion
Zoloft	sertraline

Antimanic medications

Trade Name	Chemical or generic name
Cibalith-S	lithium citrate
Depakote	divalproex sodium
Eskalith	lithium carbonate
Lithane	lithium carbonate
Lithobid	lithium carbonate
Tegretol	carbamazepine

Antianxiety medications

Trade name	Chemical or generic name
Ativan	lorazepam
Azene	clorazepate
BuSpar	buspirone
Centrax	prazepam
Dalmane	flurazepam
Klonopin	clonazepam
Librium	chlordiazepoxide
Paxipam	halazepam
Serax	oxazepam
Tranxene	clorazepate
Valium	diazepam
Xanax	alprazolam

Hospitalization: When Is It Appropriate?

The very idea of going to a psychiatric hospital is an anathema to most people. Being "locked up" in a "funny farm" or "loony bin" elicits feelings of shame and stigma. Columnist Art Buchwald recounted how he felt "humiliated" and "a total failure" when he was hospitalized for his manic depression.

There are, however, times when a person who is severely depressed or anxious should consider committing himself to a psychiatric ward for a period of time. Hospitalization may be a positive option for you when:

- You are suicidal.
- You are psychotic (hearing voices, feeling paranoid or having delusional beliefs).
- You are harming yourself in some way or are afraid you will harm others.
- You are unable to perform the tasks of daily living (for yourself and others), such as bathing, feeding yourself (or others), dressing or getting out of bed.
- You cannot handle being left alone.
- You feel that you can no longer cope.
- You lack the support you need to keep you safe.
- Your medication requires monitoring or changing.

If you need to go to the hospital, remember that it is a temporary situation that is designed to keep you safe. Try to let go of any feelings of shame or failure. You are still a worthy person regardless of your external circumstances.

Unfortunately, hospital stays are shorter than they might ideally be. When William Styron experienced his depressive breakdown in 1985, he convalesced for six weeks, a respite that he credits with saving his life. Today, in the age of managed care, such multi-week stays are unheard of, unless one has the money to pay for a private hospital that specializes in long-term residential care. While I am not advocating returning to a time when chronically mentally ill people were warehoused in large institutions, it is clear that the pendulum has swung too far in the opposite direction.*

Electroconvulsive Therapy: Beneficial or Barbaric?

By far the most controversial modality in the treatment of depression is electroconvulsive therapy (ECT), also known as electric shock therapy. Much of the public's concerns about ECT arise from the gruesome way in which the treatment has been portrayed by the popular media. Many people still cringe when they recall the memory of Jack Nicholson being punished with ECT treatments in the film "One Flew Over the Cuckoo's Nest." The idea of having electrical currents forced through one's brain inspires fear and terror while conjuring images of Frankenstein, mad scientists and electrocution. Can such a seemingly barbaric practice be effective in treating severe depression? In the following pages, we will explore the pros and cons of ECT. **

What is ECT?

Electroconvulsive therapy is a treatment for severe mental illness in which the brain is stimulated with a strong electrical current which induces a seizure, similar to those of epilepsy. In a manner that is not understood, this seizure rearranges the brain's neurochemistry, resulting in an elevation of mood.

ECT was first introduced in the United States in the 1940s and 1950s. During that time, the treatment was often administered to the most severely disturbed patients residing in large mental institutions. As often occurs with new therapies, ECT was used for a variety of disorders, frequently in high doses and for long periods.

---

* Michael Winerip, "Bedlam on the Streets," *New York Times Magazine,* May 23, 1999.

** The information for this section was taken from the National Institute of Health's Consensus Development Conference Statement, June 10-12, 1985. This statement was originally published as: *Electroconvulsive Therapy. NIH Consensus Statement,* 1985 June 10-12; 5(11):1-23. I am covering the subject in depth because of the fear and misunderstanding that still persists about ECT.

Many of these efforts proved ineffective, and some even harmful. Moreover, ECT was used as a means of managing unruly patients for whom other treatments were not then available. This contributed to the perception of ECT as an abusive instrument of behavioral control for chronically ill patients. With the introduction of effective drugs for the treatment of mental illness, the use of ECT declined. Recently, however, as safer and less traumatic ways of administering ECT have evolved, the treatment has made a comeback.

How effective is ECT in treating mental disorders?

The efficacy of ECT has been established most convincingly in the treatment of delusional and severe endogenous depressions (the latter is what I experienced), which make up a clinically important minority of depressive disorders. Some studies find ECT to be as effective as antidepressants, while others find ECT to be superior to medication. The literature also indicates that ECT, when compared with antidepressants, has a more rapid onset of action.

A nurse at one hospital reported, "I have seen severely depressed people who were unable to dress or feed themselves; I had to change their diapers because they were so regressed and withdrawn. By the end of their ECT treatments they were smiling, eating and drinking on their own. It's as if they were brought back from the dead."

ECT has also been shown to be a safe and effective treatment for mania. Before the discovery of lithium, ECT was the mainstay treatment for mania as well as for severe depression. It is still often effective for mania when lithium and antipsychotic drugs fail. For example, in one study ECT was given for eight weeks to seventeen patients who had failed to respond to lithium. All of them recovered.

After drinking alcohol and smoking marijuana, a 20-year-old college student began to act strangely and speak gibberish. He subsequently ate and slept little and was often mute and running naked at home. He was admitted to a hospital in a delusional state, with rapid, inappropriate speech. His psychotic thinking and speech persisted despite treatment with lithium, sedatives, antipsychotic drugs, and antidepressants. After one session of ECT, he began to speak coherently and sleep and eat normally. After further ECT, he recovered and was discharged.*

Although ECT can jolt people out of severe depression and mania, recovery is not necessarily permanent. Relapse rates in the year following ECT are likely to be high unless maintenance antidepressant medications are subsequently prescribed. In other instances, "maintenance doses" of ECT are given two to six times a year to prevent relapse. ECT is also useful in certain types of schizophrenia, although antipsychotic drugs remain the first line of treatment.

How is ECT administered?

Once the patient (or his or her guardians) and the physician have decided that ECT may be indicated, the patient undergoes a pre-treatment medical workup that includes a history, physical, neurologic examination, electrocardiogram (EKG), and laboratory tests. MAOI antidepressants should be discontinued two weeks before treatment, and patients should be essentially lithium-free. Because some patients may have a compromised cardiovascular status, cardiac conditions should be evaluated and monitored closely—including high blood pressure, which must be lowered before treatments can begin. It is also important to educate the patient and the family through discussion and written and/or audiovisual materials.

Typically, ECT is administered in the early morning after an eight-to twelve-hour period of fasting, although mid-afternoon treatments are also used. A number of medications and muscle relaxants are given to the patient, and stimulus electrodes are placed on the head, either on one or both temporal lobes (for unilateral or bilateral ECT, respectively). After the muscle relaxant has taken effect, the brain is stimulated with an electrical pulse lasting from a quarter of a second to two seconds. The pulse induces a seizure which usually lasts from 30 seconds to two minutes, during which time the

---

* As reported in the *Harvard Mental Health Newsletter*, June 1997, pg. 8.

patient is closely monitored. After the treatment, the patient is brought to a recovery room where he or she remains until waking.

The number of ECT treatments in a course of therapy varies between six and twelve. Treatments are given three times a week, for two to four weeks. Following ECT, most depressed patients are continued on antidepressant medication or lithium to reduce the risk of relapse. Sometimes, physicians give maintenance doses of ECT to their patients on an outpatient basis.

What are the risks and adverse effects of ECT?

ECT is clearly less dangerous than it once was. Over the years, safer methods of administration have been developed, including the use of short-acting anesthetics, muscle relaxants, and adequate oxygenation, which have reduced the risk of physical injury and mortality. Yet even under optimal conditions of administration, the ECT seizure produces two main reactions—transient post-treatment confusion, and spotty but persistent memory loss.

Immediately after awakening from the treatment, the patient experiences confusion, temporary memory loss, and headache. Some people compare their experience to having a bad hangover. The time it takes to recover clear consciousness may vary from minutes to several hours, the exact length depending on the type of ECT administered (stimulating both hemispheres produces more confusion than unilateral ECT), as well as individual differences in the patients' response patterns. Confusion is made worse by longer seizure duration, close spacing of the treatments, and increased dosage of electrical stimulation.

The second side effect of ECT is memory loss which persists after the termination of a normal course of treatment. This amnesia seems to surround events that occurred around the time of the treatment, either several weeks before or after. For example, the patient may not remember who took him to the hospital or what gifts he gave a month before the treatment. The extent of such a loss is related to the number of treatments, type of electrode placement, and nature of the electric stimulus. Greater deficit occurs from bilateral than from unilateral placement. The ability to learn and retain new information does not seem to be adversely affected, although learning difficulties may exist during the first few weeks after the treatment.

Because there is also a wide difference in individual perception of the memory deficit, the subjective loss can be extremely distressing to some and of little concern to others. For example, many patients who complain about autobiographical memory loss say that being free of depression is well worth whatever memory disruption they experience. Others insist, however, that they have suffered a terrible disruption to their memory and to their lives. Although the second group is in the minority (80 percent of people who have had ECT report that the procedure was no more frightening than going to the dentist), accounts of the suffering of those who perceive they have been harmed may add to the apprehension of many patients who consider ECT treatment.

What factors should be considered by the physician and patient in determining if ECT is an appropriate treatment?

Because of the fear surrounding ECT and the potential side effects of memory loss, a person who is considering ECT should do his or her best to make sure that ECT is truly warranted. As I stated earlier, ECT is used as the method of last resort in delusional/psychotic depressions, severe endogenous depressions, acute mania, and certain schizophrenic syndromes. If no other methods of treatment have worked and the person is incapacitated or at immediate risk of suicide, treatment is clearly indicated.

There are, of course, medical contraindications to ECT, which the patient's psychiatrist or physician should describe. Some of the better known contraindications are a history of myocardial infarctions, large aneurysms, and the presence of intracranial pressure or space-occupying lesions in the brain.

Finally, there exists the issue of informed consent. When the physician has determined that clinical indications justify the administration of ECT, the law requires, and medical ethics demand, that the patient's freedom to accept or refuse the treatment be fully honored.* The physician must make clear to the patient the nature of the ECT procedure, its possible risks and benefits (including full acknowledgment of post-treatment confusion, memory dysfunction, and other attendant uncertainties), and the alternative treatment options (including the option of no treatment at all). Special individual needs may also be relevant to some patients—for example, a personal situation that requires rapid remission to facilitate return to work and to reduce family disruption. In all matters, technical details should be translated into meaningful terms that are understood by the patient.

Once the patient consents to ECT, this informed consent should be reexamined with the patient throughout the course of the treatment. There are several reasons for this repeated consenting procedure. Since the risks of adverse effects increase with repeated treatments, the patient may want to reassess the risks versus benefits. And because of the short-term memory deficits that accompany each administration of ECT, the patient's recollection of the prior consenting transaction might itself be impaired, making it necessary to offer additional consultations reiterating the patient's treatment options.

Conclusion

ECT remains controversial despite its documented benefits. This controversy is perpetuated by the following factors: the nature of the treatment itself, its history of abuse, unfavorable media presentations, compelling testimony of former patients, special attention by the legal system, and uneven distribution of ECT use among practitioners and facilities.

---

* If a patient is catatonic or delusional, legal steps may have to be taken to ensure the patient gets the treatment he or she needs.

Nonetheless, ECT is demonstrably effective for a narrow range of severe psychiatric disorders—delusional and severe endogenous depression, manic episodes, and certain schizophrenic syndromes. There are, however, significant side effects, especially confused states and persistent memory deficits for events during the weeks surrounding the ECT treatment. Proper administration of ECT can reduce potential side effects while still providing for adequate therapeutic effects.*

Much additional research is needed into the basic mechanisms by which ECT exerts its therapeutic effects. Studies are also needed to better identify groups for whom the treatment is particularly beneficial (or toxic) and to refine techniques that will maximize the treatment's effectiveness and reduce side effects. A national survey should be conducted on how ECT is being used in the United States. To prevent misapplication and abuse, it is essential that appropriate mechanisms be established to ensure proper standards and monitoring of ECT. In this manner, ECT can be administered in the right way, at the right time, for the right patients.

Rapid Transcranial Magnetic Stimulation: Magnetic Healing of the Brain

While ECT can be an effective means of treating serious depression, its invasive nature has been a longtime source of controversy. Now there is a promising alternative that works on the same principle as ECT, but may be less traumatic. An experimental procedure known as Rapid Transcranial Magnetic Stimulation (RTMS) uses a powerful magnet to deliver an electric jolt to the brain in the same manner as ECT, but without electrical stimulation to unnecessary parts of the brain. Scientists believe that the technique works like a heart defibrillator. The electric voltage that passes through the brain causes its neurons to fire at once and somehow this action

---

* Public accounts of the success of ECT include the book *Undercurrents*, by Martha Manning, and interviews with former talk-show host Dick Cavett.

seems to reset the rate at which the brain releases its various neurotransmitters.

In clinical trials, some people who have failed to improve by using medication and other therapies have responded to RTMS treatments within six days, while the majority are significantly better after two weeks of twenty-minute treatments. Because of its newness, no one knows if these benefits will last longer than six months, but preliminary indications are promising. Like ECT, RTMS will most likely be used to "jump start" the brain so that other forms of medical care can then be used to maintain the patient's well-being over the long haul.

Magnetic therapy has been a viable medical therapy for thousands of years. Having a "gentler" form of ECT available is exciting news for people who suffer from long-term treatment-resistant depression.*

Natural Alternatives to Prozac
(and other pharmaceuticals)

In many respects, antidepressants have revolutionized the treatment of depression. By rebalancing the neurotransmitters in the brain, they impact mood at the biochemical level and allow the tormented sufferer to achieve emotional equilibrium. However, not everyone responds to these drugs favorably. For some people the side effects are too harsh, while others fail to experience the desired relief.

Fortunately, nutritionally oriented doctors and herbalists have researched a number of "natural" therapeutic approaches to depression which include herbs, vitamins and exercise. What follows is a brief summary of the most commonly used alternative modalities. While I did not use these remedies during my depressive episode, I have since tried St. John's Wort and tyrosine and have heard of positive anecdotal reports from other patients. Although scientific

---

* Schrof, Joannie M. and Stacey Schultz, "Melancholy Nation: Depression Is on the Rise, Despite Prozac. But New Drugs Could Offer Help." *U.S. News and World Report*, March 8, 1999, Volume 126, Number 9, pg. 63.

studies of St. John's Wort have been done in Germany, many of the other remedies have not been subjected to the same rigorous double-blind studies that are used with pharmaceutical drugs. This is largely because no one has put up the millions of dollars that would be needed to research the safety and effectiveness of these compounds.

Because even "natural" substances can produce strong reactions in sensitive individuals, anyone taking these remedies should do so under the supervision of a nutritionally oriented physician (psychiatrist, family doctor, chiropractor, naturopath, etc.). As with antidepressants, it is important to try one natural remedy at a time until you discover what works. Moreover, you should not switch from a prescription antidepressant to any of these supplements without first consulting your health care provider. *

St. John's Wort

St. John's Wort (Hypericum perforatum) is the star attraction in the field of natural alternatives to Prozac. The yellow flowering tops of St. John's Wort have been consumed for centuries in tea or olive oil extract for a variety of "nervous conditions." In 1994, physicians in Germany prescribed 66 million daily doses of St. John's Wort, making it the country's medication of choice for the treatment of mild to moderate depression.

Patients who respond to St. John's Wort show an improvement in mood and ability to carry out their daily routine. Symptoms such as sadness, hopelessness, feelings of worthlessness, exhaustion, and poor sleep also decrease. In one study, St. John's Wort was as effective as the prescription antidepressant Imipramine for treating mild to moderate depression (it is less effective for major depression). Moreover, St. John's Wort is relatively free of side effects when compared to pharmaceutical antidepressants (common side effects are gastrointestinal symptoms, allergy, fatigue, and increased sensitivity to light).

---

* The information for this section was gathered from the November 1997 issue of *Health Notes*, a monthly newsletter about nutrition, as well as from a number of books listed in the bibliography.

The standard dosage of St. John's Wort prescribed by the European doctors is a 0.3 percent extract of the active ingredient, hypericin, taken in 300 milligram capsules, three times a day. A person using St. John's Wort should be monitored for four to six weeks before evaluating its effectiveness. In addition, St. John's Wort should not be taken along with the traditional antidepressants. If you are already taking Prozac or another antidepressant and would like to try St. John's Wort, consult with a psychiatrist or other medical person and wean yourself from the pharmaceutical before you start the St. John's Wort.

5-Hydroxy-Tryptophan

L-tryptophan is an amino acid that serves as a precursor to the neurotransmitter serotonin (the one that is affected by SSRI drugs such as Prozac, Zoloft and the like). L-tryptophan was quite popular in treating depression and insomnia during the 1980s. However, in 1990 the substance was deemed responsible for a number of deaths and was pulled from the market in the United States. Although the deaths were later attributed to a contaminated non-pharmaceutical-grade product made by one particular manufacturer, L-tryptophan is currently available only by prescription in the United States. (Ironically, just four days after L-tryptophan was banned, the March 26, 1990, issue of *Newsweek* announced "Prozac: A Breakthrough Drug for Depression.")

However, a product similar to L-tryptophan, 5-hydroxy-tryptophan, is currently available over the counter. 5-HTP is a metabolite of tryptophan and a precursor to serotonin that may work even better than tryptophan. In a head-to-head study conducted by German and Swiss researchers in 1991, 5-HTP and the antidepressant Luvox were shown to be equally effective in treating depression over a six-week period. Since then, 5-HTP has been used by many people to lower their current dosages of antidepressants or to replace them completely. Such adjustments should be made under the care of your psychiatrist or physician.

Treating underlying metabolic and endocrine disorders

Untreated endocrine problems of all sorts are recognized as having the potential to cause mood difficulties. The most common of these is depression caused by hypothyroidism (underactive thyroid), which can be successfully treated using thyroid medication. Other medical conditions which may exacerbate or even cause depressive symptoms are chronic fatigue syndrome, candidiasis, reactive hypoglycemia, hormonal imbalances, vitamin and mineral deficiencies, and amino acid deficiencies.

Balancing mood through diet

In her book *Potatoes Not Prozac*, Kathleen DesMaisons, Ph.D., an addiction and nutrition expert, claims that many people who are prone to addictive disorders, as well as to depression, are also sugar sensitive—i.e., they have a special body chemistry that reacts in extreme ways to sugar and refined carbohydrates. The reaction throws off not only the blood sugar levels, but also the levels of serotonin and beta-endorphins (nature's pain killers) in the brain. This in turn causes an inability to concentrate; creates feelings of exhaustion, hopelessness and despair; and contributes to confusion, irritability, and low self esteem—i.e., symptoms of clinical depression!

Fortunately, DesMaisons has discovered that eating the *right foods* at the *right times* often can bring the body and emotions back into balance. Her dietary recommendations include:

- eating three regular meals a day spaced no more than five to six hours apart.
- eating the recommended amount of protein (a portion the size of your fist) at every meal.
- eating more complex carbohydrates.
- reducing or eliminating sugars (including alcohol).

DesMaisons' plan has achieved a high success rate with recovering alcoholics as well as with people with mood disorders who are striving for emotional stability. During my depressive episode, I followed these guidelines before I even discovered her work, and I continue to work with them as part of my recovery.

In addition, you may want to take a daily supplement of essential fatty acids (EFAs). EFAs help to maintain proper cell membrane functioning, which is necessary for the optimal functioning of the brain's neurotransmitters. Some preliminary studies show a link between low EFA intake and depression.

Vitamin and mineral supplementation

Many clinicians believe that supplementing your food intake with certain vitamins, minerals and amino acids may also help to balance your brain chemistry.

Vitamins B6 and B3

The entire vitamin B complex is known to maintain and promote normal mental functioning. Deficiencies of any or all of these vitamins can produce significant symptoms relating to depression, e.g., anxiety, irritability, lethargy, and fatigue. Although the research remains inconsistent, several studies indicate that vitamin B6 supplementation (100 to 300 milligrams per day) helps alleviate depression associated with premenstrual syndrome. Since oral contraceptives can deplete the body of vitamin B6, women taking birth control pills need to supplement their diets with B6 as well. In addition, niacinamide, a form of vitamin B3, has shown some success in alleviating both depression and anxiety.

Folic acid

A large percentage of depressed people have low levels of the B vitamin folic acid (*British Journal of Psychiatry;* 117:287-92). Anyone suffering from chronic depression should be evaluated by a nutritionally oriented doctor for a possible folic acid deficiency. Folic acid is usually taken with vitamin B12 and is best supervised by a physician. Large doses of folic acid may contribute to mania. Thus anyone with a bipolar disorder should be evaluated by a qualified health care provider before trying this supplement.

GABA

GABA is usually classified as an amino acid, although it actually serves as a neurotransmitter (there are more GABA sites in the brain than for other neurotransmitters, such as dopamine or serotonin). GABA basically acts as an inhibitory transmitter, keeping the brain and body from going into "overdrive." Supplementation of GABA seems to be quite effective for anxiety disorders as well as insomnia (especially the type of insomnia where racing thoughts keep the individual from falling asleep). Hence, those suffering from depression exacerbated by anxiety might want to consider taking this supplement.

Kava extract

Kava (Piper methysticum) is a member of the pepper family native to the South Pacific. Its tuberous rootstock is used to make a beverage (also called kava) that is believed to make people happy and sociable. Hence, it has been used for hundreds of years in native ceremonies and celebrations. In recent years, a number of Western pharmacologists have prepared and ingested the beverage, reporting similar tranquilizing and uplifting effects.

Like St. John's Wort, kava extracts are gaining in popularity in European countries for treating depression and anxiety. The active ingredients in kava are the kavalactones, although several other components seem to be involved as well. In a number of double blind studies, individuals taking kava extract containing 70 percent kavalactones showed improvements in symptoms of anxiety as measured by several standardized psychological tests, including the Hamilton Anxiety Scale. In addition, unlike the benzodiazepines—such as Xanax and Ativan, that are prescribed for anxiety—kava extract neither impairs mental functioning nor promotes sedation.

Another problem with benzodiazepines is that the body gradually adapts to their presence, so that it takes more of the drug to produce the same effect. This condition, known as *tolerance*, does not seem to occur with kavalactones.

Based on clinical studies, the recommended dosage for taking kava to reduce anxiety is 45 to 70 milligrams of kavalactones three times a day. For sedative effects, a dosage of 180 to 210 milligrams can be taken before bedtime. To put these dosages in perspective, the standard bowl of traditionally prepared kava beverage contains around 250 milligrams of kavalactones, and more than one bowl may be ingested at a sitting.

Finally, although no significant side effects have been reported from taking kava at the normal levels, some case reports suggest that kava may interfere with dopamine and worsen Parkinson's disease. Until this issue is resolved, kava should not be used by patients who have this illness.*

Other Amino Acids

L-tyrosine

L-tyrosine is an amino acid that serves as a precursor to the neurotransmitters norepinephrine and dopamine, which have been shown to be deficient in many depressives. The supplementation of this amino acid may help the body to form more of these substances during difficult times. Tyrosine may also be helpful in cases where clinical or subclinical thyroid disease is present.

L-phenylalynine and DL-phenylalynine

Phenylalynine is a precursor to tyrosine, and so exhibits many of the same effects. In addition, the supplementation of phenylalynine can help the body produce a substance called "phenylethylamine," which is also present in chocolate and marijuana and is created by the body in greater amounts when the individual is "in love." Phenylethylamine is supposedly present to a greater degree in the DL form of phenylalynine than the L form; however, the DL form may be more likely to increase blood pressure.

---

* Murray, Michael, *Natural Alternatives to Prozac*, New York, William Morrow and Company, 1996, pp. 140-150.

Methionine

Methionine is an amino acid that has been shown to be helpful for some individuals suffering from depression. Its metabolite, S-Adenosyl-Methionine (SAM), is intimately involved in the biochemistry of neurotransmitters and has been used in some European countries to treat depression. Recently, SAM has also become available in the United States.

Phosphatidylserine (PS)

PS is one of a class of substances known as phospholipids. The permeability of brain-cell membranes depends on adequate amounts of the substance. Some studies have shown PS to be an effective antidepressant in the elderly. PS may work by suppressing the production of cortisol, a naturally occurring steroid hormone whose levels are elevated in depressed people.

Dehydroepiandrosterone (DHEA)

DHEA is a naturally occurring androgen produced by the adrenal glands. It is abundantly found in plasma and brain tissue and is the precursor of many hormones produced by the adrenals. DHEA seems to alleviate some of the effects of aging, such as fatigue and muscle weakness. Levels of DHEA may be lower in depressed patients, while supplementation with DHEA may reduce symptoms. However, since DHEA is a hormone, you should not take it without having your doctor check your blood level of the hormone. Also check with your physician before adding it to your diet if you are on an antidepressant, a thyroid medication, insulin, or estrogen.

Alternative Medical Therapies

In addition to the herbs, vitamins, minerals and amino acids listed above, there exist a number of alternative medical therapies such as homeopathy, Chinese medicine (including acupuncture and herbal medicine), chiropractic, Bach flower remedies (and other flower essences), therapeutic gemstones, etc. Although these modalities lie outside of mainstream medicine, I have seen them alleviate depression in certain individuals, especially those people who are sensitive to subtle energies and for whom traditional medicine has not worked.

If you are interested in trying one or more of these alternative approaches, consult first with the health provider who is treating you for depression. Because of their non-invasive nature, you may be able employ these therapies at the same time that you are receiving standard treatment (medication and/or psychotherapy).

Neurological reorganization

A little known alternative treatment modality that fits into the category of alternative therapies is called "neurological reorganization." For anyone suffering from a chronic mental illness, this procedure may be helpful in investigating possible neurological problems—e.g., those brought on by a head injury or other trauma to the nervous system—as the underlying cause of symptoms. (This is especially true if physical or personality changes began to manifest after a physical trauma.)

The process begins when historical information is gathered about the mother's pregnancy, the birth process, early development, and injuries and accidents. If the evaluation reveals a dysfunction, the patient is then assigned daily activities that *replicate the normal neurological development which takes place in infancy.* These activities trigger the reflexes which stimulate the growth of desired nerve connections and consequently re-establish brain function. Symptoms such as anxiety, depression, schizophrenia have been reduced or eliminated using these exercises.

Neurological reorganization is practiced at specialized clinics in America, one of which is the Northwest Neurodevelopmental Training Center (503-981-0635). Its address and Internet site can be found in Appendix C, Resources for Wellness.

ADDITIONAL COPING STRATEGIES

The following are some additional coping strategies that can help you or a loved one to respond to and survive a major mood disorder.

Prayer

"Ask and ye shall receive. Seek and ye shall find.
Knock and the door shall be opened. For everyone who asks receives,
and he who seeks finds, and to him who knocks, it shall be opened."
Matthew 7: 1-3

As far as I know, there are no scientific studies that document the efficacy of prayer in the healing of depression or other forms of mental illness. There do exist, however, documented cases about the success of prayer in physical healing.*

If prayer can alter physical matter, and the brain is made of material substance, then it seems reasonable that prayer can impact the brain chemistry that creates depression. (I have my own experience to testify to this truth.) Thus, I would encourage anyone with depressive illnesses to combine prayer with the traditional treatment modalities. There are two approaches you can take: 1) pray for your own healing and 2) ask others to pray for you.

As I learned in my own healing, group energy seems to increase prayer's potency and effectiveness. If you can't get your support people to meet as a single group, you can still ask those in different locations to pray for you (preferably at a specific time of day). In addition, you may place your name on a prayer list where it will be prayed over for thirty days or more (see the list of prayer ministries in Appendix C).

---

* One such example is a survey by Daniel J. Benor, M.D., of 131 examples of spiritual healing, which appears in the appendix of Larry Dossey's book, *Healing Words*.

Affirmative Prayer

This five-step affirmative prayer is based on a process developed by Ernest Holmes, the founder of a school of philosophy known as Religious Science.

Step One: Recognition (*God is*)

I recognize the existence of a Power and a Presence greater than myself. This creative intelligence is known by many names: "God", "Higher Power", "Spirit", "Light", "Cosmic Consciousness", "Christ Consciousness", "The Divine", "The Is", " The Universe", "The Force", "I Am", "Higher Self".

Step Two: Unification (*I am in God, God is in me*)

I surrender myself to this Presence and merge my will with its will.

Step Three: Realization (*Making it real*)

I invoke the power of the word for my situation by stating carefully chosen words of truth. I make a statement of this truth, as if it has already happened—e.g., I may say, "I am in perfect health. Every cell in my body is bathed in the Light and Love of God. I am whole and well."

Step Four: Acceptance and Thanksgiving

(*I have faith that my word has power*)

I accept that my words are acted upon by the law of the Divine mind. I forgive myself and all others for thoughts conscious and unconscious, that would interfere with the acceptance of my greater good. I feel a sense of peace, and my heart is filled with gratitude.

Step Five.: Release (*I let go and let God*)

I release this affirmative prayer into the action of the law of creation. I let go, and ask my Higher Power to do its perfect work. I realize that clinging or worrying about the outcome may hold back the healing process. And so I turn the ultimate outcome over to my Higher Power, knowing that it will bring the perfect outcome, for my highest good and the highest good of all concerned.

The success of prayer does not depend on one's religious persuasion. (As AA puts it, "there are no atheists in foxholes.") If the word "prayer" seems too religious, think of the process as asking people to send you positive thoughts of love and support.

There is a type of prayer that I was taught in my spiritual studies called "affirmative prayer" or "positive prayer" (refer to sidebar on the facing page). It was used by many members of my support group at LEC. In this type of prayer, one connects with one's Higher Power, creates an inner picture of wellness, and then affirms its reality, as if it were already happening.

Affirmative prayer is just one of many forms of prayer—there is no right way to pray. The sincerity of your request and your intention to heal is more important than the outer structure you use. If you bring a pure heart to your inner altar and remain open to the presence of grace, who knows what miracles may occur?

The 12 Steps of AA Applied to Recovery From Depression
"Religion is for people who are afraid of going to hell.
Spirituality is for people who have already been there."
Alcoholics Anonymous

Although I have never suffered from a drug or alcohol addiction, during my episode of depression I often turned to the principles of the recovery movement and the 12 Steps of AA as a source of healing and inspiration. This was no accident, for I now see a direct correlation between recovery from alcoholism/addiction and recovery from mental illness.

To begin with, a substantial number of people with mental illness also suffer from drug and/or alcohol abuse. (The lifetime incidence of mental disorders is 22.3 percent for alcoholism and 14.7 percent for drug abuse, compared to 13.5 percent and 6.1 percent in the general population.)* One reason for this relationship is that

---

* Lisa Dixon and Jane DeVeau, "Dual Diagnosis: The Double Challenge," *NAMI Advocate*, April/May 1999, Volume 20, Number 5, pg. 16.

dopamine, a chemical that drives the brain's reward systems, is implicated in both addictions and depression. As Kathleen DesMaisons explains in her book *Potatoes Not Prozac,* the same diet that was developed to prevent relapse into alcoholism also works to heal depression. In fact, the parallels between the two conditions are so great that some people see them as underlying aspects of the same disorder.

In addition to their physical similarities, both addiction and depression have a number of psychological and spiritual parallels. In both disorders, the sufferer is dealing with a force that is outside his or her control. As step one of the 12 steps states, "We admitted we were powerless over alcohol—and that our lives had become unmanageable." This leads the alcoholic to surrender to "a Higher Power" as a way to restore order in his life. In a similar fashion, I realized that I could not heal my depression through willpower alone, and so I turned to spiritual help.

In addition, healing from addiction/depression is not a one-time event. The person who has stopped drinking does not refer to himself as a recovered alcoholic or an ex-alcoholic but a *recovering* alcoholic. Similarly, staying free from depression is an ongoing process. This understanding leads both the alcoholic and the depressive to live life "one day at a time," doing what is necessary to stay sober and emotionally stable for each 24 hours.

To accomplish this end, the relapse prevention strategies of AA are wonderfully suited for helping the previously depressed person take care of himself or herself. The widespread healing of alcoholism did not begin until those who suffered from the disease came together in community. By the same token, people who suffer from depression are now coming together in mutual support groups.

Another key to recovery from addiction is the Serenity Prayer—"God, grant me the serenity to accept the things I cannot change, the courage to change the things I can, and the wisdom to know the difference." Likewise, the depressive must learn to accept those things that are outside his or her personal control—for instance, genetics and temperament—and then change the things that he or she can

The Twelve Steps

1. We admitted we were powerless over our addiction (and depression)—that our lives had become unmanageable.

2. Came to believe that a Power greater than ourselves could restore us to sanity.

3. Made a decision to turn our will and our lives over to the care of this Higher Power, as we understood Him, Her or It.

4. Made a searching and fearless moral inventory of ourselves.

5. Admitted to our Higher Power, to ourselves and to another human being the exact nature of our wrongs.

6. Were entirely ready to have our Higher Power remove all these defects of character.

7. Humbly asked our Higher Power to remove our shortcomings.

8. Made a list of all persons we had harmed, and became willing to make amends to them all.

9. Made direct amends to such people wherever possible, except when to do so would injure them or others.

10. Continued to take personal inventory, and when we were wrong, promptly admitted it.

11. Sought through prayer and meditation to improve our conscious contact with our Higher Power as we understood Him, Her or It, praying only for knowledge of our Higher Power's will for us and the power to carry that out.

12. Having had a spiritual awakening as a result of these steps, we tried to carry this message to others and to practice these principles in all of our affairs.

control—attitudes, behaviors, diet, exercise, openness to treatment, reactions to other people, and so on.

Finally, people in recovery who also suffer from depression report that "working the program"—i.e., applying each of the 12 steps—heals their depression as well as addiction. (It certainly has worked for me.) Many of the aphorisms from the recovery movement—"one day at a time," "easy does it," "utilize, don't analyze," "act as if," "first be willing, then get busy," and "don't give up five minutes before the miracle"—contain practical wisdom that can help those with mood disorders to stay serene, productive and at peace, one day at a time.

Adjustments to Make During a Depressive Episode

Like any serious chronic illness, major depression can seriously compromise one's normal ability to function. Hence, if you are afflicted with major depression, you will need to readjust your expectations of what you can and cannot do. Here are some simple guidelines:

1. Do not set unreasonably difficult goals for yourself, or take on too much responsibility. Break large tasks into small ones and do what you can, as you can.
2. Attempt to postpone major life decisions, such as starting a new relationship, moving, quitting a job, beginning a new career, etc., until the depression has passed. If you feel you must make a major change, solicit feedback from people who can objectively assess your situation.
3. Do not expect too much from yourself right now. Striving to meet unrealistic expectations can exacerbate feelings of failure or worthlessness.
4. Focus on activities that will help you to feel better—e.g., mild exercise, socializing with friends, attending a play or movie, etc.
5. If you feel guilty because you are not being more productive, congratulate yourself for what you are doing—staying alive! That in itself is a major accomplishment.

In general, the simpler and less complex you can keep things, the better. Since your inner life is in turmoil, your outer world should be as stable and stress-free as possible. Think of this period as "down time" or as taking a sabbatical from the rigors of the external world. One day, you will come to fully participate in life again.

Managing Anxiety that Often Accompanies Depression

Over 60 percent of major depressions are accompanied by varying levels of anxious feelings and behavior. (During my illness, my extreme anxiety interfered with my recovery and increased the risk of suicide.) These symptoms may be diagnosed as generalized anxiety disorder, panic disorder, obsessive-compulsive disorder, or post-traumatic stress disorder (PTSD). Here are some techniques that are commonly used to treat mild to severe anxiety.

1) **Medications.** The medications most often used to treat anxiety are a class of drugs known as benzodiazepines (also called "minor tranquilizers"). These include Xanax, Ativan and Klonopin. The main problem with these substances is their potential for tolerance, physical dependence, and the likely recurrence of panic and anxiety symptoms when the medication is stopped. Hence, they are best used for treating short-term anxiety and panic. Because anxiety is so often associated with depressive disorders, it is essential to treat the underlying depression along with the anxiety disorder. When the depression is healed, symptoms of anxiety often diminish.

2) **Exercise and relaxation techniques**. Because anxiety clearly has a physical component (especially when it manifests as a panic attack), techniques for relaxing the body are an important part of the treatment plan. These include abdominal breathing, progressive muscle relaxation (relaxing the body's muscle groups) and biofeedback. You can learn these practices from any mental health professional who teaches relaxation or stress reduction. Regular exercise also has a direct impact on several physiological conditions that

underlie anxiety. Exercise reduces skeletal muscle tension, metabolizes excess adrenaline and thyroxin in the bloodstream (chemicals which keep one in a state of arousal) and discharges pent-up frustration and anger.

3) **Cognitive-behavioral therapy**. Cognitive-behavioral therapy is a psychotherapy that helps you to alter anxious self-talk and mistaken beliefs that give the body anxiety-producing messages. For example, saying to yourself, "What if I have an anxiety attack when I'm driving home?" will make it more likely that an attack will ensue. Overcoming negative self-talk involves creating *positive counterstatements* such as "I can feel anxious and still drive," or "I can handle it." What often underlies our negative self-talk is a set of negative beliefs about ourselves and the world. Examples of such mistaken beliefs are, "I am powerless," "Life is dangerous," and "It's not okay to show my feelings." Replacing these beliefs with empowering truths can help to heal the roots of anxiety (see "cognitive distortions" sidebar on pg. 165).

4) **Monitoring diet and nutrition**. Stimulants such as caffeine and nicotine can aggravate anxiety and leave one more prone to anxiety and panic attacks. Other dietary factors such as sugar, certain food additives and food sensitivities can make some people feel anxious. Seeing a nutritionally oriented physician or therapist may help you to identify and eliminate possible offending substances from your diet. He or she can also help you to research supplements and herbs (e.g., GABA, kava, B vitamins, chamomile and valerian teas) that are known to calm the nervous system.

If you are suffering from a serious anxiety disorder, you may want to locate a clinic in your area that *specializes* in the treatment of anxiety. Your local hospital or mental health clinic can give you a referral. In addition, you may wish to call (800) 64-PANIC to receive helpful material from the National Institute of Mental Health. Books and Internet sites on anxiety disorders can be found in Appendix C and in the Recommended Reading section.

How to Cope with Suicidal Thoughts and Feelings
—In Yourself and Others

The ultimate tragedy of mood disorders is suicide. Suicide is a double disaster. Not only does it prematurely end a life, it wreaks havoc on the lives of those left behind. Devastated survivors can be traumatized by feelings of grief, guilt, anger, resentment, and confusion.* "There was no time to say good-bye," and "Perhaps I could have done more," are examples of comments that are made by shell-shocked friends and relatives. Moreover, the stigma surrounding suicide makes it very difficult for family members to talk about what has happened.

Suicide has been defined as a "permanent solution to a temporary problem." For the person caught in the black hole of depression, however, there is nothing temporary about the hell he or she is experiencing. The resulting sense of hopelessness is the *major trigger* for suicidal thoughts, feelings and attempts. This hopelessness includes:

- no hope for the future.
- no hope that things will ever change.
- no hope that I will ever be well or stable.
- no hope that I will be able to meet my goals in life (or even have goals).
- no hope that the pain will ever stop.
- no hope that I can do anything to change it.

When the psyche is assailed by this level of despair, suicide feels like the only way out. If you are feeling suicidal, here are some thoughts that can help you to counter the suicidal urge:

1. Remember that you are under the influence of a "drug" called depression which is distorting your view of reality. As a result, your feelings of hopelessness do not accurately reflect your true potential for recovery.

---

* A good friend of mine told me that her heart "shut down" for *thirty years* after her older brother committed suicide when she was nineteen.

2. Depression, like everything else in the physical world, is cyclic. In most cases, it comes and goes; it has a beginning and an end. A useful affirmation to repeat is, "Nothing stays the same forever. This, too, shall pass."

3. An *overwhelming majority* of people who have suffered from suicidal feelings have fully recovered. The *odds* that you will get better are *in your favor.*

4. If you have family and/or friends in your life, realize that they will be devastated by losing you. Their suffering will only add to the existing suffering in the world.

5. Use the techniques described in the depression survival plan in this book to increase your coping resources and to keep yourself safe.

6. Remember that feelings and actions are two different things. Just because you feel like killing yourself, it doesn't mean you have to act on it this minute. This is one time when procrastinating is a good idea.

7. Do not remain alone when you are feeling suicidal. If you are feeling overwhelmed, ask for help. Set up a suicide support system with people who can spot your mood swings even before you do, and will take action to keep you safe. Make a pact that you will contact them when you are feeling suicidal. If you don't have friends who can do this, try to locate a depression support group at a hospital or clinic.

8. Use your local crisis hotline as a resource. Their job is to support you through your struggle, one day at a time. If you don't have a local hotline, call (888) SUICIDE—(888) 784-2433.

9. Regulate anything in your environment that may be used to harm you. Flush old medications down the toilet, keeping only small quantities of those you take regularly. Dispose of all firearms you have, or give them to a support person for safekeeping.

Finally, remember, people do get through this, even when they feel as bad as you do right now. Here is a passage from Kathy Cronkite's *At the Edge of Darkness* that was very helpful in restoring my hope.

Part of the anxiety and dread of depression is that "storm in the brain" that blocks out all possibility of sunlight. In the depths of despair that by definition murders faith, courage may have to suffice. Keep slogging. Even if you don't believe it at the moment, remind yourself of the existence of good. Reassure yourself: "Once I enjoyed 'X,' I will again." The *disease* may have turned off the spigot of love, but it will come back.

When someone you know is suicidal

Many Americans have mistaken ideas about the suicidal feelings that result from major depression. Depressed people who say they are suicidal are often not taken seriously by their friends and family. (For example, a day before a 14-year-old boy went on a shooting spree in a Georgia school, he told his friend that he wanted to kill himself. "You're crazy," came the reply.) What follows are some do's and don'ts on what to say to a suicidal individual.*

DO ask people with suicidal symptoms if they are considering killing themselves. Contrary to popular opinion, it will not reinforce the idea. "In fact, it can prevent suicide," says Dr. Joseph Richman, professor of psychiatry at the Albert Einstein College of Medicine in New York. Since the suicidal person feels isolated and alienated, the fact that someone is concerned can have a healing effect.

DON'T act shocked or disapproving if the answer to the question "Are you suicidal?" is "Yes." Don't say that suicide is dumb or that the person should "snap out of it." Suicidal feelings are part of being clinically depressed, just as a high white blood cell count is a symptom of an infection.

DON'T lecture a suicidal individual about the morality or immorality of suicide, or about responsibility to the family. A person in a state of despair needs support, not an argument.

---

* Taken from Caryl Stein, "Why Depression is a Silent Killer," *Parade Magazine*, September 28, 1997, pp. 4-5.

DO remove from easy reach any guns or razors, scissors, drugs or other means of self-harm.

DO assure the person that although it may not feel like it, suicidal feelings are temporary.

DO ask the person if he or she has a specific plan. If the answer is yes, ask him to describe it in detail. If the description seems convincing, urge the person to call a mental-health professional right away. If he or she is not seeing a therapist or psychiatrist, offer a ride to the emergency room for evaluation, or call the local crisis line— or (888) SUICIDE—(888) 784-2433.*

DO make a "no-suicide" contract. This means that the person agrees (in words or in writing) that if he feels on the verge of hurting himself, he will not do anything until he first calls you or another support person. You in turn promise that you will be available to help in any way you can. Ideally, it is best if the suicidal person has prepared a list of people (three or more is ideal) that he or she can contact in the midst of a crisis.

DON'T promise to keep the suicidal feelings a secret. Such a decision can block much-needed support and put the person at greater risk. If a person needs help from a medical professional or a crisis-intervention center, make sure that he or she gets it, even if you have to go along.

DO pay particular attention to the period after a depressive episode, when the person is beginning to feel better and has more energy. Ironically, this may be a time when he or she is more vulnerable to suicide.

DO assure the person that depression is a treatable illness and that help is available. If the individual is too depressed to find support, do what you can to help him or her find support systems— e.g., psychotherapy, medical treatment, and support groups that are described in this book.

DO call a suicide hotline or crisis hotline if you have any questions about how to deal with a person you think may be suicidal. Help is available for you, the caregiver.

---

* If the person is drunk or high, the risk of self-harm is greatly increased.

Finally, there exist a number of telephone hot lines and Internet sites that can provide immediate support and relief for anyone who is struggling with feelings of suicide.

1. **American Suicide Survival Line** (888) SUICIDE—(888) 784-2433. This nationwide suicide telephone hotline provides free 24-hour crisis counseling for people who are suicidal or who are suffering the pain of depression.
2. **The Samaritans Suicide Hotline** (212) 673-3000 or e-mail: jo@samaritans.org. They will respond to your e-mail within 24 hours.
3. **Covenant House Nineline** (800) 999-9999
   http://www.covenanthouse.org
   This hotline provides crisis intervention, support and referrals for youth and adults in crisis, including those who are feeling depressed and suicidal.
4. **Internet site:** http://www.metanoia.org/suicide/
   This is an excellent Web site which I visited when I was suicidal. I credit it with being one of the factors that prevented me from taking my life.
5. **Internet site**: http://www.save.org/index.html
   This is the Web site for SA\VE (Suicide Awareness Voices of Education), whose mission is to educate others about suicide and to speak for suicide survivors. I also frequented this Internet site when I was suicidal and found it to be extremely helpful.

These phone numbers and Internet addresses are repeated in Appendix C, along with other resources.

Facts About Suicide

Statistics

- More than 32,000 people in the U.S. kill themselves every year.
- Suicide is the eighth leading cause of death in the U.S.
- Each day, 85 people commit suicide and about 2,000 attempt it.
- A person commits suicide about every 15 minutes in the U.S., but it is estimated that an attempt is made once a minute.
- 60 percent of all people who commit suicide kill themselves with firearms.
- There are four male suicides for every female suicide. However, at least twice as many females as males attempt suicide.
- 75 percent of all suicides are committed by white males.

Youth

- Suicide is the second leading cause of death among college students.
- Suicide is the third leading cause of death among all those 15 to 34 years old.
- Suicide is the fourth leading cause of death among all those 10 to 14 years old.
- The suicide rate for young men (15 to 24) has tripled since 1950, while for young women (15 to 24) it has more than doubled.
- The suicide rate for children (10 to 14) has more than doubled over the last 15 years.

Facts About Suicide

Depression

- More than 60 percent of all people who commit suicide suffer from major depression. If one includes alcoholics who are depressed, this figure rises to over 75 percent.
- About 15 percent of the population will suffer from clinical depression at some point in their lives. 30 percent of all clinically depressed patients attempt suicide; half of them succeed.

Alcohol and Suicide

- 96 percent of alcoholics who commit suicide continue their substance abuse up to the end of their lives.
- Alcoholism is a factor in about 30 percent of all completed suicides.
- 18 percent of alcoholics die by suicide; 87 percent of these deaths are males.

Firearms and Suicide

- Death by firearms is the fastest growing method of suicide.
- Firearms are now used in more suicides than homicides.
- States with stricter gun control laws have lower rates of suicide.

Figures are based on 1995 United States statistics.

Source: American Foundation for Suicide Prevention.

Are You a Survivor?

When people are confronted by extreme trauma, they can respond in a number of ways. Some individuals are broken by their experience. Others limp their way through. But a small minority actually emerge in a stronger and better state. These "triumphant survivors" have been able to overcome disastrous childhoods or major setbacks in their lives.

Researchers such as psychologist Al Siebert (author of *The Survivor Personality*) have found that such people are endowed with certain attitudes or emotional resources—such as a sense of humor, flexibility, the ability to be empathetic, the ability to pick the most positive and useful interpretation for any situation, and—perhaps most importantly— the ability to reach out for help. Surgeon Bernie Siegel worked with people suffering from cancer who exhibited these attributes and called them "exceptional patients."

When questioned about their recovery, triumphant survivors state, "The critical issue for me was not what has happened, but *What am I going to do about it?*" After their ordeal has passed, survivors are often inspired to share their story with others. Part of their message is this: "Out of misfortune, some good can emerge."

Many of the qualities of the survivor personality can be applied by people who are suffering from depression.

WHERE HAS ALL THE INSURANCE GONE?
FINANCIALLY SURVIVING A DEPRESSIVE EPISODE

E xperiencing a depressive episode in our society is not cheap. Hospital rooms run $800 a day, psychiatrists charge from $150 to $180 an hour, and antidepressants may cost as much as $2.80 a pill. During my depressive episode, I was fortunate to be covered by the group insurance plan from my previous job, which paid for a majority of my hospitalization and outpatient costs. Most individuals are not so lucky. As a rule, insurance plans are structured so that the money allotted for mental health treatment is far less than the funds given for physical health benefits. This means that many people who suffer from depression run out of insurance before they run out of illness.

This lack of parity is most discriminatory for the self-employed. For example, as a self-employed writer, I purchase my insurance from the Providence Health Plan, one of the premier managed care companies in the Pacific Northwest. If I were in a car accident, had a heart attack, or developed an acute infection, my insurance would pay for 80 percent of my hospitalization costs. But if I suffered a relapse into depression and needed to be hospitalized, the Providence Health Plan would pay *absolutely nothing* for my treatment! Moreover, I cannot sign up for better mental health coverage. As incredible as it seems, mental health inpatient benefits for the self-employed are *unavailable* in the state of Oregon.

Day treatment coverage is not much of an improvement. Under current law, the state of Oregon mandates a maximum of $1,000 worth of benefits (which pays for only one week of outpatient care) every 24 months. When I attended the day treatment program at the Pacific Counseling Center, it took nine months before I got well.

Fortunately, I was covered by my employer's group health plan. But what if I were to have a relapse now? Where would I go? What of other self-employed people who are currently in the hell of depression? How many them are literally dying because they cannot get the care they deserve? *

These discriminatory policies reflect a long-held societal stigma against mental illness. This stigma is reflected in the fact that for every $100 of cost created by mental disorders, 30 cents is spent on research (compare that to $1.63 for cancer research). We will know that attitudes have changed when we see "depression awareness" booths (just like today's blood-pressure stations) set up in airports and other public facilities, in which individuals can receive free screenings to determine if they suffer from clinical depression or a related mood disorder.

Fortunately, a shift in attitudes is slowly taking place. In the first White House Conference on Mental Health (June 7, 1999), President Clinton stated, "As a nation founded on the principles of equality, it is high time that our health plans treat all Americans equally." He then announced that the federal government, the largest self-insured institution in the country, would amend its insurance coverage so that mental health services are *on a par* with physical health treatments. Under the new policy, private health plans covering federal employees and their families *could not* set limits on the number of outpatient visits or days spent in a hospital for treatment of "recognized mental health disorders" such as schizophrenia, bipolar or manic-depressive disorder, and major or clinical depression. Moreover, the policy would bar making co-payments higher for mental health disorders than those for the treatment of physical illnesses. The administration hopes that this policy will be a model for the rest of the health care industry. **

---

* While there have been reports in the media on people dying from physical illnesses that were neglected by the managed care system, no one has reported on suicides due to untreated mental illness. I can assure you that it happens, since untreated depression is the leading cause of suicide.

** To learn more about the government's support of mental health reform, visit the White House Web site on mental health (http://www.mentalhealth.gov).

In this vein, I plan to join with the National Alliance for the Mentally Ill (NAMI) in lobbying the Oregon legislature to pass a law mandating that insurance companies in this state provide equal coverage for mental illness. If you have similar concerns about your state's insurance coverage for mental health, I encourage you to get involved. It is time to put benefits for mental and physical health on an equal playing field, thereby guaranteeing that those who suffer from the terrible malady of mental illness can receive the same compassionate care that is offered to other patients with "physical" problems.

Replacing lost income

A second economic challenge that many people suffering from depression face is replacing lost income, especially when the illness is so disabling that one can no longer work. For those individuals who do not have insurance and/or independent resources, financial support is available, thanks to Social Security benefits provided by the federal government.

A person who can document that he or she is suffering from a disabling mental illness is eligible for SSD (social security disability income), and, if his or her income is low enough, for SSI (supplemental security income). After benefits have begun, he or she can then receive Medicare, which pays for inpatient psychiatric care and some outpatient services.

Although the monthly income from SSD and SSI is extremely modest, recipients do seem to get by. During my stay at day treatment, I saw many people get well because they were supported by disability income and their therapy was paid by Medicare. To learn more about obtaining assistance, you can call the Social Security Administration at (800) 772-1013. In addition, a number of attorneys and social workers specialize in helping people with disabilities to apply for Social Security benefits. Ask for a referral from a local mental health center or consult the Yellow Pages. Locate the section advertising attorneys, and then look for lawyers who are listed under the subheading, "Social Security."

A Special Letter of Support

This letter was written to me by my partner Joan three months after the beginning of my major depressive episode.

Douglas   12-25-96

Love is truly the greatest healing power. May the power of love work through you to do the work it needs to do to move you towards your healing.

May you be led to the right medicine to bring you into balance. I have great compassion for what you are going through. There is a *mystery* to this illness that your mind can't understand. There is a *higher force* at work here.

Honor and respect the divine feminine within. Please honor and respect it, for it can guide you in your healing journey. You are receiving love and support from the feminine externally. May you be able to receive that same love and support from your inner feminine.

I send you so much love and healing and light on this Christmas day! Douglas, please don't give up. May you receive the inspiration you need to keep going from day to day and moment to moment— especially when you feel the deepest despair and loss of faith. There is a way out. Somehow, some way, you will be led to the light!

I am here in love and support for you during this healing crisis.

May your soul hear this.

Love,

Joan

WHEN SOMEONE YOU LOVE IS DEPRESSED

The pain of seeing a loved one in the depths of clinical depression is almost as torturous as being depressed oneself. If you are the partner, parent, child or friend of someone who is undergoing a depressive episode, your understanding of the illness and how you relate to the patient can either support or deter his or her ability to get well. Here are some important ways in which you can help the healing process.

1) If a friend or family member's activity and outlook on life starts to descend and stays down not just a few days, but for weeks, depression may be the cause. The first way you can be of support is to **help the person to recognize that there is a problem**. This is especially crucial, since many people fail to realize that they are depressed. Begin by encouraging your friend to share his or her feelings with you and by showing him or her the self-rating scale for depression on page 135. Contrary to myth, talking about depression makes things better, not worse. Once it becomes clear that something is amiss, you can suggest that he or she seek professional help. (This is critical since only one third of people with mood disorders ever receive treatment.)

You can be of further support by accompanying your friend to his initial doctor's or therapist's appointment and subsequently monitoring his or her medication. In addition, explain that seeking help for depression does not imply a lack of emotional strength or moral character. On the contrary, it takes both courage and wisdom to know when one is in need of assistance.

2) **Educate yourself about the illness**, whether it is depression, manic depression, anxiety, etc. Learn about symptoms of the illness and how to tell when they are improving. Your feedback to

the psychiatrist or therapist about how your friend is faring will help him or her to assess if a particular treatment is working.

3) **Provide emotional support**. Remember, what a person suffering from depression needs most is compassion and understanding. Exhortations to "snap out of it" or "pull yourself up by your own bootstraps" are counterproductive. The best communication is simply to ask, "How can I be of support?" or "How can I help?"

4) **Provide physical support**. Often this means participating with your friend in low-stress activities—taking walks, watching movies, going out to eat—that will provide an uplifting focus. In other instances you can ease the depressed person's burden by helping with the daily routines—running errands, doing shopping, taking the kids out for pizza, cooking, vacuuming the carpet, etc.

5) **Monitor possible suicidal gestures or threats**. Statements such as "I wish I were dead," "The world would be better off without me," or "I want out" must be taken seriously. The belief that people who talk about suicide are only doing it for the attention is just plain wrong. If the person you care about is suicidal, make sure that his or her primary care doctor is informed. Use the suggestions listed on pp. 215-217 to keep the patient safe. Don't be afraid to talk with the person about his or her suicidal feelings. Meanwhile, hold on to the possibility that your loved one will get better, even if he or she does not believe it.

6) **Don't try to talk the depressed person out of his feelings**, even if they are irrational. Suppose the depressive says, "My life is a failure," "Life is not worth living," or "All is hopeless." Telling him he is wrong or arguing with him will only add to his demoralized state. Instead, you might want to say, "I'm sorry that you are feeling so bad. What might we do right now to help you feel better?"

7) **Maintain a healthy detachment.** You may become frustrated when your well-meaning advice and emotional reassurance are met with resistance. Do not take your loved one's pessimism personally—it is a symptom of the illness. When the light you shine is sucked into the black hole of depression, you may become angry or disgusted. Direct your frustration at the *illness*, not the person. People who suffer from depression complain that their families' resentment over their condition often leads to neglect or outright hostility.

8) If prayer is something you believe in, then **pray for your friend's healing.*** Turn his or her welfare over to the care of a Higher Power. In addition, you may wish to place his or her name on any prayer lists that you can locate (see pp. 281-83 for a listing of prayer ministries). Prayer goes directly to a person's unconscious where it will not meet the negative thinking so commonly found in depression. To respect the person's confidentiality, it is best to pray privately. Moreover, if you put a loved one's name on a prayer list, use first name only.

9) **Establish communication with other people** in the person's support network—e.g., family members, friends, physicians, therapists, social workers, clergy, etc. By talking to other caregivers, you will obtain additional information and perspective about the depressed person. If possible, arrange for all of the caregivers to meet together in one room for a brainstorming/support session. In this way, you will be working as part of a team—and not in isolation.

10) **Take good care of yourself and your needs.** It is easy to get immersed in your friend's care and lose your own sense of self. You may also experience "contagious depression"—i.e., taking

---

* Here is a prayer of protection you may wish to use. See your friend surrounded with light and say, "The light of God surrounds you. The love of God enfolds you. The power of God protects you. The presence of God watches over you. Wherever you are, God is. And all is well."

on the other person's depressive symptoms. Here are some ideas on how to "inoculate" yourself so that you can stay centered enough to truly help.

- *Take good care of your body.* Make sure that you are getting adequate food and rest.
- *Find a safe place to process your feelings.* In the role of being a caregiver, you may feel powerless, helpless, worried and scared (when you hear talk of suicide), or resentful and frustrated (at your inability to heal the pain). Discharge your frustrations with a trained therapist or a friend; you will be less likely to dump your negative mood (anger, fear or sadness) on the person who is suffering. Remember, it is okay to have negative thoughts as long as you don't act on them.
- *Maintain your routine as much as possible.* Although you may need to adjust your work schedule or other routines to accommodate helping a depressed person, keep your life as regular as possible. Don't become so involved that you lose touch with friends and social support.
- *Learn to set limits,* especially when you are feeling overwhelmed by the depressed person's pain and tales of woe. To avoid burning out or experiencing hostility towards the depressed person, encourage him or her to seek professional help. Your role is that of a friend or family member, not a therapist or a medical doctor.
- *Take breaks.* When you start to feel emotionally or physically drained, ask other friends and support people to relieve you. Then do things to nurture yourself.
- *Continue to pursue activities that bring you pleasure.* Having fun will replenish you so that you can keep on giving.
- *Give yourself credit for all that you are doing*—and realize that you cannot do everything. No matter how much you love another person, you cannot take responsibility for his or her life. Try to distinguish between what you can control (your

Best Things to Say to Someone Who Is Depressed

It is not always easy to know what to say when a person you care about is clinically depressed. Here are some words to say that will show your support, while acknowledging the person's right to feel his or her feelings.

1. "I love you!"
2. "I care."
3. "You're not alone in this."
4. "I'm not going to leave/abandon you."
5. "Do you want a hug?"
6. "When all this is over, I'll still be here and so will you."
7. "Would you like hold my hand and talk about it?"
8. "I can't fully understand what you are feeling, but I can offer my compassion."
9. "I'm sorry you're in so much pain."
10. "I have empathy for what you are going through."
11. "I am not going to leave you. I am going to take care of myself, so you don't need to worry that your pain might hurt me."
12. "I can't imagine what it's like for you. I just can't imagine how hard it must be."
13. "You are important to me."
14. "If you need a friend, I am here."

own responses) and what you cannot (the course of the illness). To this end, you may wish to meditate on AA's "Serenity Prayer."*
- *Attend support group meetings* for families who are dealing with
  mental illness. The local chapters of the following organizations can provide you with times and locations of such groups:
  National Alliance for the Mentally Ill, (800) 950-NAMI;
  National Depressive and Manic Depressive Association,
  (800) 82-NDMDA; and the Depression and Related
  Affective Disorders Association, (410) 955-4647.

11) Finally, **encourage the person you are caring for to
create a support system** such as the one that I outlined in my
personal narrative (pp. 33–49), or help him or her to do so. It takes a
whole village to see someone through a dark night of the soul. You
cannot transform the illness of depression by yourself, but you can
be an integral part of the healing process.**

---

* The serenity prayer is, "God, grant me the serenity to accept the things I cannot
change, the courage to change the things I can, and the wisdom to know the difference."

** Unfortunately, there are times that despite one's best efforts, healing does not occur.
In extreme cases, the depressed person may end his life. If this occurs, the caregiver needs
to work on dealing with guilt and self-blame—through counseling or joining a survivors
of suicide group. Visit the SA/VE Web site (http://www.save.org/index.html) to find out
more about such support groups.

LIVING IN AN AGE OF MELANCHOLY: WHEN SOCIETY BECOMES DEPRESSED

*"Depression is not just a private, psychological matter.
It is, in fact, a social problem... The fact that depression seems
to be "in the air" right now can be both the cause and result
of a level of a societal malaise that so many feel."*
Elizabeth Wurtzel, *Prozac Nation*

*"One cannot be deeply responsive to the world
without being saddened very often."*
Erich Fromm

As we begin the new millennium, the occurrence of depression around the world is expanding at an alarming rate. In the following pages, I will address what I believe are the collective forces that are contributing to this increase. It is important to understand that depression is not just an isolated phenomenon limited to a few poor souls with dysfunctional brain chemistry. Depression is a collective problem, and we who suffer from it should release the guilt and shame that comes from feeling that we are uniquely afflicted.

Acknowledging depression's social roots has another benefit. As we strive to improve the societal conditions that foster depression—whether it be through mentoring wayward adolescents, delivering meals to shut-in elderly, working for equality between mental and physical in health care, or defending the environment—we are lifted out of our self-contained suffering and freed from the prison of self.

With this in mind, let us turn our focus outward and examine the social context in which depression is taking place.

The Social Causes of Depression
"Where there is no vision, the people perish."
Proverbs 29:18

The 1990s may well be remembered as the decade of the brain. Advancements in neuroscience have enabled researchers to more clearly understand the workings of the brain's chemistry and to identify the biological roots of mood disorders. Ironically, as pharmaceutical companies create new and better "designer" antidepressants, the rates of depression around the world are increasing. According to *Psychology Today*, depression is the second most disabling ailment (after heart disease) in Western countries, and the fourth most disabling illness in the world (this ranking could rise to second by the year 2020). It appears that melancholy has replaced anxiety as our culture's prevailing discontent. *

Evidence to support this trend comes from a study of 9,500 adults which found that people born near the end of the 20th century were three times more likely to develop depression than those born earlier. A person born in the 1930s was likely to have his or her first depressive episode between the ages of thirty and thirty five. If you were born in 1956, your initial episode occurred between 20 and 25.** This phenomenon—the early onset of depression and the greater prevalence of depression in young people—is reflected in a 300 percent increase in the youth suicide rate in one generation.

This trend of higher rates of depression in children is occurring not just in the United States, but in other Western countries such as Canada, Germany, Sweden, and New Zealand. And it's not just confined to cities, but occurs in suburban and rural areas as well. Like canaries in the mine shaft whose fatal reaction to underground gas portends an impending explosion, the decline of our children's mental well-being should tell us that something in our society is terribly amiss.

---

* Hara Estroff Marano, "Depression: Beyond Serotonin," *Psychology Today*, Volume 32, #2, p. 30, March-April 1999.

** Gerald Klerman and Myrna Weissman, "Increasing Rates of Depression," Journal of the American Medical Association 261(15): pp. 2229-2235, 1989.

When changes of this magnitude occur within a fifty-year period, social forces are clearly at work. Myrna Weissman, epidemiologist of Columbia University, blames such societal factors as an increase in stress, fewer family and community ties, and even nutritional deficiencies.* Buddhist psychologist John Wellwood, whom I quote at length, provides his own compelling analysis of depression in our time:

> Our materialistic culture helps foster depression. Not only do we lack a living wisdom tradition to guide modern society, but we find it more and more difficult to achieve even the ordinary worldly satisfaction of adult life: finding rewarding work, maintaining an intimate long-term relationship, or imparting a meaningful heritage to our children. Our sense of personal dignity and worth is quite fragile in a society where stable families, close-knit communities, commonly held values, and connection with the earth are increasingly rare. In a society such as ours where the motivating ideal is to "make it" through social status and monetary success, depression is inevitable when people fail to find the imagined pot of gold at rainbow's end.
>
> Furthermore, many in the psychiatric profession seem determined to view depression as an isolated symptom that can be excised from the psyche with the help of modern technology. The fact that drugs have become the treatment of choice indicates that we as a society do not want to directly face the existential meaning of this pathology. If we believe that depression is primarily physiological and treatable by drugs, we will not confront the ways in which we create it, both as individuals and as a culture. The view that depression is an alien force that descends on the psyche actually interferes with genuine possibilities for healing. **

---

* Quoted in Shorpf, "Melancholy Nation," *U.S. News and World Report*, March 8, 1999, Volume 126, Number 9, pg. 56.

** John Wellwood, "Depression as a Loss of Heart," an essay from Nelson and Nelson, *Sacred Sorrows: Embracing and Transforming Depression*, New York, Tarcher/Putnam, 1996.

The theme of disconnection lies at the heart of the societal imbalance described by Wellwood. People who are depressed describe themselves as disconnected—from their bodies, their emotions, their spirits—i.e., from their core selves. The roots of this disconnection are to be found not only within the individual, but within society and its institutions. Here are just a few examples of how the values and lifestyles of Western culture promote and foster disconnection.

We are disconnected from our feelings

In the chapter "Overcoming the Stigma of Depression," I shared how in our intellectual culture, feelings are devalued and considered a sign of weakness. Family therapist John Bradshaw describes the "no-talk, no feel" that is prevalent in family systems. Children are raised to suppress their feelings, especially those of anger and sadness. But when we are conditioned to lose touch with our so-called "negative" feelings, so too do we lose touch with our joy.

We are disconnected from one another

Mother Teresa called America "the loneliest place in the world." This loneliness is created by many factors: the dissolution of extended families (the number of Americans living in extended families has gone from 80 percent in 1945 to three percent in 1990), the breakdown of traditional communities, and our hurried way of life. Instead of true community, we now have *pseudo-communities* like malls (where children frequently hang out) and the Internet. While people on the Internet would like to think that they are experiencing community, sitting in front of a computer terminal for long periods, like watching television, can be isolating. Thus, a recently released study found that the more time a person spends on-line, the more likely he or she is to experience symptoms of depression.

We are disconnected from time

In her seminal book, *The Overworked American,* Harvard psychologist Juliette Schor documents that the average American works an extra 163 hours a year (or the equivalent of an extra month) compared to thirty years ago. As a result of the decline of leisure, we have less time to devote to our families and to our children. Child neglect has become endemic to our society. Children are increasingly left alone to fend for themselves while their parents work. Even when the parents are at home, overwork may leave them with little time or energy for their kids.

We are disconnected from our sense of morality

In 1991 and 1992, the Joseph and Edna Josephson Institute of Ethics conducted a survey of the ethical behavior of 8,965 young adults. They found that six in ten high school students and one in three college students admitted to cheating on exams in the previous year. Moreover, one in three high school students took something from a store without paying. (An extreme example of this behavior recently occurred in my neighborhood; the student-body president of the high school where I tutor was sentenced to 12 years in prison for committing 19 armed robberies. According to his friends, he did it to gain "thrills and excitement.") The authors of the study concluded that such a precipitous decline in ethics has been caused by two factors—a pervasive cynicism about the need for ethical conduct in order to succeed, and the failure of parents, schools and businesses to consistently impose natural consequences for unethical behavior.

Moral and ethical values are usually imparted to children in their families. When parents abdicate responsibility for raising children, their children are more likely to be influenced by the pernicious violence and nihilism that infects much of the entertainment industry—i.e., video games, music, and TV. *

---

* To underscore the problem of violence in this culture, consider these astonishing facts. In 1996, handguns were used to kill two people in New Zealand, 15 in Japan, 30 in Great Britain, 106 in Canada, 313 in Germany and 9,390 in the United States! At last count there were 192 million firearms in the hands of private citizens in the United States. (*New York Times*, April 22, 1999, pg. A31.)

We are disconnected from curiosity and a sense of wonder

Anyone who has spent a day with a five-year-old child knows that children possess an innate love of learning. Somehow, between kindergarten and the sixth grade, this natural curiosity gets stamped out. In his acclaimed book *Dumbing Us Down: The Hidden Curriculum of Compulsory Schooling*, award-winning teacher John Taylor Gatto asserts that public schools (which he calls "jails for children") suppress the self-knowledge, curiosity and solitude that are essential to learning—replacing them with emotional and intellectual dependency, conditional self-esteem and fear of self-expression. Gatto poses the question, "How can we restore children's love of learning and put them back in touch with their special genius?" In searching for an alternative to public schools, he prescribes a combination of independent study, community service, large doses of solitude, and learning through apprenticeships.

We are disconnected from the earth

Nowhere is our disconnection more evident (and more dangerous) than in our relation to Mother Earth. In his book, *Earth in the Balance: Ecology and the Human Spirit*, Al Gore diagnoses our ecological problem as being a symptom of a dysfunctional, addictive civilization. Gore writes:

> I believe that our civilization is addicted to the consumption of the earth itself. This addictive relationship distracts us from the pain of what we have lost: a direct experience of our connection to vividness, vibrancy, and aliveness of the rest of the natural world. The froth and frenzy of industrial civilization masks our deep loneliness for communion. The price we pay is the loss of our spiritual lives.

We are disconnected from our spirit

As Gore says, the ultimate disconnection in this culture is the disconnection from our spirit. This is why Mother Teresa repeatedly stated, "The main problem facing the Western world is that of spiritual deprivation." In trying to fill that inner void, we vainly turn to alcohol, sex, drugs, workaholism, compulsive gambling, and a host of other addictions. Yet no amount of money, status, power, or sensual pleasure can create the connection to the deeper spiritual self that alone grants us peace.

Many of the ills I have listed are, I believe, a misapplication of capitalism as practiced by the corporate culture. The threefold human crisis of deepening poverty, environmental destruction and social disintegration can be traced to economic models that make growth the ultimate goal and that treat people as mere means. While the profit motive is not inherently evil, when money is worshipped as a false god (i.e., when it becomes an all-consuming priority, to the detriment of living systems and the natural world), evil deeds result—the exploitation of young children in overseas sweatshops; the oppression of American workers in electronic sweatshops; the unequal distribution of the earth's resources, so that 20 percent of the earth's people are chronically hungry or starving, while the rest of the population, largely in the North, consume 80 percent of the world's wealth; the marketing of cigarettes to teenagers; the inhumane treatment of farm animals in factory farming; the decimation of the rainforests; and ultimately, the destruction of the earth's biotic capacity to produce life.

There is, however, another way. Business can move towards sustainability and create a real ecological economic system. In his visionary book, *The Ecology of Commerce*, Paul Hawken writes:

> The ultimate purpose of business is not, and should not be, simply to make money. Nor is it merely a system of making and selling things. The promise of business is to increase the general well-being of humankind through service, creative invention and ethical philosophy.

Hawken argues that we have the capacity to create a new and different economy, one that can "restore ecosystems and protect the environment, while bringing forth innovation, prosperity, meaningful work and true security." Among other things, Hawken's "restorative economy" would:

- Reduce absolute consumption of energy and natural resources in the North by 80 percent in the next half century (the technology already exists to accomplish this).
- Provide secure, stable and meaningful employment for people everywhere.
- Honor market principles.
- Exceed sustainability by restoring degraded habitats and eco-systems to their fullest biological integrity.
- Be fun and engaging, so that people eagerly participate in cultural transformation.

Paul Hawken and other visionaries such as E.F. Schumacher (*Small is Beautiful*), David Korten (*The Post Corporate Era: Life After Capitalism*) and David Suzuki (*The Sacred Balance*) lay out clear and practical road maps that can lead us to sustainability.

Martin Luther King, Jr. preached that injustice anywhere is a threat to justice everywhere. I would paraphrase King's words to say that emotional illness anywhere is threat to emotional serenity everywhere. We can no longer afford to view depression as a problem of the individual. To end the worldwide epidemic of depression, we must implement a new social, economic, and spiritual vision, one that touches the hearts and souls of humanity. Such models already exist. What is needed is the political will to implement them.

Whatever the solution to our social malaise, one thing is clear: we cannot heal in isolation. We are part of the fragile web of life, and our individual salvation is inextricably connected to that of our fellow human beings. Perhaps this is what the anonymous author was thinking when he wrote:

> *"I sought my soul, but my soul I could not see.*
> *I sought my God, but my God eluded me.*
> *I sought my brother [and sister], and I found all three.*
> *My God, my brother [and sister] and me."*

Depression and the Young

"At the height of Nirvana's popularity, when they managed to both
top the charts and smash their instruments on Saturday Night Live,
I remember thinking that American youth must be really
pissed off to have turned something like this into a hit."
Elizabeth Wurtzel, *Prozac Nation*

Growing up has never been easy. Today's children, however, face problems far more serious than those of previous generations. For example, a recent *Parents Magazine* study compared the major concerns of children in 1949 with those today. Fifty years ago, children worried about talking out of turn, chewing bubble gum, making noise, running in the halls, and cutting in line. Now they list their major concerns as drugs, alcohol, teen pregnancy, AIDS, suicide, rape, child abuse, poverty, and homelessness. In the book *Breaking the Patterns of Depression*, psychologist Michael Yapko writes:

> When I was eight years old, my biggest concern is whether I'd be the starting pitcher on my Little League baseball team. I didn't have to choose between Mom or Dad for my primary residence. I didn't have to set up a complex visitation schedule following their divorce, because they never divorced. No one instilled in me a fear of people who wanted to do "bad touches" to me. No one tried to scare me away from drugs, because drugs weren't a kid's issue. No one lectured me in fourth grade about safe sex and AIDS. No one brought guns to school and opened fire. It *is* a different and tougher world for today's youth, who do face these sorts of things every day.

With weighty concerns such as these to deal with, children are at risk as never before. According to a recent report by the American Medical Association, today's youngsters "are having trouble coping with stresses in their lives and have more serious psychological problems" than the previous generation. In one school system, one of

Moments in America, for All Children

Every 1 second	a public high school student is suspended.
Every 9 seconds	a high school student drops out.
Every 9 seconds	a public school student is corporally punished.
Every 16 seconds	a child is arrested.
Every 25 seconds	a baby is born to an unmarried mother.
Every 37 seconds	a baby is born to a mother who is not a high school graduate.
Every 40 seconds	a baby is born into poverty.
Every 1 minute	a baby is born without health insurance.
Every 1 minute	a baby is born to a teen mother.
Every 2 minutes	a baby is born at low birth weight (less than 5 pounds, 8 ounces).
Every 3 minutes	a baby is born to a mother who had late or no prenatal care.
Every 3 minutes	a child is arrested for drug abuse.
Every 6 minutes	a child is arrested for a violent crime.
Every 10 minutes	a baby is born is born at very low birth weight. (less than 3 pounds, 4 ounces).
Every 18 minutes	a baby dies.
Every 40 minutes	a child or youth under 20 dies from an accident.
Every 1 hour	a child or youth under 20 is killed by a firearm.
Every 2 hours	a child or youth under 20 is a homicide victim.
Every 4 hours	a child or youth under 20 commits suicide.
Every 11 hours	a young person under 25 dies from HIV infection.

Source: Children's Defense Fund, *The State of America's Children Yearbook*, 1999.

every four children exhibited behavioral or emotional problems within the space of the school year.

The American Academy of Child and Adolescent Psychiatry now estimates that at least 3.4 million children younger than 18 suffer from depression. In addition, in a 1997 Youth Risk behavior survey, conducted by the National Centers for Disease Control and Prevention, more than one in five students reported they had seriously considered suicide in the previous year, while 7.7 percent admitted that they had tried one or more times. (This led to over a million suicide attempts, says the U.S. Department of Education.)

Children who suffer depression exhibit a wide variety of symptoms, sometimes making it hard to diagnose. Some kids with depression look like unhappy adults; they're sad, despondent, tearful, and have a loss of appetite. Others, however (especially boys), react in an opposite manner; they become aggressive, hyperactive, break rules, get in fights, and use drugs and alcohol. Moreover, depression in children often coexists with other problems such as learning disabilities, eating disorders, anxiety disorders and substance abuse. In addition, 20 percent of children who have ADHD (attention-deficit hyperactivity disorder) also have depression, and it is believed that these disorders may be both genetically and neurologically related.

The problems of children in our culture can be further analyzed as the problems of boys. At the turn of the millennium, boys in America drop out of school, are considered emotionally disturbed, and commit suicide four times as often as girls. They get in twice as many fights, commit 10 times more murders, and are the victims of violent crime 15 times more often. They are less likely than girls to go to college (because they haven't done as well in high school), are labeled "slow learners" and assigned to special-ed classes twice as often, and are far more likely to be labeled as having attention-deficit disorders and placed on powerful prescription drugs.*

---

* Brad Knickerbocker, "Young and Male in America: It's Hard Being a Boy," *Christian Science Monitor*, April 29, 1999, p.1.

Symptoms of Depression in Children

1. They act badly or are irritable for no apparent reason. They are demanding and difficult to please. Since nothing makes them happy, they complain about everything. Their attitudes and behavior alienate the adults and peers around them.

2. They frequently look sad, tired, ill or tearful. They do not seem to have the usual amount of childhood energy and curiosity, or they lack the sense of humor and fun that most children have.

3. They complain of not feeling good or of stomachaches, headaches or other physical ills.

4. The have little tolerance for frustration. They are easily stressed out and overwhelmed and tend to worry a lot or have exaggerated fears.

5. They become upset, clinging and overly dependent when they are separated from their parents. They may experience some form of regression, such as sucking their thumbs or wetting their pants.

6. They lose interest in activities they used to enjoy, such as sports, hobbies, or attending clubs.

7. They are overly shy and have difficulty making friends. They are nervous about interacting with others and may refuse to engage in social situations, or may become increasingly withdrawn.

8. Their grades are declining.

9. They talk of death and dying.

One reason that boys are so much more at risk lies in the way they are socialized. According to therapist Pia Mellody, "Boys in our culture are taught that real men are stoic. The ability to not complain, endure pain, and strive in the face of adversity is admired and celebrated in story and in song. The price paid for this isolation is depression." For a comprehensive analysis of how boys are socialized to become depressed and act out through violence, please refer to Terrance Real's *I Don't Want to Talk About It: Overcoming the Secret Legacy of Male Depression*, listed in Recommended Reading.

Depression and Teenagers

With the spate of killings that has led to 251 "school-associated" violent deaths between the 1992-93 and 1998-99 school years, national attention has been focused on the troubled world of a particular subset of children—teenagers. Researchers have discovered that millions of teens in America suffer from "serious, untreated mood disorders"—*especially depression*. Many of these adolescents are socially isolated and immersed in violent video games, and find access to guns to be as easy as obtaining a six-pack of beer. This combination has created a ticking time bomb that has too often exploded in our nation's schools.

Here is a list of some of the classic symptoms of depression in adolescents:

- being ill-tempered, "touchy," overreactive, or difficult to get along with.
- aggressive, disruptive, or delinquent behavior.
- falling grades.
- loss of interest in clubs, athletics, spending time with friends, or other activities they were formally interested in.
- compulsive partying, boy or girl chasing, or thrill seeking; or they may be just the opposite—withdrawn, inhibited, and overly serious.
- compulsive studying (never taking a break and relaxing) or compulsive exercising.

- low self-worth and low self-esteem.
- having unrealistic concerns that they are unattractive or are disliked by others.

The increase in depression among teens is partially caused by the steady decline in the amount of time parents spend with their children. Two-thirds of school-age children have working parents who are often unavailable during the hours directly after school, leaving an alarming *thirty-five* percent of 12-year-olds to fend for themselves. (Researchers call this the "3-6 p.m. teen alone zone.") A University of Illinois study found that children who are unsupervised after school are more likely to use drugs and alcohol. The FBI reports that during the "teen alone zone," youths are most likely to commit crime or be crime victims. It is also when they are most likely to commit suicide.

Teenage suicide

Suicide is the third leading cause of death among teenagers (after motor vehicle accidents and homicides) and has increased three-fold in the last generation. Depression is the major risk factor for suicidal behavior in adolescents, as it is with adults. Research reveals that children with mood disorders such as depression are five times more likely to commit suicide than children not affected by such problems. Other risk factors for suicide include:

- substance abuse (drugs and alcohol can exacerbate depression and increase the likelihood of impulsive behavior).
- previous suicide attempts (a person who tries once may try again).
- coexisting psychiatric conditions such as eating disorders.
- significant losses and separations.
- physical or sexual abuse.
- conflict among family members.
- family history of suicide.
- poor social relationships.
- the presence of a firearm in the home.
- stressful life events.

Fortunately, clear markers often exist to indicate that a teen-ager is at risk for suicide. They include:

Verbal hints of impending suicide
- I won't be a burden to you much longer.
- Nothing matters. It's no use.
- I feel so alone.
- I wish I were dead.
- That's the last straw.
- I can't take it anymore.
- Nobody cares about me.

Changes in behavior
- accident proneness.
- drug and alcohol abuse.
- violence towards self, others and animals.
- dangerous or risky behavior.
- loss of appetite.
- sudden alienation from family and friends.
- worsening performance in school.
- dramatic highs and lows.
- lack of sleep or excessive sleeping.
- giving away valued possessions.
- letters, notes, poems with suicidal content.

Changes in life events
- death of a family member or friend, especially by suicide.
- separation or divorce.
- loss of an important relationship, including a pet.
- public humiliation or failure.
- serious physical illness.
- getting in trouble with the law.

Caring adults and the prevention of suicide

The presence of one or more caring adults in the life of a suicidal adolescent—a person whom the child can turn to for advice—can decrease the likelihood of suicide from 50 to 75 percent. Here is what a concerned adult can do when this advice is sought.

Listen:
- Stay calm. Don't be outwardly shocked, as this may put distance between you and the child.
- Don't assume the teen is just trying to get attention. Don't try to argue him out of feeling suicidal.
- Show concern. Encourage the child to talk to you or some other trusted person.
- Allow for the full expression of feelings. Don't give advice or feel obligated to find simple solutions.

Share feelings:
- Accept the child's feelings, letting him know that he or she is not alone.
- Discuss how you have felt when you were sad or depressed.
- Be nonjudgmental. Don't debate whether suicide is right or wrong.
- Don't challenge the teen to "go ahead and do it." It is possible that he or she might take your advice.
- Show interest and support.

Be honest:
- Talk openly about suicide.
- If the child's words or actions scare you, tell him or her. If you're worried or don't know what to do, say so. Simply being a witness to the child's pain can promote healing.
- Offer hope that alternatives are available. Reassure the child that you know how to locate assistance.

Tips for Effective Parenting

Experts agree that all positive parenting rests on the attribute of love. The National Center for Kids Overcoming Crisis offers parents these seven guidelines:

1. **Value your child.**
   Supply honest praise, work to build self-esteem, and be loyal to the child's best desires.

2. **Nurture your child.**
   Display love through hugs, eye contact and encouraging words. Spend time with your child.

3. **Teach your child.**
   Treat your child as you'd like him to treat himself—and you. Encourage him or her to talk about problems; share how you've dealt with your own struggles.

4. **Speak the truth to your child.**
   Do not deceive. It is sometimes better to say little or nothing and allow the child to trust, than to lie and undermine confidence. A trusting relationship makes it easier for your child to confide in you.

5. **Discipline your child.**
   Offer compassionate, consistent correction when a child transgresses guidelines. A quick temper or holding grudges won't replace gentle but firm actions.

6. **Encourage your child.**
   Always put the child's needs and interests first, ahead of your own. As the child develops interests, encourage him to explore them.

7. **Never give up on your child.**
   Challenge yourself to find new solutions to problems. When unsure what is right, follow your intuition. Ask others for advice.

Get help:
- Don't be sworn to secrecy.
- Professional help is crucial. Assistance may be found from a local mental health clinic, school counselor, suicide prevention center, or family physician.
- Take action. Remove means of self-harm such as guns or pills. Call the American Suicide Survival Line: (888) SUICIDE—(888) 784-2433.
- Stay close to the person until he or she is under professional care.

Despite the susceptibility to depression among young people, the good news is that once diagnosed, depression in children and teens is highly treatable. Most depressed children respond quite well to a combination of individual therapy, family therapy, and medication. In more serious cases, day treatment programs, home-based therapy, therapeutic foster care and/or residential treatment are recommended. In addition, many of the coping strategies and healing modalities discussed in this book can be directly applied to help kids with mood disorders.

But while treating individual children for depression is important, it is not sufficient to reverse the rising trend in childhood depression. We must address the social and economic conditions that have turned the lives of too many young people into a struggle for physical and emotional survival. Here are some suggestions that, if implemented, would radically change our children's quality of life:

- Create economic and social support for children and their families through prenatal and maternity care, parenting leave, and more affordable child care.
- Encourage couples to take parenting classes before they have children. Just as driving a car is considered to be a privilege and not a right, parenting should likewise be seen as a privilege that requires knowledge and training.

- Reduce the hours parents spend working so that they can spend more time with their children.
- Encourage children—especially boys—to express a full range of emotions without the fear of ridicule or disapproval.
- Increase access to mental health counseling through granting parity between mental and physical health benefits.
- Develop greater awareness of and early treatment for depression and other mood disorders.
- Increase the number of school counselors and reduce classroom size.
- Teach young people principles of good communication, active listening and conflict resolution.
- As part of the school curriculum, teach children about values and ethics.
- Model good conflict resolution for children through respectfully working out adult disagreements.
- Reduce violence in the media and children's exposure to sexually exploitative media.
- Set limits with children and let them experience the natural consequences of their actions.
- Return to more traditional forms of moral development—through exposing children to ethical values and religious traditions.
- Rebuild local communities so that "the whole village" is once again available to raise a child.
- Establish a more balanced and respectful relationship with the earth and its inhabitants.

Childhood should be a time of innocence, discovery and joy. We owe it to our children and their children to create a safe, structured and nurturing environment in which young people can grow and flourish. Let us dedicate our ourselves, our communities and our country to transforming "Prozac nation" into a humane, just and loving society where children's health is the norm rather than the exception.

Depression and Suicide in the Elderly

It is not only the young who are at risk. Growing old in the modern society has become hazardous to one's health. The social causes of depression in the elderly seem clear. The old are horribly isolated—a consequence of our youth-worshipping culture and the breakdown of the extended family. In traditional societies, elders have been venerated and taken care of by the community. Now they live in understaffed, sometimes abusive nursing homes or alone in decrepit apartments.

One manifestation of this phenomenon is the alarming increase in the number of older Americans who are attempting suicide—and succeeding. Although the elderly make up 13 percent of the population, they account for 20 percent of all suicides—more than any other age group.

There are many reasons, of course, why an older person might want to commit suicide—failing physical health, chronic pain, or an unwillingness to be a burden to the family. But studies show that up to 90 percent of those who kill themselves are acting not out of a logical despair, but because they are suffer from clinical depression.

Eighty percent of older people who commit suicide are white males, and most use firearms. Other suicides go totally unreported. For example, many elderly people may kill themselves by refusing to eat or by stopping their medications. On the death certificates, these deaths are usually blamed on pneumonia or heart failure. With proper treatment, their lives could have been saved.

Fortunately, the elderly rarely kill themselves on impulse; hence there is a better chance to identify and to help those at risk. People who have recently retired, who have lost a loved one, or who have entered a nursing home (thereby losing their home, privacy and personal freedom) are among the groups who are most likely to become depressed—and then suicidal. If you have an older friend or relative you think might be suicidal, here are some signs to look for:

- **Changes in behavior**. Symptoms include more drinking and less interest in friends, family, hobbies or churchgoing; giving away money and prize possessions; buying a gun or stockpiling guns.
- **Carelessness about personal appearance**. Symptoms include hair uncombed, clothes not cleaned or pressed.
- **How they feel**. Symptoms include lethargy, loss of appetite (many people simply stop eating), having no joy in life, anger expressed towards self or others, a sense of hopelessness and despair.
- **What they say**. Words include "I'd be better off dead," "My family would be better off without me" and "I won't be around much longer."

Experts fear that elderly suicides will soar as the baby boom generation ages. Fortunately, when older people are treated for depression through therapy, medication, or ECT, they often get well quickly and go on to years more of productive living. This is why it is critical to recognize the early signs of depression so that the tragedy of suicide can be averted.[*]

In addition, changes in the social milieu can be implemented so that our elders are reintegrated into the community. The current trend towards co-housing—a situation where people pool their resources and live in individual dwellings on a shared piece of land—is very encouraging. Perhaps, out of economic necessity, aging baby boomers will begin to recreate community. And what is good for the pocketbook will be beneficial for the emotions and spirit as well.

---

[*] Caryl Stein, "Why Depression Is a Silent Killer," *Parade Magazine*, September 28, 1997, pp. 4-5.

Let Your Light Shine

Our deepest fear is not that we are inadequate.
Our deepest fear is that we are powerful beyond measure.
It is our Light, not our Darkness, that most frightens us.
We ask ourselves, who am I to be brilliant, gorgeous,
    talented, fabulous?

Actually, who are you NOT to be?

You are a child of God. Your playing small does not serve the world.
There is nothing enlightened about shrinking so that other people
    won't feel insecure around you.
We were born to make manifest the glory of God that is within us.
It is not just in some of us; it is in everyone.
As we let our own Light shine, we unconsciously give people
    permission to do the same.
As we are liberated from our fear, our presence automatically
    liberates others.

Nelson Mandela
1994 Inaugural Speech

AFTERWORD

"Wherever a person's deepest wound exists,
that is where his greatest gift to the community lies."
Robert Bly

I n contrast with the blackness of my mood, it was a sunny spring day in May of 1997. Using more willpower than faith, I dragged myself to the usual LEC Sunday morning service. Afterwards, I found myself in the office of associate minister Michael Moran, a colleague at whose church I had spoken five years before.

"It is the cruelest of ironies," I lamented, "that as students of New Thought spirituality, we understand that thought is creative, that 'whatever the mind can conceive and believe, it can achieve.' But now I suffer from a disease that renders this God-given faculty inoperative! How can I heal myself with the principles that you and Mary teach, when the mind, the instrument of creative imagination, is itself diseased?"

"Do you remember Martin Luther King's words," Michael said, "that for those who are on the spiritual path, suffering can be redemptive?"

"Yes," I replied, "but I can't imagine what good can result from this seemingly insurmountable affliction."

Michael swiveled his chair to the right and gazed out the window. Outside, a robin had just alighted upon a budding lilac tree. Putting his head in his hands, Michael pondered my words for what seemed an interminable length of time, until at last he turned towards me and spoke.

"You are going through this ordeal so that one day you can write about it."

" Are you dreaming?" I replied. "I haven't been able to write a word in five years."

"I know it sounds far-fetched, but that's what Spirit told me."

Two years later, by the grace of God, Michael's uncanny prophecy has come true. Before she died, my therapist and mentor Anne Zimmerman made a similar request—that my next book should emerge from the depths of my inner torment.

And so it appears that I have been called, though not willingly, to share my ordeal as part of the "wounded healer" tradition. I pray that what I have portrayed—the account of my own struggle with depression, as well as the clinical information offered in the second half of the text—has been of support to you or a loved one. I hope that this book has shone a light into the darkness that may have engulfed you. Most importantly, I wish that your suffering, like mine, can be redemptive—that out of the pain of your struggle, some unexpected good may emerge.

May the blessings be.

PROMISES OF DELIVERANCE

When I was caught in the despair of depression, I could not see my way out of the darkness. To bolster my faltering faith, I collected "messages of hope" from the Bible's Book of Psalms, from my own book, *I Am With You Always*, and from other inspirational writings. I present a sample of them here, in the hope that they may similarly be used by others who are wanting to believe that there is a light at the end of the tunnel.

"God is our refuge and strength, a very present help in trouble.
Therefore will we not fear, though the earth be removed,
and the mountains be carried to the midst of the sea."
Psalm 46:1-2

"The Lord is my light and my salvation; whom shall I fear?
The Lord is the strength of my life; of whom shall I be afraid?"
Psalm 27:1-2

"Though I walk through the shadow of the valley of death, I will fear no
evil; for thou art with me; thy rod and thy staff they comfort me."
Psalm 23

"The will of God will never take you where the grace of God will not
protect you. Don't give up five minutes before the miracle."
Alcoholics Anonymous

"In the midst of winter, I found within me an invincible summer."
Albert Camus

"The Lord is near to them that are brokenhearted,
and He saves those that are humble in spirit.
Many are the afflictions of the righteous,
but the Lord delivers him out of them all."
Psalm 34:19-20

"I will turn their mourning into joy, and will comfort them,
and will make them rejoice from their sorrow."
Jeremiah 31:13

"Remember, no human condition is ever permanent; then you will not be
overjoyed in good fortune nor too sorrowful in misfortune."
Socrates

"Fear not, for I have saved you. I have called you by name because you
are mine. When you pass through the sea I will be with you; and through
the rivers, they shall not overwhelm you; and when you walk through the
fire you shall not be burned. Neither shall the flame kindle upon you."
Isaiah 43: 1-2

"Our greatest glory is not in never falling,
but in rising every time we fall."
Buddha

"Though he fall he shall not be utterly cast down,
for the Lord upholds him with His hand."
Psalm 37:24

"Although the world is full of suffering,
it is also full of the overcoming of it."
Helen Keller

"For I reckon that the sufferings of this present time are not worthy to be compared to the glory which shall be revealed in us."
Romans 8:18

"There never has been a miracle that did not first start out as a problem."
Jack Boland

"Enlightenment begins on the other side of despair."
Sartre

*"But they that wait upon the Lord shall renew their faith:
they shall mount up with wings as eagles.
They shall run and not be weary, and they shall walk and not faint."*
Isaiah 40:31

*"Sometimes I get discouraged and feel my work's in vain;
But then the Holy Spirit revives my soul again."*
Martin Luther King, Jr.

*"Faith is a bird that feels the light
and sings while the dawn is still dark."*
Cancer survivor

*"The Light of God surrounds me.
The Love of God enfolds me.
The Power of God protects me.
The Presence of God watches over me.
Wherever I am, God is.
(And all is well)"*
The Prayer of Protection

"Fear not, I am with thee, O be not dismayed,
For I am thy God, I will still give thee aid;
I'll strengthen thee, help thee, and cause thee to stand.
Upheld by My gracious omnipotent hand.

When through fiery trials thy pathway shall lie,
My grace, all sufficient, shall be thy supply;
The flame shall not hurt thee; I only design
Thy dross to consume and thy gold to refine."
Christian Science hymn

"Let nothing disturb thee,
Nothing affright thee.
All things are passing,
God never changes.
Patient endurance
Attaineth to all things.
Who God possesses,
In nothing is wanting.
Alone God suffices."
St. Theresa of Avila

THE MASTER MIND PROCESS

One of the most powerful tools that I use to maintain my recovery from depression is being a part of a Master Mind group. A Master Mind group consists of two or more persons (two to six is ideal) who meet regularly in an atmosphere of trust and harmony for the purpose of providing mutual support and encouragement.

A Master Mind group is not established so that individual members can solve one other's problems. The group is based on the Master Mind principle—that when two or more people come together to support each other, a third energy, the Master Mind (God, Higher Power, etc.) is present. Moreover, Master Mind partners are able to believe for one another things which each person alone might find difficult to embrace.

Master Mind meetings may be held in a home, place of business, church or any agreed-upon location that provides quiet and privacy. During the meetings, each member is encouraged to surrender to the Master Mind any of his or her problem areas, challenges, needs for healing, or other heartfelt desires. When such requests are fully and properly made to the Master Mind, answers and solutions occur in the most amazing way.

One person should serve as facilitator for the meetings, which can occur once a week or every other week. Normally, a meeting begins with a moment of silence, a prayer, or some agreed-upon ritual. Then, the group members read aloud the following "Eight Steps Into the Master Mind Consciousness," which are derived from the 12 steps of Alcoholics Anonymous:

1. I surrender. I admit that of myself, I am powerless to solve my problems, powerless to improve my life. I need help.

2. I believe. I have come to believe that a power greater than myself—the Master Mind—can change my life.

3. I am ready to be changed. I realize that erroneous, self-defeating thinking is the cause of my problems, unhappiness, fears and failures. I am ready to have my beliefs and attitudes changed so that my life can be transformed.

4. I decide to be changed. I make a decision to surrender my will and my life to the Master Mind. I asked to be changed at depth.

5. I forgive. I forgive myself for all my mistakes and short-comings. I also forgive all other persons who may have harmed me.

6. I ask. I make known my specific requests, asking my partners' support in knowing that the Master Mind is fulfilling my needs.

After step six, each member makes known his or her personal request and receives the full attention and support of every other member. The requests may pertain to the areas of health, relationships, finances, vocation, spiritual growth, or any subject that is a goal or issue for the requester. (My initial request was, of course, healing from my depression.)

When the request has been completed, the group responds with an affirmation, such as, "I know the Master Mind has heard you, and is providing what you have asked for, or something better."

Then steps seven and eight are read to conclude the meeting.

7. I give thanks. I give thanks that the Master Mind is responding to my needs, and I assume the same feelings I would have if my requests were fulfilled.

8. I dedicate my life. I now have a covenant in which it is agreed that the Master Mind is supplying me with an abundance of all things necessary to live a successful and happy life.

I dedicate myself to be of maximum service to God and to those around me; to live in a manner that sets the highest example for others to follow; and to remain responsive to God's guidance.

I go forward with a spirit of enthusiasm, excitement and expectancy. I am at peace. *

At this point, the meeting may be concluded. Between meetings, members may stay in contact via the phone or in person to ask for additional support or to share the good news when requests have been answered.

My Master Mind group has been going strong for over a year. Each of the eight members has benefited greatly in his or her spiritual growth and uplifting.

To learn more about the Master Mind process, or to receive reprints of the "Eight Steps Into the Master Mind Consciousness," you may contact Master Mind Publishing, PO Box 1830, Warren, Michigan 48090-1830; or call (800) 256-1984.

---

* Reprinted from the book *1999 Master Mind Goal Achiever's Journal*, © 1999. Permission granted by Master Mind Publishers.

RESOURCES FOR WELLNESS

"Give a man a fish and you feed him for a day.
Teach a man how to fish and you feed him for a lifetime."
Japanese proverb

C linical depression is a serious, complex and often deadly illness. Fortunately, many excellent books, organizations and Web sites now exist that can lead the sufferer and his family out of the darkness. What follows is a compilation of resources that I have found to be particularly helpful in my recovery. I recommend these materials in the hopes that you, too, may receive healing and inspiration from them.

Healing On-line: Internet Sites
for Depression and Other Mood Disorders

I am a lover of books. As a writer of 21 years, books are my favorite means of learning about the world. But when I became depressed and my ability to concentrate was limited, I discovered another pathway to knowledge—the Internet. In the late evening when the black cloud lifted enough to give me few moments of respite, I would turn on my Macintosh computer and surf the Net to gain valuable tips from my fellow sufferers.

The Internet is one of the best sources of information about depression and mental disorders (if not *the* best) that is available to the general public. Hundreds of sites (as well as support groups) offer compassionate, common-sense, and clinically up-to-date help and support.

The following sites will start you on your journey towards healing. I have personally visited each of these locations and testify to their excellence. Many of them have links to other sites, which have links to more sites—and so on. The resources are endless.

One final note. Internet sites are constantly being updated and revised. These URL addresses are current as of November 1999. If you discover that any of them have changed, please E-mail me (dbloch@teleport.com) and I will make the appropriate corrections for the next edition of this book.

Mental Health Net
http://mentalhelp.net/

This award-winning site lists over 7,000 resources in the mental health field. It offers straightforward information on an easy-to-navigate site. The information is targeted towards both the lay public and professionals. A Reading Room offers access to books, articles, advice columns, opinion polls, roundtables and an index of discussion forums.

Mental Health Net suicide prevention links
http://mentalhelp.net/guide/suicidal.html

This Web site offers an extensive collection of links provided by Mental Health Net. It is incredibly comprehensive and gives you the opportunity to be on a suicide support mailing list.

Internet Mental Health
http://www.mentalhealth.com

This site functions as a World Wide Web mental health page. The goal of this site is to improve understanding, diagnosis, and treatment of mental illness throughout the world. One of its special features is that it offers descriptions, treatments, and research findings for the 52 most common mental disorders. It also lists the 67 most common psychiatric drugs, including: indications, contraindications, warnings, precautions, adverse effects, dosage, and research findings. This site also has a links page that will connect you with over 100 other mental health Web sites that offer free mental health information.

Dr. Ivan's Depression Central
http://www.psycom.net/depression.central.html

This site is one of the Internet's central clearinghouses for information on all types of depressive disorders and on the most effective treatments for individuals suffering from major depression, manic depression (bipolar disorder), cyclothymia, dysthymia and other mood disorders. It contains an amazing amount of information, more than I have seen in any single book volume.

Mental Health Infosource
http://www.mhsource.com

This has several excellent features, including the invitation to submit questions to an expert clinician on any aspect of mental health. It also has an excellent on-line directory of mental health resources on the Internet.

Psych Central: Dr. John Grohol's Mental Health Page
http://psychcentral.com/

Since 1995, a personalized one-stop index for psychology and mental health issues, resources, and people on the Internet. Another comprehensive, compassionate source of information.

Dr. Grohol's Suicide Help Line
http://www.grohol.com/helpme.htm

Dr. Grohol's suicide help line, a part of his excellent mental health home page.

Alt.Support.Depression FAQ
http://stripe.colorado.edu/~judy/depression/asdfaq.html

Alt.support.depression is a newsgroup for people who suffer from all forms of depression, as well as for others who may want to learn more about these disorders. This Web site contains frequently asked questions (FAQs) about depression, including its causes, its symptoms, its medication and treatments—as well as things you can do to help yourself. In addition, it contains information on where to get help, books to read, a list of famous people who suffer from depression, Internet resources, and instructions for posting anonymously.

the Anxiety Panic internet resource (tAPir)
http://www.algy.com/anxiety/index.html

This is a grassroots project involving thousands of people interested in anxiety disorders such as panic attacks, phobias, shyness, generalized anxiety, obsessive-compulsive behavior and post-traumatic stress disorder. It is a self-help network, replete with an on-line bookstore, that is dedicated to overcoming and curing anxiety disorders.

Depression.com
http://depression.com

Another good Web site that contains a wide array of information on depression. The site is supported in part by a grant from Bristol-Meyer-Squibb, so there may be a slight bias towards medication.

Haveaheart's Home
http://www.geocities.com/HotSprings/3628/index.html

This Web site contains several articles on depression and manic depression, written by someone who has struggled with his own depression and suicidal thoughts.

Suicide Help
http://www.metanoia.org/suicide/

This is an excellent resource which I read when I was suicidal. The writer compassionately takes you by the hand and describes why and how you should hold on to life, even in the face of overwhelming pain. This site was one of the factors that prevented me from taking my life.

SA\VE (Suicide Awareness Voices of Education)
http://www.save.org/index.html
E-mail: save@winternet.com
(612) 946-7998

This is the Web site for SA\VE (Suicide Awareness Voices of Education), whose mission is to educate others about suicide and to speak for suicide survivors. I also visited this Internet site when I was suicidal and found it to be extremely helpful.

http://www.save.org/question.html

Visit this link of SA\VE to get the answers to the most frequently asked questions about suicide prevention.

The Samaritans
http://mentalhelp.net/samaritans/

The Samaritans United States home page, which describes their services in support of suicidal individuals.

Depression After Delivery, Inc.
http://www.behavenet.com/dadinc

Information and support for women who are experiencing postpartum depression, as well as for health care professionals.

Wing of Madness
http://www.wingofmadness.com/

Another good Web site that contains a plethora of information on depression and mood disorders.

Pendulum Resource Center for Bipolar Illness
http://www.pendulum.org/

A great site for everything you would want to know about manic depression.

Internet Depression Resource List
http://www.execpc.com/~corbeau

Has great links to other pages.

Andrew's depression page
www.blarg.net/~charlatn/Depression.html

Another good resource.

Famous people who have suffered from depression or manic depression
http://www.frii.com/~parrot/living.html

Society for Light Treatment and Biological Rhythms
http://www. websciences.org/sltbr

Visit this site to learn about the current research on light therapy for the treatment of biological rhythm disorders.

The Web of Addictions
http://www.well.com/user/woa/

This group is dedicated to providing accurate information about alcohol and other drug addictions. It is also a resource for teachers, students and others who need factual information about abused drugs.

The National Clearinghouse for Alcohol and Drug Information Line
http://www.health.org/links/reglink.htm

This site provides great links to other Web sites with information on healing from drug and alcohol abuse.

Finally, here are two Web sites on sleep and sleep disorders.
http://www.sleepnet.com
http://www.stanford.edu/~dement/

Mental Health Advocacy and Consumer Organizations

Many organizations are dedicated to providing healing information and support to those who suffer from mood disorders and other types of emotional pain. Contact the following agencies for information about depression, sources of treatment, and local community support groups.

Depression Awareness, Recognition, and Treatment Program
(D/ART) National Institute of Mental Health
5600 Fishers Lane, Room 10–85
Rockville, MD 20857–8030
(800) 421–4211
(301) 443–4513
http://www.nimh.nih.gov

Write or call for free informational brochures about depression and anxiety disorders.

National Alliance for the Mentally Ill (NAMI)
200 N. Glebe Rd., Suite 1015
Arlington, VA 22201
(800) 950-NAMI
http://www.nami.org

The nation's voice on mental illness, NAMI is the national umbrella organization for more than 1,000 local support and advocacy groups for families and individuals affected by serious mental illnesses. Contact them to learn more about groups in your area, as well as how to connect with local affiliates.

Depressive and Related Affective Disorder Association (DRADA)
Johns Hopkins Hospital
Meyer 3-181
600 North Wolfe Street
Baltimore, MD 21287
(410) 955-4647
http://www.med.jhu.edu/drada

Call to be put in touch with support groups in your area.

National Foundation for Depressive Illness
PO Box 2257
New York, NY 10016
(800) 248-4344
http://www.depression.org

Refers people to physicians who treat depression using biological (i.e., antidepressant) therapies.

National Depressive and Manic Depressive Association (NDMDA)
730 North Franklin, Suite 501
Chicago, IL 60610
(800) 82-NDMDA
http://www.ndmda.org

A nonprofit group that provides educational information about depressive and manic depressive illness. Call for support groups.

The Dana Alliance for Brain Initiatives
745 Fifth Avenue, Suite 700
New York, NY 10151
(212) 223-4040
http://www.dana.org/brainweb

This organization supports cutting-edge research on a number of brain diseases and disorders, including depression.

National Alliance for Research on Schizophrenia and Depression (NARSAD)
60 Cutter Mill Rd., Suite 200
Great Neck, NY 11021
(516) 829-0091
http://www.narsad.org

Raises funds for research on mental illness. Also provides informational brochures.

National Mental Health Association
1021 Prince Street
Alexandria, VA 22314
(800) 969-NMHA
http://www. nmha.org

Established in 1909 by former psychiatric patient Clifford W. Beers, the NMHA is dedicated to promoting mental health and preventing mental disorders through advocacy, education, research, and service. Over 330 affiliates nationwide. Call for literature.

Depression After Delivery, Inc.
P.O. Box 278
Belle Mead, NJ 08502
(908) 575-9121; (215) 295-3994 (professional inquiries)
(800) 944-4PPD (information request line)
http://www.behavenet.com/dadinc

Offers education, information, and referral for women and families coping with mental health issues associated with childbearing, both during and after pregnancy. Be sure to visit their Web site to learn about postpartum depression and its treatment.

Anxiety Disorders Association of America

11900 Parklawn Dr., Suite 100
Rockville, MD 20852
(301) 231-9350
http://www.adaa.org

A non-profit organization that contains a number of excellent self-help publications, books and tapes on healing from anxiety disorders.

Holistic Depression Network

9550 Roosevelt Way NE, #302
Seattle, WA 98115
(206) 528-9975
(206) 528-9832 fax
http://www.holisticdepression.net
E-mail: info@holisticdepression.net

Holistic Depression Network is committed to educating, supporting and connecting those interested in the holistic care of depression. It offers educational material, support groups, workshops/training and well-being services—such as Reiki clinics and yoga classes—and membership benefits.

National Self-Help Clearinghouse

365 Fifth Ave., Suite 3300
New York, NY 10016
(212) 817-1822
http://www.selfhelpweb.org
http://www.cmhc.com/selfhelp (This Web site puts you in direct contact with self-help groups.)

Refers people to local self-help clearinghouses, who then refer to local self-help groups.

National Mental Health Consumer Self-Help Clearinghouse

1211 Chestnut St., Suite 1207
Philadelphia, PA 19107
(800) 553-4539
(215) 751-1820
http://www.mhselfhelp.org

This organization disseminates information to mental health consumers on how to start one's own mental health self-help group and how to locate self-help groups in your local area.

Enviro-Med

1600 SE 141st Ave.
Vancouver, WA 98683
(800) 222-3296
http://www.bio-light.com
e-mail: info@bio-light.com

Offers light systems for the treatment of biological rhythm disorders—e.g., seasonal affective disorder and sleep disturbances due to jet lag and change in work schedules.

SunBox Company

19217 Orbit Drive
Gaithersburg, MD 20879
(800) 548-3968
http://www. sunboxco.com
e-mail: sunbox@aol.com

Offers bright light therapy units for the treatment of biological rhythm disorders, as well as dawn simulators that will create the experience of sunrise indoors.

For information about light therapy contact:

NIMH Seasonal Studies Program
Building 10, Rm 4S-239
9000 Rockville Pike
Bethesda, MD 20892
(800) 421-4211

The Northwest Neurodevelopmental Training Center
P.O. Box 406
Woodburn, OR 97071
(503) 981-0635
email: nntc@open.org
http://www.open.org/nntc

This center investigates possible brain injuries or developmental dysfunctions in the nervous system as possible causes of mental and emotional disorders.

Suicide Prevention Organizations

The following groups are dedicated to providing information about suicide prevention, and support for those who are suicidal.

American Association of Suicidology
4201 Connecticut Ave. NW, Suite 408
Washington, DC 20008
(202) 237-2280
(202) 237-2282 fax
http://www.suicidology.org

This group offers books, pamphlets, journals and workshops on suicide prevention.

American Foundation for Suicide Prevention
120 Wall Street, 22nd Floor
New York, NY 10005
Toll free (888) 333-AFSP
(212) 363-6237 fax
http://www.afsp.org

This foundation funds research, education and treatment programs aimed at the prevention of suicide.

SA\VE (Suicide Awareness Voices of Education)
PO Box 24507
Minneapolis, MN 55424
(612) 946-7998
http://www.save.org/index.html

This mission of this organization is to educate others about suicide and to speak for suicide survivors. I also visited their Internet site when I was suicidal and found it to be extremely helpful.

American Suicide Survival Line
Toll free (888) SUICIDE—(888) 784-2433

The nationwide toll-free suicide hotline provides free 24-hour crisis counseling for people who are suicidal or who are suffering the pain of depression. Confidentiality is assured. Case management is also offered to connect people with healing resources in their local communities.

The Samaritans Suicide Hotline
(617) 247-0220; (212) 673-3000; (401) 272-4044
Email: jo@samaritans.org
http://mentalhelp.net/samaritans/ (U.S. Web site)
http://www.samaritansnyc.org (New York Web site)

The Samaritans are a UK (United Kingdom) charity, founded in 1953, which exists to provide confidential emotional support to any person who is suicidal or despairing, and to increase public awareness of issues around suicide and depression. This service is provided 24 hours every day by trained volunteers. It is free. You are guaranteed absolute confidentiality and that you will not be judged. Your email will be answered within 24 hours. I have also listed some phone numbers that can be called from anywhere in the United States.

Covenant House Nineline
346 W. 17th Street
New York, NY 10011
(800) 999-9999
http://www.covenanthouse.org

This hotline provides crisis intervention, support and referrals for youth in crisis—i.e., for runaways, abandoned youth, and those who are depressed or suicidal. Help is also available for adults.

Surgeon General's Call to Action to Prevent Suicide
(202) 690-7694
(202) 690-6960 fax
http://www.surgeongeneral.gov

In June of 1999, the Surgeon General of the United States defined suicide as a "major public health problem." Consequently, the surgeon general's office has developed a national strategy for suicide prevention. For a free copy of the report, visit the Web site or call.

National Institute of Mental Health (NIMH)
Suicide Research Consortium
http://www.nimh.nih.gov/research/suicide.htm

This branch of the National Institute of Mental Health coordinates program development in suicide research across the country and disseminates science-based information on suicidology to the public, media, and policymakers.

12-Step/Recovery Groups
Call these groups for meeting locations in your area.

Alcoholics Anonymous World Service Office
475 Riverside Drive
New York, NY 10115
(212) 870-3400
http://www.aa.org

Narcotics Anonymous World Service Office
P.O. Box 9999
Van Nuys, CA 91409
(818) 773-9999
http://www.na.org

Cocaine Anonymous World Service Office
P.O. Box 2000
Los Angeles, CA 90049
(310) 559-5883
(310) 559-2554 fax
e-mail: cawso@ca.org
http://www.ca.org

Al-Anon and Alateen Family Group Headquarters
1600 Corporate Landing Way
Virginia Beach, VA 23454
(800) 344-2666
(757) 563-1655 fax
http://www.al-anon.alateen.org

Al-Anon and Alateen are offshoots of AA, and are designed to support families and friends of alcoholics or those dealing with substance abuse. Call for meeting locations in your area.

Emotions Anonymous World Service Office
P.O. Box 4245
St. Paul, MN 55104
(651) 647-9712
(651) 647-1593 fax
http://www.mtn.org/EA

Emotions Anonymous is a 12-step fellowship composed of people who come together in weekly meetings for the purpose of working towards recovery from a wide variety of emotional difficulties, including depression and anxiety. Call for meeting locations.

Overeaters Anonymous World Service Office
6075 Zenith Court NE
Rio Rancho, NM 87124
(505) 891-2664
(505) 891-4320 fax
e-Mail: overeatr@technet.nm.org
http://www.overeatersanonymous.org

National Clearinghouse for Alcohol and Drug Information
(NACDI)
111426-28 Rockville Pike
Rockville, MD 20852
(800) 729-6686
http://www.health.org/index.htm

NCADI is the world's largest resource for current information
and materials concerning substance abuse.

Associations of Mental Health Professionals

These professional organizations can be contacted for referrals
to mental health professionals in your area.

American Psychiatric Association
1400 K Street NW
Washington, DC 20005
(202) 682-6220
http://www.psych.org

American Psychological Association
750 First Street NE
Washington, DC 20002
(202) 336-5800
http://www.apa.org

National Association of Social Workers
750 First Street NE
Washington, DC 20002
(800) 638-8799
http://www.socialworkers.org

American Society of Clinical Hypnosis
33 West Grand Avenue
Chicago, IL 60610
(312) 645-9810

American Association for Marriage and Family Therapy
1133 Fifteenth Street NW, Suite 300
Washington, DC 20005
(202) 452-0109
http://www.aamft.org

American Association of Pastoral Counselors
9504-A Lee Highway
Fairfax, VA 22301
(703) 385-6967
http://www.aapc.org

American Mental Health Alliance (AMHA)
e-mail: AMHA@mental-health-coop.com
(877) 264-2007 (toll free)
http://www.mental-health-coop.com/index.html

AMHA is a growing grassroots national alliance of over 2,000 mental health practitioners, including psychiatrists, psychologists, licensed social workers, and other licensed mental-health practitioners. Its goal is to develop a caring and respectful mental healthcare delivery system that provides an alternative to the managed care systems.

Telephone Prayer Ministries

The turning point in my healing from depression came when a group of people started to pray for me. In addition to receiving support from the LEC group, I called a number of telephone prayer ministries and asked them to hold a vision of my wellness.

I believe that such telephone ministries perform a valuable service to all who seek prayer support. Having a prayer partner is not only consoling, the presence of "two or more" souls activates an energy field that can attract Divine healing and grace. Please feel free to use the following resources as Spirit directs you.

Silent Unity

1901 NW Blue Parkway
Unity Village, MO 64065
(800) 669-7729
(816) 251-3554 fax
e-mail: unity@unityworldhq.org

The granddaddy of prayer ministries was founded in 1890 by Charles and Myrtle Fillmore as the "Society of Silent Help." Initially, all requests for prayer arrived by mail, but soon people turned to the telephone and called in their prayers. Today, telephone lines are open 24 hours a day, seven days a week. When you call, you will speak to a live person who will respond to your request with an affirmative prayer treatment. Your request will be prayed over for 30 days by the Silent Unity prayer team. In addition, you may ask to be sent a healing affirmation and support literature.

World Ministry of Prayer
3251 West Sixth Street
P.O. Box 75127
Los Angeles, CA 90075-0127
(213) 385-0209
(213) 388-1926 fax
(800) 421-9600
e-mail: inquiry@wmop.org
http://www.wmop.org

Run by the Church of Religious Science, this live 24-hour prayer line functions like that of Silent Unity. When you call, a person will pray with you over your request. The prayer team will hold you in the light for the next 30 days and will send you a letter of support, as well as two or three affirmations. This is an excellent prayer ministry.

Inspiration for Better Living
24 Hour Ear-to-Ear Prayer Ministry
11901 S. Ashland Avenue
Chicago, IL 60643
(773) 568-1717
(800) 447-6343

Another fine 24-hour prayer line. Someone will speak to you in person and send you a prayer response, including an affirmation. You might also request their "Daily Inspiration for Better Living," a series of daily affirmations and meditations for each month.

Christ Church Unity Prayer Ministry
3770 Altadena Avenue
San Diego, CA 92195
(619) 282-7609

Run by the Christ Church Unity in San Diego, this 24-hour telephone prayer line was designed to serve the congregants of the church, but receives requests from the entire Southern California area, as well as the rest of the country. I have visited their Prayer Tower, which is filled with a consciousness of light and love. You will receive a written response to your prayer request which will be prayed over for 30 days.

Living Enrichment Center Ministry of Prayer
29500 SW Grahams Ferry Road
Wilsonville, OR 97070
(503) 582-4218
(503) 682-4275 fax
e-mail: prayer@lecworld.org
http://www.lecworld.org

This is not a telephone ministry per se, but I list it because it is the ministry where I work in the Pacific Northwest. When you call, you will hear a taped inspirational message and will have the opportunity to leave your prayer request on a message line. Although you will not speak to a live person, your prayers will be answered by mail (if you leave your address) and will be prayed over for 30 days. You can also send your requests by e-mail.

RECOMMENDED READING

For those people whose depression and/or anxiety has not impaired their ability to read, I wish to recommend some excellent books and articles on the subject of depression and other mood disorders. I have organized my bibliography around specific themes so that you can easily locate the appropriate book to speak to your particular needs. In addition, I have annotated some of the listings, offering my specific reasons for recommending a particular book.

Memoirs of Melancholy

Each of the following works presents a beautiful and compelling account of the author's unique struggle with the hell of depression, and how he or she made it through to the other side.

Callahan, Steven, *Adrift: Seventy-Six Days Lost at Sea*, Boston, Houghton Mifflin, 1986. A book about situational depression brought on by a life-death struggle. The book-on-tape read by Dick Estelle is must listening.

Cronkite, Kathy, *On the Edge of Darkness: Conversations About Conquering Depression*, New York, Doubleday, 1994.

Danquah, Meri Nana-Ama, *Willow Weep for Me: A Black Woman's Journey Through Depression*, New York, WW Norton, 1998.

Dravecky, Jan, *A Joy I'd Never Known*, Grand Rapids, Zondervan Publishing House, 1996. An evangelical account of God's role in healing depression.

Duke, Patty and Gloria Hochman, *A Brilliant Madness: Living With Manic Depressive Illness*, New York, Bantam Books, 1992.

Janet Filips, "Father John's Resurrection: A Priest Credits Prozac and Prayer for Pulling Him Out of His Depression," *The Oregonian*, February 10, 1995, Section B, pp. 1-2.

Hampton, Russell, *The Far Side of Despair: A Personal Account of Depression*, Chicago, Nelson-Hall, 1975. (Out of print, but available in libraries.)

Jamison, Kay Redfield, *An Unquiet Mind*, New York, Alfred A. Knopf, 1995. The classic memoir about manic-depressive illness.

Kaysen, Susanna, *Girl, Interrupted*, New York, Random House, 1993. A compelling account of the author's two-year stay at McLean Hospital, at a time when psychiatric hospitals still provided long-term care.

Manning, Martha, *Undercurrents: A Therapist's Reckoning With Her Own Depression*, San Francisco, HarperSanFrancisco, 1994. A moving story that describes the author's recovery from major depression through ECT.

Smith, Jeffery, *Where the Roots Reach for Water: A Personal and Natural History of Melancholia,* New York, North Point Press, 1999. A literary and psychological account of depression.

Andrew Solomon, "Anatomy of Melancholy," *New Yorker*, January 12, 1998, Volume 73, Number 42, pg. 46 (14). An excellent melding of memoir and informational reporting.

Styron, William, *Darkness Visible: A Memoir of Madness*, New York, Vintage Books, 1990. During my depressive episode, this book was my bible. Here was someone who truly understood what my hell was like, and described it in exquisite detail.

Thompson, Tracy, *The Beast: A Reckoning with Depression,* GP Putnam and Sons, New York, 1995. A *Washington Post* reporter vividly portrays her experience with depression and the road to healing.

Thorne, Julia, *You Are Not Alone: Words of Experience and Hope for the Journey Through Depression*, New York, HarperPerennial, 1993. The author, who suffered from depression, has compiled short first-person accounts by fellow sufferers.

Wurtzel, Elizabeth, *Prozac Nation: Young and Depressed in America*, Boston, Houghton Mifflin Company, 1994. A funny, witty, and poignant tale.

Books and Articles on the Treatment of Depression and Other Mood Disorders

Beck, Aaron, *Cognitive Therapy of Depression*, Guilford Press, New York, 1979.

Berger, Diane and Lisa Berger, *We Heard the Angels of Madness: A Family Guide to Coping With Manic Depression*, New York, William Morrow, 1992.

Bloomfield, Harold and Peter McWilliams, *How to Heal Depression*, Prelude Press, Los Angeles, 1994.

Bourne, Edmund J., *The Anxiety and Phobia Workbook*, Oakland, New Harbinger Publications, 1995. An excellent resource for coping with panic and anxiety.

Callahan, Rachel and Rea McDonnell, *God Is Close to the Broken-hearted: Good News for Those Who Are Depressed,* Cincinnati, Ohio, St. Anthony Messenger Press, 1996.

Carrigan, Catherine, *Healing Depression: A Guide to Making Intelligent Choices About Treating Depression,* Santa Fe, NM, Heartsfire Books, 1997.

Cobain, Bev, *When Nothing Matters Anymore: A Survival Guide for Depressed Teens*, Minneapolis, Free Spirit Press, 1998. Bev Cobain, the cousin of rock star Kurt Cobain, who took his own life in 1994, has created a much-needed resource for young people with depression.

Cohen, David B., *Out of the Blue: Depression and Human Nature,* WW Norton, New York, 1994.

Conroy, David L., *Out of the Nightmare: Recovering from Depression and Suicidal Pain*, New Liberty Press, New York, 1991. Promotes the theory that suicide occurs when pain exceeds one's coping resources.

Copeland, Mary Ellen, *The Depression Workbook: A Guide to Living with Depression and Manic Depression,* Oakland, New Harbinger Publications, 1992. A superb resource.

DesMaisons, Kathleen, *Potatoes Not Prozac*, New York, Simon and Schuster, 1998. Controlling depression through diet.

Elkins, Rita, *Depression and Natural Medicine: A Nutritional Approach to Depression and Mood Swings*, Pleasant Grove, Utah, Woodland Publishing, 1995.

Engler, Jack and Daniel Goleman, *A Consumer's Guide to Psychotherapy*, New York, Simon and Schuster, 1992. A truly comprehensive manual.

Fassler, David and Lynne S. Dumas, *Help Me, I'm Sad: Recognizing, Treating and Preventing Childhood and Adolescent Depression*, New York, Viking, 1997. A comprehensive and compassionate work for children and their parents.

Garbarino, James, *Lost Boys: Why Our Sons Turn Violent and How We Can Save Them*, New York, Simon and Schuster, 1999.

Garland, Jane. E., *Depression is the Pits, But I'm Getting Better: A Guide for Adolescents*, Washington, DC, Magination Press, 1997. An easy-to-understand guide to teenage depression.

Gilbert, Binford W., *The Pastoral Care of Depression*, Haworth Press, Binghampton, NY, 1998.

Daniel Goleman, "The Rising Cost of Modernity: Depression," *The New York Times*, December 8, 1992, p. B5.

Gorman, Jack M., *The Essential Guide to Psychiatric Drugs*, New York, St. Martin's Griffin, 1997.

Hirschfield, Robert, *When the Blues Won't Go Away: New Approaches to Dysthymic Disorder and Other Forms of Low-Grade Chronic Depression*, Macmillan, New York, 1991.

Kindlan, Dan and Michael Thompson, *Raising Cain: Protecting the Emotional Life of Boys*, New York, Ballantine Books, 1999.

Kleiman, Karen R., and Valerie D. Raskin, *This Isn't What I Expected: Recognizing and Recovering from Depression and Anxiety after Childbirth*, New York, Bantam, 1994.

Klerman, Gerald and Myrna Weissman, *Interpersonal Psychotherapy of Depression*, Northvale, NJ, Aronson Press, 1994.

Hara Estroff Marano, "Depression: Beyond Serotonin," *Psychology Today*, March–April 1999, Volume 32, #2, p. 30.

Brian Meehan, "Shedding Light, Hope on Dark Side of Teen Years," *The Oregonian*, May 17, 1999, pg. A-1.

Rick Moody, "Why I Pray," *Esquire*, October 1997, Volume 128, #4, pg. 92 (5). A moving account of one person's healing from depression through the power of prayer.

Murray, Michael, *Natural Alternatives to Prozac*. New York, William Morrow and Company, 1996. A comprehensive and well-researched account of the most common natural remedies for depression.

Nelson, John, and Andrea Nelson, editors, *Sacred Sorrows: Embracing and Transforming Depression*, Tarcher/Putnam, New York, 1996. A fine compilation.

Norden, Michael J., *Beyond Prozac: Brain-Toxic Lifestyles, Natural Antidotes and New Generation Antidepressants,* New York, ReganBooks (HarperCollins), 1995.

O., Jack, *Dealing with Depression in 12-Step Recovery*, Seattle, Glen Abbey Books, 1990.

O'Connor, Richard, *Undoing Depression*, Little, Brown and Co., Boston, 1997.

Owen, Patricia, *I Can See Tomorrow: A Guide to Living with Depression*, Hazelden, Center City, MN, 1995.

Papolos, Demitri and Janice Papolos, *Overcoming Depression*, New York, HarperPerennial, 1992.

Rosen, Laura Epstein and Xavier Francisco Amador, *When Someone You Love Is Depressed: How to Help Your Loved One without Losing Yourself*, New York, The Free Press (Simon and Schuster), 1996. A well-researched and helpful book on how to support a friend or loved one who is depressed.

Quinn, Brian P., *The Depression Sourcebook,* Chicago, Contemporary Books, 1997.

Quinnett, Paul, *Suicide: The Forever Decision*, Crossroad, New York, 1997. A helpful treatise on suicide prevention.

Real, Terrance, *I Don't Want to Talk About It: Overcoming the Secret Legacy of Male Depression*, New York, Scribner, 1997. An exceptional book that explores the world of men's depression.

Rosenthal, Norman, *Winter Blues*, Guilford Publications, New York, 1998. The classic book on seasonal affective disorder.

Schrof, Joannie M. and Stacey Schultz, "Melancholy Nation: Depression is on the rise, despite Prozac. But new drugs could offer help," *U.S. News and World Report*, March 8, 1999, Volume 126, #9, pg. 57.

Seligman, Martin, *Helplessness: On Depression, Development and Death*, San Francisco, W.H. Freeman and Company, 1995. *Learned Optimism*, New York, Alfred A. Knopf, 1990.

Sheffield, Anne, *How You Can Survive When They're Depressed*, New York, Harmony, 1998. An excellent guide for learning how to cope with a loved one's depression.

Slagle, Patricia, M.D., *The Way Up from Down: A Safe New Program that Relieves Low Moods and Depression with Amino Acids and Vitamin Supplements*, New York, St. Martin's Press, 1987.

Smyth, Angela, *Seasonal Affective Disorder*, Thorsons, San Francisco, 1992.

U.S. Public Health Service, *The Surgeon General's Call to Action to Prevent Suicide*, Washington, DC, 1999.

Valenstein, Elliot S., *Blaming the Brain: The Truth Abou Drugs and Mental Health*, New York, Free Press, 1998.

Harriet Washington, "Infection Connection," *Psychology Today*, July/August 1999, pg. 43 (5).

Wemhoff, Rich (editor), *Anxiety and Depression: The Best Resources to Help You Cope*, Seattle, Resource Pathways, Inc., 1998. A well-done review of many fine books and Web sites.

Whybrow, Peter, *A Mood Apart*, New York, Basic Books, 1997. A profound and eloquent introduction to the science of mood.

Wolfe, Sidney M., Larry D. Sasich, Rose-Ellen Hope and Public Citizens' Health Research Group, *Worst Pills, Best Pills: A Consumer's Guide to Avoiding Drug-induced Death or Illness*, New York, Pocket Books, 1999.

Yapko, Michael D., *Breaking the Patterns of Depression*, New York, Doubleday, 1997.

Zuess, Jonathan, *The Wisdom of Depression*, Harmony Books, New York, 1998.

General Health—Physical and Psychological

Davis, Martha, R. Eschelman and Matthew McKay, *The Relaxation and Stress Reduction Workbook*, Oakland, CA, New Harbinger Publications (fourth edition), 1995. The classic book on stress management.

Dossey, Larry, *Healing Words: The Power of Prayer and the Practice of Medicine*, San Francisco, HarperSanFrancisco, 1993.

Dreher, Henry, *The Immune Power Personality,* E.P. Dutton, New York, 1995.

Dufty, William, *Sugar Blues,* New York, Warner Books, 1986.

Frankl, Victor E., *Man's Search for Meaning*, New York, Simon and Schuster, 1984. A philosophy of meaning developed in the concentration camps. One of the most important books of the 20th century.

Hauri, Peter, *No More Sleepless Nights*, New York, John Wiley, 1990.

Hutschnecker, Arnold, *The Will to Live*, New York, Simon and Schuster, 1986.

Kabit-Zinn, Jon, *Full Catastrophe Living: Using the Wisdom of Your Body and Mind to Face Stress, Pain and Illness,* New York, Dell Publishing, 1990.

Kaplan, Harold I., Benjamin J. Saddock and Jack A. Grebb, *Kaplan and Saddock's Synopsis of Psychiatry*, seventh edition, Baltimore, Williams and Wilkens, 1994.

Ornish, Dean, *Love and Survival: The Scientific Basis for the Healing Power of Intimacy*, New York, HarperCollins, 1987.

Peck, M. Scott, *The Road Less Traveled*, New York, Simon and Schuster, 1979. My all-time personal favorite.

Siebert, Al, *The Survivor Personality*, Portland, OR, Practical Psychology Press, 1993.

Siegel, Bernie, *Love, Medicine, and Miracles: Lessons Learned About Self-Healing From a Surgeon's Experience with Exceptional Patients*, New York, Harper & Row, 1986.

Stearns, Ann Kaiser, *Living Through Personal Crisis*, Chicago, The
    Thomas More Press, 1984.
Viorst, Judith, *Necessary Losses*, New York, Simon and Schuster,
    1986.
Weil, Andrew, *Spontaneous Healing: How to Discover and Enhance
    Your Body's Natural Ability to Maintain and Heal Itself,* New
    York, Alfred A. Knopf, 1995.
Zi., Nancy, *The Art of Breathing,* ViVi Company, 1997.

Spiritual Inspiration

This is by no means a complete listing of the many inspiring
books that are in print. They have, however, been of particular comfort to me over the years, and especially so during my dark night of
the soul.

Bach, Marcus, *The Power of Serendipity: The Art of Finding Valuable or
    Agreeable Things not Sought For*, Marina del Rey, CA, Devorss
    Publications, 1970.
Eadie, Betty, *Embraced by the Light*, Carson City, NV, Gold Leaf
    Press, 1994. A stirring account of a near-death experience.
Fahy, Mary, *The Tree that Survived the Winter*, Mahwah, NJ, Paulist
    Press, 1989.
Fox, Emmet, *The Sermon on the Mount,* San Francisco,
    HarperSanFrancisco, 1992.
    Power through Constructive Thinking, Cutchogue, NY,
    Buccaneer Books, 1994.
Freeman, James Dillet, *The Story of Unity*. Unity Village, MO, Unity
    Books, 1991.
Kuhlman, Katherine, *I Believe in Miracles*, Bridge-Logos Publishers,
    North Brunswick, NJ, 1992.
Paulus, Trina, *Hope for the Flowers*, Mahwah, NJ, Paulist Press, 1972.
    An allegory about the meaning of life, told by a caterpillar.
Saint-Exupery, Antoine de, *The Little Prince*, New York, Harcourt,
    Brace, Jovanovich, 1971.

Taize Monks, *Songs and Prayers from Taize*, Chicago, GIA Publications, 1991.

Wilber, Ken, *Grace and Grit: Spirituality and Healing in the Life and Death of Treya Killam Wilber*, Boston, Shambhala Publications, 1991. A masterful and moving account of a courageous woman's battle with cancer.

Books on Social and Ecological Change

We cannot separate our mental health from the health of the social and physical environments in which we live. Self-transformation and societal transformation go hand in hand. The following books point the way towards a sustainable and just future for ourselves and our children.

Brown, Lester R., *State of the World*. A yearly Worldwatch Institute report on progress toward a sustainable society, New York, WW Norton & Co.

Callenbach, Ernest, *Ecotopia*, New York, Bantam, 1973.

Capra, Fritjof, *The Web of Life: A New Scientific Understanding of Living Systems*, New York, Doubleday, 1996.

Eisler, Riane, *The Chalice and the Blade*, Cambridge, MA, Harper & Row, 1987.

Fox, Matthew, *The Reinvention of Work: A New Vision of Livelihood for Our Time*, San Francisco, HarperSanFrancisco, 1994.

Gore, Al, *Earth in the Balance: Ecology and the Human Spirit,* Boston, Houghton Mifflin, 1994.

Greider, William, *Who Will Tell the People: The Betrayal of American Democracy*, New York, Simon & Schuster, 1992.

Hartmann, Thom, *The Last Hours of Ancient Sunlight*, New York, Harmony Books, 1999. A call to planetary transformation.

Hawken, Paul, *The Ecology of Commerce: A Declaration of Sustainability,* New York, HarperCollins, 1993. Required reading. The first book to design a comprehensive system that makes conservation profitable, productive and possible.

Huxley, Aldous, *Brave New World & Brave New World Revisited,* New York: HarperPerennial Library, 1965. Huxley's brilliant satire about a socially engineered pseudo-utopia is more relevant today than ever.

Korten, David, *The Post-Corporate World: Life After Capitalism,* Hartford, CT, Kumarian Press, 1996. Provides specific alternatives to the present economic system.

Mander, Jerry, *In the Absence of the Sacred: The Failure of Technology and the Survival of the Indian Nations,* San Francisco, Sierra Club Books, 1991. Mander speaks passionately about the plight of indigenous cultures, whose wisdom we need to create a sustainable future for our planet.

New Dimensions Foundation, *Deep Ecology for the 21st Century,* San Francisco, 1999. Thirteen hours of interviews, with Dr. David Suzuki, Fritjof Capra, Paul Ehrlich, Arne Naess, George Sessions, Paul Shepherd, Gary Snyder, Ted Roszak, Edward Abbey, Cecelia Lanman, Tim Hermach, John Seed, Julia "Butterfly" Hill, Dave Foreman. To order the whole set or individual tapes, call (800) 935-8273.

Peck, M. Scott, *The Different Drum: Community-Making and Peace,* New York, Simon and Schuster, 1987.

Robbins, John, *Diet For a New America,* Tiburon, CA, H.J. Kramer, 1998.

Schaef, Anne Wilson, *When Society Becomes an Addict,* San Francisco, Harper & Row, 1987.

Schor, Juliet B., *The Overworked American: The Unexpected Decline of Leisure,* New York, Basic Books, 1991. Schor advocates a scaling back of consumerism so that people can escape the cycle of "work and spend" and reclaim their leisure.

Schumacher, *Small Is Beautiful: Economics As If People Mattered,* New York, Harper and Row, 1973.

Suzuki, David, *The Sacred Balance: Rediscovering Our Place in Nature,* Amherst, NY, Prometheus Books, 1998. A comprehensive and highly readable book from a leading environmental writer.

CREDITS

Grateful acknowledgment is made for permission to reprint the following:

"The Scream," Edvard Munch (© ARS). Used by permission of Erich Lessing/Art Resource, NY.

"The Sleep of Reason Produces Monsters," Francisco de Goya and Lucientes. Used by permission of Victoria and Albert Museum, London/Art Resource, NY.

"The Scream, Woodcut." Edvard Munch. Used by permission of Foto Marburg/Art Resource, NY.

"Guernica," Pablo Picasso, © 1999 Estate of Pablo Picasso/Artists Rights Society (ARS), New York.

"Creation of Adam," Michelangelo Buonarroti, Sistine Chapel. Used by permission of Alinari/Art Resource, NY.

"Job and His Family Restored to Prosperity," William Blake, *Illustrations of the Book of Job*, III, 45, pl. 21. Used by permission of The Pierpont Morgan Library/Art Resource, NY.

"The Invisible Helper," Courtesy of the Rosicrucian Fellowship, Oceanside, California.

"Melancholy," Albrecht Durer. Used by permission of Giraudon/Art Resource, NY.

Mood Chart (pp. 166-67), reprinted from *When Nothing Matters Anymore*, by Bev Cobain, © 1998. Used with permission from Free Spirit Publishing, Minneapolis, MN. 1-800-735-7323; *www.freespirit.com*; ALL RIGHTS RESERVED.

ABOUT THE AUTHOR

Douglas Bloch is an author, teacher and counselor who writes and speaks on the topics of psychology, healing and spirituality. He earned his B.A. in Psychology from New York University and an M.A. in Counseling from the University of Oregon. He is the author of ten books, including the inspirational self-help trilogy *Words That Heal: Affirmations and Meditations for Daily Living*; *Listening to Your Inner Voice*; and *I Am With You Always*, as well as the parenting book, *Positive Self-Talk for Children*.

Douglas lives in Portland, Oregon with his partner Joan and his two cats and muses, Gabriel and Athena. He is available for *lectures* and *workshops*. You may contact him at:

4226 NE 23rd Ave.
Portland, OR 97211
(503) 284-2848; fax: (503) 284-6754
e-mail: dbloch@teleport.com
http://www.teleport.com/~dbloch

Feel free to communicate your feedback and comments about how this book has impacted your life. If you wish to purchase additional copies of *When Going Through Hell...Don't Stop* or any of my other inspirational books, you may photocopy the order form on the facing page, or write or call us.

If you have any uplifting stories concerning how you or someone you know recovered from depression, anxiety or any "dark night of the soul" experience, please write or send me an e-mail. I look forward to hearing from you.

TOOLS FOR TRANSFORMATION
By Douglas Bloch, M.A.

When Going Through Hell...Don't Stop. An inspirational story of one person's healing from major depression. Part Two is a self-help manual on recovering from depression, which includes a comprehensive list of Internet sites on depression and other mental disorders.

Words That Heal. Both a self-help primer on affirmations and a source of daily inspiration. Contains 52 meditations that provide comfort, upliftment and support. Endorsed by John Bradshaw and Jerry Jampolsky.

Listening to Your Inner Voice. The sequel to *Words That Heal.* How to discover the truth within you and let it guide your way.

I Am With You Always. A treasury of inspirational quotations, poems and prayers from history's great spiritual teachers, philosophers and artists.

Positive Self-Talk for Children. How to use affirmations to build self-esteem in children. A guide for parents, teachers and counselors (in bookstores only).

ORDER FORM

Name _____

Street Address _____

City, State, Zip _____

When Going Through Hell...Don't Stop # ___ x \$15/copy = _____

Words That Heal   # ___ x \$12/copy = _____

Listening to Your Inner Voice   # ___ x \$10/copy = _____

I Am With You Always   # ___ x \$12/copy = _____

Postage (\$3.50 for the first item; \$1.00 for each additional)   _____

TOTAL COST (make check payable to Pallas Communications)   _____
Please mail the order and payment to:
Douglas Bloch, 4226 NE 23rd Ave., Portland, OR 97211 (503) 284-2848
Delivery will take 7-10 days.

If you are on the edge of the abyss, don't jump.
If you are going through hell, don't stop.
As long as you are breathing, there is hope.
As long as day follows night, there is hope.
Nothing stays the same forever.
Set an intention to heal,
reach out for support, and you will find help.